Administration
NVQ Level 1

£3-00

GE

08/9

D1324788

Administration
NVQ Level 1

Second edition

Lynda Bourne and
Pamela Scott

PITMAN
PUBLISHING

PITMAN PUBLISHING
128 Long Acre, London WC2E 9AN

A Division of Pearson Professional Limited

© Longman Group Limited 1994

First published in Great Britain 1993
Second edition published 1994
Reprinted 1995, 1997

British Library Cataloguing in Publication Data
A CIP catalogue for this book is available
on request from the British Library

ISBN 0-273-60618-2

Typeset by ⋏ Tek-Art, Croydon, Surrey
Printed and bound in Singapore

The Publishers' Policy is to use paper manufactured from sustainable forests.

CONTENTS

Contents

INTRODUCTION

This book has been developed to provide trainers and trainees with a fully comprehensive, easy to understand and logically sequenced text for NVQ 1 Administration. Each unit has been written in accordance with the performance criteria, range statements and knowledge/understanding required by awarding bodies such as RSA, LCCI and City & Guilds.

Do-it-yourself tasks are included throughout each unit and can be selected to assess a particular skill or provide evidence of understanding for APL (accreditation of prior learning) purposes. Units can be selected and used as discrete, stand-alone modules, or as part of a complete text giving a guide towards a full NVQ award. The authors have used, wherever possible, DIY tasks that are different to those used in the previous NVQ1 publication.

Completion of DIYs will build a comprehensive work folder, supported by evidence of practical assessment carried out in the workplace. It is important to remember that NVQ assessment is based upon a trainee's demonstration of practical ability over a period of time and cannot therefore be proved by written work alone. However, evidence must be provided that supports the trainee's practical ability and proves underpinning knowledge.

Unit and element numbers follow those in the NVQ assessment folder or book provided by the awarding body. DIY tasks have been given a reference number to help trainers and trainees record progress. Questions that may be asked by assessors and verifiers have been included throughout each unit. Each element concludes with information on the evidence required for completion and how to claim competence. Sample competence record statements are also provided but should be used only as a guide by trainees and not copied word for word.

ACKNOWLEDGEMENTS

During the writing of this book we have had the support of company representatives, colleagues and friends. In particular we would like to mention Mr R D Dyer, Environmental Health Department, Poole Borough Council, and Martin Bedford, Customer Services Centre, Royal Mail Letters, Bournemouth.

We would also like to thank Dennis Scott for his endless proof-reading, Sharon and Jayne for typing and printing, and Jerry, Pete, Kris, Carly, Natalie, Leila and Perri for their patience.

APEX; BT; M Flanagan; Gestetner Limited; GBC (United Kingdom) Ltd; Her Majesty's Stationery Office; Hewlett-Packard Ltd; IBM (United Kingdom) Ltd; R B Jackson; Pitney Bowes plc; The Post Office; Rank Xerox (UK) Ltd; The Royal Society for the Prevention of Accidents (RoSPA); and Twinlock plc.

Finally, our thanks to Carolyn Lyne at Pitman Publishing for her direction and guidance.

GUIDELINES FOR SIMULATED ACTIVITY

The term 'workplace' refers to an area where naturally-occurring administrative activities are carried out. This should include the normal day-to-day constraints, pressures, deadlines, working relationships and activities experienced in a working office environment. Work being assessed can take the form of 'real' work or 'structured activities' carried out for the purpose of assessment.

If competence is to be assessed outside the workplace, eg in a model office, training office or training centre, the structured activity must be carried out in realistic working conditions which reflect those found in the workplace. This must include facilities, equipment and materials appropriate for the activities being assessed. The activities must include the relationships, constraints and pressures met in the workplace.

Simulation should be treated as a second choice mode of assessment. Only high quality simulations which reflect the reality of a workplace are acceptable. When using this mode of assessment the following guidelines should be observed:

a Simulation must allow the candidate to carry out activities to the required standard.
b Activities must reflect those that would be carried out in the workplace.
c The activity must take place in a complete working situation.
d Simulation must include constraints, time and work pressures, contingencies, work patterns, demands on personal responsibility and accountability in the job role.
e Paper-based projects, assignments, case studies, etc, may contribute towards evidence of competence but should not form the main evidence.

UNIT 1
Contribute to the efficiency of the work flow

■ Element 1.1
ORGANISE OWN WORK

Performance criteria

- *Own method of working makes the most effective use of time*
- *Own work is co-ordinated with colleagues' work*
- *Wastage of materials is minimised*
- *Work practices are in accordance with established procedures*

One of the most valuable types of person in any organisation is the person who can organise his or her own work, sort work into an order of importance and fit in urgent work from colleagues when necessary.

To be able to organise your own work, you must know the job well – so it is unlikely that you will be able to do this until you have been in the same job for a month or so. During the first few weeks of a new job it is important that you start to recognise which are the daily routine jobs, which are the weekly jobs and which are the ones that occur regularly at other times. You should then be able to start to organise a routine for your work to ensure that you have a continual workflow. On some occasions you may find that you have too little work or too much, but this should not happen too often if you are prepared.

▶ *What kind of jobs may need doing on a daily basis?*

Sorting, opening and distributing the post

It may not be your responsibility to sort the post for the whole organisation, but you may be responsible for opening and sorting the

1

Fig 1.1 Being disorganised takes longer!

post in your section or department. This job should be done first thing in the morning, or as soon as the post arrives from the mail room. The post may contain cheques, orders, confirmations, requests or complaints – all of which need prompt action. Make sure that any enclosures are firmly attached to the letters and that payments made are recorded according to the company rules.

Telephone calls

You are likely to receive telephone calls throughout the day. It is important that these are answered immediately. Some organisations have an agreed standard – such as 'All telephone calls will be answered within 4 rings'. You may work for such an organisation, and therefore must work to the agreed standards. If you do not, you may be replaced with someone who will!

Greeting customers

Apart from answering the telephone, you may also be responsible for greeting customers. Once again the customer should never be kept waiting. If you are on the telephone when a customer enters, always look up and show that you know they are waiting. If you are talking to a customer and the telephone rings, you will need to excuse yourself, in order to answer the telephone. The customer can hear the phone ringing, but the caller on the other end of the phone does not know that you are with a customer. Therefore the telephone should be answered as quickly as possible. However, do not have a long conversation and keep you customer waiting. If the call is likely to be complicated or rather long, take a name and number and call back in a few minutes. The way in which you deal with the prioritising of calls and customers may mean the difference between more business and loss of business for your organisation. Never leave a reception area unstaffed or an office with a telephone with no one to answer it – especially during busy times. There is usually a way to switch the calls through to another office or you could inform the switchboard operator that you are unavailable for a while.

■ DIY 1.1.1

You work in the main reception and are responsible for receiving visitors coming into the company and also have the main switchboard to answer. 'You are talking on the phone to one customer and there are 2 more calls waiting to be answered. In addition, you have already asked one caller to wait. Then another 2 customers enter and a delivery man wants you to sign for a package.' Write down what you would say to each of the people, in which order you would deal with them, and why.

Processing of correspondence – external and internal

You may be responsible for replying to letters or memos and these tasks would be carried out in between answering calls and dealing with customers.

External correspondence could be letters requesting details of products, prices or supplies. Letters from customers should be dealt with as quickly as possible. A quick, efficient response shows customers that the organisation is efficient. However, the letters must be error-free, with no spelling mistakes and with good grammar.

Internal correspondence is usually in the form of a memo, which may be handwritten, typed or electronically sent using an electronic mail box system. Once again these should be error-free. Some of the memos you receive will be urgent, others may be left for a day or so. You will need to read the content of the memo and decide how quickly you need to reply. If you have little work in progress you may reply immediately; on the other hand, you may have heaps of work – all more urgent than the memo. You must decide.

Photocopying

There is usually quite a lot of copying that needs to be done each day. When you do the copying will depend on the quantity and urgency of each job. If you need to copy documents for a meeting next week, this may be done any time before the meeting. However, if today's letters are waiting for a copy of the price list, then this should be done as quickly as possible – in order to get the letters in the outgoing post.

Filing

How quickly you need to file will depend on the type of files you keep and who uses them. If the filing system is one used by the whole department it is important to keep it up to date every day. There is nothing worse than using a file which is out of date because someone could not be bothered or did not have the time to file. It may result in a customer being given incorrect information and may lead to costing the company more money – as errors could be made. Filing systems which only you use, may not need such a high priority – once again only you can decide which is most important. Many people leave the filing until the end of the day; however, if an urgent phone call or difficult customer arrives at this time, the filing may not be completed unless you stay late at work. Try to keep the filing to a minimum – quite often it is just as easy to put a document away in the right place as it is to throw it into the filing tray.

The way in which you prioritise your own work may depend on what your colleagues' responsibilities are. If you are relying on others to give you work then you will need to tell them when you do not have any work or when you are too busy. Discuss the flow of work with your colleagues so that you have an even share throughout the day. It is no good if you have a colleague that works all day preparing correspondence to go out in the post and then gives you the letters to prepare envelopes 5 minutes before the post is due to leave. It is your responsibility to ensure that the work is passed to you as quickly as possible, then you can prioritise and work out a routine to meet the deadlines set by your colleagues and supervisor, other departments, mailing times and the office hours.

All the tasks you carry out should be done to the best of your ability. As we mentioned earlier many companies are now setting standards. These are usually called quality standards and may be contained in a

Fig 1.2 Organised calm. Be in control – get organised

customer charter. A customer charter is a document which states how the organisation will deal with the requests etc from their customers. It may say that 'all customer's orders will be processed within 24 hours'. It will be partly your responsibility to make sure that all the work carried out by the section meets the quality standards agreed. If you have a regular problem in meeting the deadlines or standards, then it may be that you have too much work, or you are not organising yourself and your work correctly. Do not leave it until it is too late – talk to your supervisor who will help you arrange your work more efficiently.

▶ *How could you arrange your work more efficiently?*

Many people find it easier to organise their work with the use of office aids such as **diaries, timetables, checklists** and **work schedules**. If you know that an important job is due on Thursday, then you should try to keep Thursday as free as possible from all other work. This may mean working quicker and harder on Wednesday and leaving some work until Friday. Ensure that you write in a diary or use a bring forward file (*see* page 178) to remind yourself of important work and deadlines.

■ DIY 1.1.2

You arrive at work to find that you have the following jobs to do. Write yourself a checklist in the order in which you would tackle these jobs.

● Return a phone call to a customer whom you did not get through to yesterday.

- Process six orders for goods through to the sales department.
- Answer two letters of complaint about late deliveries.
- Write to personnel to tell them when your holidays will be this year.
- Open and sort the post.
- Photocopy a report (10 pages) for this afternoon's section meeting (there are 7 people attending, including you).
- Get the room ready for the meeting (2.00–4.00), order the tea/coffee from the secretary and photocopy the agenda.
- File yesterday's orders and correspondence.
- Call the central photocopying section to find out when the monthly report will be ready.
- Telephone the railway station to find out what times the trains leave for Halesowen, as you want to visit a friend at the weekend.

In between carrying out these tasks you will also be receiving 3 customers who have made appointments to see your supervisor, answering the telephone and carrying out requests from your colleagues.

When organising your work you should link tasks together whenever possible to save time. For instance if you have several pieces of work to photocopy, copy them at the same time – do not take them one at a time to the copier. Filing should be sorted through prior to filing, to ensure that you only need to get each file out once. Do not waste time hand delivering items to other sections if they are not urgent, they can go through the internal mail system or wait until there are other things to go to the section. These are only simple ideas but can result in quite a saving in time, time left for doing other things and becoming a more efficient member of the team.

■ DIY 1.1.3

Make a list of the work you carry out in one day on a chart like the one in Fig 1.3. When completed, look at the list and identify 3 areas which could be

Name of Trainee:	
Task carried out	**Improvement that could be made**

Fig 1.3

6

improved. It may be that you did not photocopy everything together, you wasted time delivering a memo which could have waited, you left filing which could have been carried out at the time, etc.

▶ Why is it important to work as a member of a team?

Everyone employed in a company relies on someone else to make sure that the work flow is smooth and uninterrupted throughout the company. There is no one department or person that is more important, everyone makes a contribution. If one person does not fit into the smooth running of the work flow then this can cause disruption, delay and reduce the amount of work that the team could otherwise get through.

All organisations are looking to get the best from their workers and increase the amount of work carried out (this is called increasing productivity). The more work carried out the more profit the organisation should earn. How you co-ordinate your work with your colleagues is an important part of this process. If you have completed Unit 4.1 on creating and maintaining effective working relationships you will already know about making teams work effectively (*see* page 83).

▶ How can you minimise wastage of materials?

Many organisations are now taking into consideration the amount of materials regularly wasted by their employees every day. The materials wasted are a cost to the organisation and will be reducing profits. Some wastage is bound to occur, but even this could be channelled for recycling or put to further use. Every day paper, pens and pencils, paperclips and other consumables are wasted. This may be through carelessness, laziness or thoughtlessness. When people work in an untidy and messy way they are more likely to lose materials and waste items. The person who does not check the work on the computer carefully before printing out will waste paper and printer consumables (either ribbon, cartridge or toner). Using a spell check or reading carefully through before printing may avoid wasting paper and printer consumables unnecessarily. If you do need to print a letter or document to read or to get someone else to read, then try to use paper that has already been used. You should not use creased, stapled or spoiled paper in printers, as you may cause damage to the printer. Whenever possible print using a draft or medium quality of print instead of high quality: this will save the printer ink and extend the life of the ribbon or cartridge. In the same way as in printers, recycled paper may be used in photocopiers, but only if it is in good condition.

Paper should be stored correctly within the section or department. If it is not stored flat it will crease and creased paper cannot be used in machinery.

Employees should not be encouraged or allowed to take stationery or consumables for their own use at home.

▶ *Working within the health and safety rules*

No matter how urgent the duties are or demanding your job becomes, you must always work safely. You should not take shortcuts that may cause hazards and accidents to yourself or your colleagues. Do not try to carry too much at one time, and do not speed up the pace of equipment to such an extent that you cannot cope. Always use the correct equipment to reach high shelves or storage cupboards. Never run in the corridors or down stairs in order to get somewhere on time – walking briskly will get you there just as quick and in one piece! The requirements of all the health and safety legislation should be followed at all times. The details of these requirements can be found in Unit 2 on pages 24–40.

■ DIY 1.1.4

Copy the table in Fig 1.4 on to A4 paper. Over the next few weeks write down the work that you organise and prioritise. Get your supervisor to sign it when it is finished.

Completing Element 1.1

To complete this element on organising your own work you will need to put all DIY tasks in your folder and carry out a final assessment. Competence must be proven by arranging, co-ordinating and carrying out your own work activities

Name of Trainee:	
Name of Organisation:	
Dates worked: From.................................... to	
Date	Work organised and prioritised

I confirm that the above work has been completed by ....

This work was carried out according to organisational procedures and within the health and safety guidelines.

Signed ....(Supervisor) Date ....

Fig 1.4

under supervision and instruction. Acceptable evidence will include copies of your checklists, diaries and notes of discussions with your colleagues and supervisor.

Claiming credit

Once you have completed your final assessment, you will need to write in your record book or folder how, when, where and what you have done to prove that you are competent.

The following is an example of how one trainee completed this claim:

I have been working at Coles & Co for the last month. During this time I have worked in the Sales Department as a member of their team. Apart from my supervisor, there were 3 sales staff and 1 other assistant. I carried out the usual duties of a junior in the sales office which included photocopying, typing, sorting the post and filing. In the morning I would look through my tray and see what work was needed for the day; I also looked in the diary to see if there were any appointments or meetings for the day. Quite often I was asked to do urgent jobs which meant I had to stop what I was doing. Sometimes I was asked to do several things at once and this meant I had to do the most urgent thing first. I made sure that I told the sales staff that there would be a slight delay when I was too busy to do something straight away. I have made a log book of some of the duties carried out during my work and this is in my folder.

■ Element 1.2
DEVELOP SELF TO IMPROVE PERFORMANCE

Performance criteria

- *An action plan for self-learning is agreed and regularly reviewed with supervisor*
- *A personal portfolio of learning and job experience is established and maintained*
- *Opportunities for improving own competence are actioned in agreement with appropriate persons*
- *Own needs for information and advice are identified and discussed with appropriate persons*

Before starting work it is likely that you will have carried out training, either at school or at a training centre or college. This training is called 'off the job' as it is carried out away from any job of work. The type of training you receive is usually to teach you the basic skills required for a job. This may include typewriting, word processing, using a database and spreadsheets, filing, answering the telephone, dealing with the post, etc. When you have a part-time or full-time job you will need training on how to use your skills within the organisation you are working for. For example, you may be capable of creating a database, but you may not be familiar with the structure of the database used in the organisation or the packages they use on their computers. The training you receive whilst working in the company is called 'on-the-job' training. It makes sure that you are totally familiar with the organisation's rules, regulations and procedures.

▶ *What are records of achievement?*

Part of your training at school or college will probably be recording your achievement. You will usually have a **Record of Achievement** issued by your tutor in which you write all the qualifications and experience you have gained whilst training. This should be the start of your record of self-development which should be added to when you achieve further qualifications or carry out more training.

▶ *Action plans*

Who uses action plans?

Many companies are taking training more seriously than in the past and are introducing **action plans** to their staff. Action planning and training has the advantage of ensuring that the employees cover everything they need and want to know. They are taught how to carry out tasks properly – and this usually means more efficiently, therefore saving time. Action planning has become widely used as a method of planning what you and your company need to do to ensure you receive the right kind of training.

▶ *What period of time does an action plan cover?*

An action plan may be short, medium or long term, or include all 3. A short-term plan may cover the areas of training needed in the next 6 months, medium term up to 1 year and long term 1–5 years. When written, however, the action plan may well alter to take into account changes in your circumstances. When writing your short-term action plan you will need to think about:

1 What you want to achieve in the next 6 months.
2 What you need to know and be able to do to achieve your aim.
3 Who you need to contact and what equipment and materials you will need.
4 What time you will have to commit to your plan and what arrangements need to be made.

For example, let's say that your action plan for the next 6 months is going to be 'obtaining the Administration Level 1 qualification'. You may complete your action plan as follows:

ACTION PLAN

Name ————————————————————————————————————

Start date ————————————Expected completion date ————————————

Aim: Administration Level 1 qualification

1 I require the knowledge and information to carry out all the units for the qualification.

2 I will need access to the necessary equipment and procedures detailed in the units.

3 I will need to talk to my tutor and supervisor at work.

4 I will need to:

(a) talk to my tutor at college and learn some of the basics, such as keyboarding;

(b) spend time at work learning new procedures and using different equipment;

(c) read up at home about some of the procedures.

Once you have a skeleton plan such as this you can start to break it down into sections. For instance, you may look through the units of the qualification and identify which ones you can carry out quite quickly with only a little training, because you are already doing those particular jobs at work.

■ DIY 1.2.1

Complete a short-term action plan for one of the units or elements in Administration that you have not yet completed. List down what you need to know, the equipment you need to use and who can help you achieve this. Follow the layout of the action plan above or use one that you already have.

▶ *Off-the-job training*

What are the advantages of off-the-job training?

Most training centres have qualified specialist staff to train and assess you in skills and knowledge covered. The equipment available is selected for training purposes and you will have uninterrupted time to learn the new skills and procedures. The training staff will also negotiate action plans with you and help you to develop a programme to suit you and enable you to acquire your qualifications. If you have special needs then these are usually provided for with special equipment or specially trained staff. Textbooks will be available as well as special training manuals; in addition, resource centres containing books, computers, videos, tapes and other facilities will be on hand. You will be able to mix with others who are learning the same procedures and skills. In addition, the skills you gain are general and can be adapted to suit any organisation or company.

What are the disadvantages of off-the-job training?

Although the staff are qualified trainers they may not have experience of working in an organisation and carrying out the procedures and skills that they are teaching. The equipment at the centre may become dated and faulty through over-use and by careless handling by inexperienced trainees. Individual attention may not be available in large groups of trainees. Some of the procedures and skills may be difficult to learn in a training room, such as greeting and assisting visitors. It is difficult to learn how to become part of a team and learn how to deal with unexpected interruptions such as telephone calls and visitors.

▶ *On-the-job training*

What are the advantages of on-the-job training?

The procedures and skills are learnt whilst carrying out the job. A supervisor will usually spend time with you demonstrating how the job is done and then watch while you have a go. If you make mistakes the supervisor will correct you and, if necessary, demonstrate again. Once you are able to carry out the task without supervision you will be able to do the job. You are in the company of the people you work with and will be able to see how your part of the job fits into the section or department you are working for. You will be able to see the everyday problems that occur during work, ie the interruptions, the telephone calls and visitors, and deal with them accordingly.

What are the disadvantages of on-the-job training?

The supervisors are not usually qualified trainers. They may know how to do a job but they may not necessarily have the knowledge and understanding that surrounds the task. The information that they pass on may be relevant to the organisation worked in but it may not be useful when changing jobs to another company. The interruptions, such as the telephone, visitors, urgent work and the demands of other staff, may cause the training to stop and start. Quite often you need a quiet period of time to get to learn a new skill or procedure. In addition, people expect you to get all your work finished as well as carry out the training. The duties carried out in one job are unlikely to cover all the areas you wish to develop. For instance, if you wished to acquire your Administration qualification, there might be some units that are not dealt with by the section in which you work.

As you can see there are many advantages/disadvantages of on- and off-the-job training and you can probably think of more. Some large companies have the advantage of having their own training section, where staff can be released from their normal place of work to attend on a day or half-day basis. The staff within these training centres may be fully qualified trainers but may also have worked within the company on everyday duties.

■ DIY 1.2.2

Write down a list of advantages and disadvantages of the training that you are currently carrying out. If this includes on- and off-the-job training, make 2 separate lists.

Ideally a trainee can arrange to link both types of training. As we have seen, some things are better learnt in a specialist training centre, others in the workplace. Quite often you will be the only person that sees both places and will be in the best position to decide which things you learn in the training centre and which you learn at work. This will become an important part of your action planning.

This means that if you have the opportunity of going to work, even if it is only for a few weeks, you must take full advantage of the facilities that will be available to you. Make sure that you list everything that you want to know and cover whilst on work placement and talk to your supervisor about it. Do not be too disappointed if you cannot do everything. If you do not have a definite action plan you may well be disappointed with the work that is given to you.

In the same way, if you have the opportunity of going to a training centre, one day a week or during the evening, make sure you have an action plan. Only you will know what opportunities you have at work and what you need to be included in your off-the-job training. You should complete an action plan and discuss it with your centre trainer to make sure that the training programme you are entering will fulfil your requirements.

■ DIY 1.2.3

Draw up an action plan for your own requirements covering the next month. Discuss it with your supervisor and trainer to see if your requirements can be met. Negotiate changes if necessary and ensure that you meet the agreed plan as far as possible.

Most action plans will need changing on a regular basis because you and your circumstances change. You may change your job at work, move from the area, face something upsetting at home – literally anything may affect your action plan. When these changes occur you should update your action plan to take account of the changes. Discuss any problems with your supervisor and trainer and make sure they are aware of your new action plan – especially if you are expecting them to help.

▶ *What should you do when you have completed your action plan?*

One of the first things to do will be to update your Record of Achievement. If you have gained a new qualification then the certificate, or a copy, should be placed in your record and your curriculum vitae updated. If you have attended a training course or learnt a new skill a statement from you, signed by your trainer or supervisor, would be a suitable document to put in your record. Always include the dates of training on your record – this will ensure it is accurate and up to date. Later it may be difficult to remember exactly when and what you did.

Your Record of Achievement should not contain any spelling errors as you may wish to use it at future interviews. The way in which you organise your records will reflect the type of person you are. One with documents and certificates falling out, or dirty and torn statements will not impress a future employer. Your record should be something you are proud to show anyone.

▶ *Do all organisations include training?*

Unfortunately not – most organisations can see the benefit of training and action planning, but not all will offer it to their staff. If you wish to carry out personal development without the assistance of your company you may need to attend training sessions in the evenings or at weekends. You will still need to complete an action plan and identify who and what you need to access to achieve your aims. There are several places that you can go for information. First start with your supervisor or personnel department, if you have one. They will advise you as to whether the company will support you in what you wish to do. Sometimes a company will pay for the training course, but only after the employee has been successful. If the company will not support you, then you will be able to find out further information from your local Careers Guidance Office, local training centres and colleges, council libraries, job centres and local Training Enterprise Councils (TECs). Many of these contacts now have a computer-based information system that lists all the training and support (including grants) available within the county. There are usually projects run by the government to support individuals wishing to attend training and development programmes. Some of these are supported financially – which means the cost to you will be kept to a minimum.

■ DIY 1.2.4

Find out where your sources of information on training are locally. Write down the names and addresses of the organisations that may be useful. Keep these on file, or as part of your action plan documentation.

▶ *What else can you get from your organisation?*

Some companies and organisations have appraisal or review systems in place. This is a regular review (usually once a year) of your progress and where your future development may be. It is at this time that you will have a chance to identify any opportunities or training that you wish to follow. Do not be afraid of discussing your ambitions at an appraisal interview. It is also an opportunity for identifying any training and development needs that you feel are required to help you in your work. It is unlikely that the company will be able to help everyone do everything but there is usually a system to ensure that the assistance given by the organisation is fairly distributed around the staff.

■ DIY 1.2.5

Draw up a medium (up to 1 year) and long-term (up to 5 years) action plan for yourself. Identify what achievements you would like to make, and who and what you need to assist you to meet these achievements. Keep your action plans on file and review them in 6 months (make a note in your bring forward file or diary).

Completing Element 1.2

To complete this element on developing yourself to improve performance you will need to put all DIY tasks in your folder and carry out a final assessment. Competence must be proven in dealing with on- and off-the-job training programmes, and involve discussions with your colleagues and supervisor (keep notes of these meetings). Include the action plans that you have agreed and reviewed. Your Record of Achievement will also be needed as evidence of your competence for this element. You may also ask your trainer to provide evidence that you have regularly reviewed your progress and negotiated your action plans.

Claiming credit

Once you have completed your final assessment, you will need to write in your record book or folder how, when, where and what you have done to prove that you are competent.

The following is an example of how one trainee completed this claim:

I made an action plan when I started on my training programme which included the qualification I wanted to get and the type of job I wanted. This action plan was discussed with my mum and my trainer to make sure that it included all the things that I wanted and that they were possible. I then started on a training programme and was supplied with action plans to use as a review with my tutors. I kept up to date my Record of Achievement that I was given at school, although I have tidied it up quite a bit since. My CV has been updated since I got my qualification in typing and word processing. I also included my part-time job.

When I went on work experience I agreed an action plan with the supervisor. It was important to me that I carried out the jobs that I could not do at the training centre. These included answering the phone and dealing with the post. The work I carried out also included some training, especially on the telephone equipment that I had to use.

I have found that the action plans have made me organise myself better, and I have been able to complete things that I started.

Copies of the action plans are in my folder.

■ Element 1.3
MAINTAIN OWN WORK AREA TO ASSIST WORK FLOW

Performance criteria

- *Work area is orderly and safe*
- *Material not in use is appropriately stored for easy reference*
- *Required resources are placed for ease of access*
- *Working conditions which affect own efficiency and are outside own control are reported to the appropriate person*
- *Items surplus to requirements are disposed of safely and appropriately*

Generally most people prefer to work in a neat and tidy way, so that they know exactly what work they have to complete. There are a few people who are happy to work in a mess and they may be able to manage. However, if they have to share a workload with anyone it is not fair to other people to impose an untidy work area on them. Work areas that are always untidy do not impress visitors and clients, therefore it is important to keep your work area as tidy and safe as you can. It is your responsibility to ensure that there is nothing in the work area that may cause a hazard or an accident. If you see anything you should try to put it right or report it to your supervisor. You have a legal duty to report such hazards, and if you do not report them, you could be sued if anyone is injured. The Health and Safety at Work Act is one which you should be familiar with (*see* page 28).

▶ *What would your work area include?*

This is the area directly in your responsibility and any general areas that you use. This would include your chair and desk, filing cabinets and cupboards, and any electrical equipment that you are responsible for. The floor, walls and any noticeboards next to your work area would also be included. There are obvious things that you should look for, such as keeping wires away from the area that people walk in or through. Never place liquids, such as tea; coffee, or soft drinks, near electrical equipment.

Most organisations supply trays for keeping work in – generally there is an IN and an OUT tray, and you may also have a PENDING or FILING tray. The work in these trays should be stacked neatly and not thrown in at all angles. Files should be kept neatly and any damaged ones repaired or replaced. People normally place the trays in the most sensible order, which will depend on how the work flows through the area. For instance, the IN and OUT trays would not be kept in a place which was difficult for people to reach. On the other hand, your PENDING and FILING trays may be placed conveniently for you to use, but not others.

Always keep the items that are used frequently in a place that is easy to reach. Items such as the stapler, paper clips, pens and pencils are likely to be left on the desk; on the other hand, the hole punch, ruler and adhesive tape may be kept in your drawer.

There will be other things that you use regularly, perhaps the internal telephone directory or your customer lists. Some of these items you may share with other people in the office and they would need to be handy for anyone to reach.

■ DIY 1.3.1

In a table, like the one in Fig 1.5, make a list of all the items you have available all the time and those which are kept in your drawer or desk, and are used only occasionally.

In your own work area, or perhaps in one of the more general areas, there will be larger items of equipment or resources that you will use. These may include computers, typewriters, printers, binding machines, lettering machines and photocopiers. Some of these may usually be kept in a cupboard or in another office and only brought out when required. You should make an effort to return the equipment to the correct storage place when it is not in use. This will enable others to find it when they need it and keep your work area free from unnecessary equipment.

Resources used daily	Resources used occasionally

Fig 1.5

▶ *What else should I keep tidy?*

The area around the photocopier is one place where there is generally a bit of a mess. People that copy something wrongly, may just leave the waste paper at the side of the machine. Spare paper ready to be placed in the machine may get pushed and shoved about unless there is a special place for it to be stored out of the way. Paper that jams in the machine may be left at the side or even on the floor. All of this will need tidying up. It is normal practice to keep a waste bin (preferably one for recycling) by the side of the photocopier so that rubbish can be thrown away immediately. If one is not available and you notice that a mess tends to occur most days, then it would be worth asking your supervisor if a suitable waste bin could be ordered.

The printer may also be a place where waste paper tends to collect. Used paper should be kept available for 'trial runs' but it should be stored neatly and in a place which is handy for those using it.

■ DIY 1.3.2

Copy the table in Fig 1.6 and make a list of all the large moveable equipment you use. Against each item state where it should be stored.

Type of equipment	Normal storage place	Is it usually put away in the correct place? Yes/No

Fig 1.6

You may be responsible for keeping the noticeboard up to date. Check the noticeboard on a regular basis – about once a week is enough. Take down any information which is out of date, or any document which has been tampered with. If damage has occurred to any of the notices, they should be repaired and put back again. Make sure that the most important items are at eye level and can be easily seen by everyone – do not cover them with other items. Health and safety notices can become quite tatty as they have to be displayed all the time. When they get beyond repair, order some more from your supervisor or health and safety officer.

▶ *How can filing and storage systems be kept tidy?*

Any filing and storage system should be kept up to date to ensure that the work flow is not hindered. If one of your colleagues needs a file which you have not yet returned, they will not be too pleased, and they will have wasted time looking for it. Keep the files and folders in good order and repair any that get torn or split. You are responsible for doing everything you can to help your supervisor and colleagues to complete their work as efficiently and quickly as possible. This means making sure that all the items they use are always put back in their proper place when they are finished with.

When sorting out the 'dead' files (the ones no longer required) they should be stored in the correct place and not left on the floor next to the cabinets. The organisation may have a room in the basement or elsewhere which is used for the storage of archive material.

▶ *What else may be disposed of?*

You may have equipment that gets replaced – for example, old manual typewriters may get replaced with new electronic ones. It may be up to you to arrange for the old equipment to be removed and disposed of safely. Occasionally organisations may sell the old equipment to staff that want it. It is important to follow the correct procedures in case you throw out something that should have been sold. The organisation may have arrangements with a local trader who comes to remove any items that are no longer needed. If extra items are left around the work area they will only be left to gather dust and could become a hazard. Whatever the arrangements are for disposing of old equipment, it will be necessary to record the fact that the equipment is no longer part of the company. This is because equipment may be rated as an asset, and the accounts department will need to know if it no longer exists.

As well as old equipment you may have to get rid of extra stationery supplies or stock. Stationery and supplies should not sit in a cupboard for years – there should be a regular turn round of stock to ensure that the quality remains good.

■ DIY 1.3.3

Find out how you would dispose of the following in your organisation and who you need to inform:

1 a manual typewriter
2 10 reams of A4 headed paper
3 3 boxes of window envelopes
4 an old computer and printer which has been replaced.

▶ *What else may affect your work flow?*

You should report any difficulties you may have with the surroundings. This will include the lighting, heating, windows and noise. If the work area becomes too hot or too cold, then you will be unable to work to the best of your ability. However, remember that it is difficult to get the temperature just right for everyone. Some people prefer always to have a window open, even on the coldest of days. If this is the case and you are constantly cold, if the person refuses to compromise, then you should inform your supervisor of the problem.

Building maintenance is usually carried out in the evenings and weekends but there may be occasions when the workers have no choice but to work during office hours. If the noise or disruption is too great then you should inform your supervisor of the problem. Generally though, the building workers try to keep any disruption to a minimum. Your organisation may have a building manager who is responsible for all the contractors that work in the building. They will generally have a schedule of work to be carried out. If you have any special event in the future, it is best to check whether there will be any work being carried out at that time. This will give you the chance to negotiate with the manager.

■ DIY 1.3.4

Find out who is responsible for the building maintenance in your organisation and who you would need to tell if there was faulty heating or lighting.

Completing Element 1.3

To complete this element on maintaining your own work area to assist work flow you will need to put all DIY tasks in your folder and carry out a final assessment.

Competence must be proven in dealing with materials, equipment and storage systems. You must demonstrate that you can keep your work area orderly and safe, that material not in use is stored correctly for easy reference and that required resources are easily reached. If problems arise affecting your efficiency, which you cannot control, you should know who to inform. Lastly you must know how to dispose in a safe and correct way of items that are not required.

Claiming credit

Once you have completed your final assessment, you will need to write in your record book or folder how, when, where and what you have done to prove that you are competent.

The following is an example of how one trainee completed this claim:

During my 6 months of training and work I have made sure that my work area was kept neat and tidy. I made sure that there were no trailing leads and that any hazards were put right or reported. I put back on the shelf the dictionary, telephone and fax directories and other reference books used so that others could find them. I also made sure that my desk was kept clean and that people knew where to place items for filing or for my attention. On one occasion when I arrived for work the heating had not come on. I reported it to the main desk, who informed me that someone was already working on it. It took about an hour to get the office back to normal temperature. When I removed the old files from the cabinets I made sure that they were collected and taken to the archives as quickly as possible.

I have made a personal statement about my work which has been signed by my colleague and my supervisor. My tutor has visited me at work and agrees that my desk and work area were tidy at the time. I have also taken photographs of my work area and the surrounding general area to show the type of equipment and space involved.

UNIT 2

Contribute to the health, safety and security of the workplace

■ **Element 2.1**
CONTRIBUTE TO THE PREVENTION OF HAZARDS IN THE WORKPLACE

Performance criteria

- *Potential hazards to the well-being of self and others are correctly identified and dealt with within limits of individual authority and in accordance with approved procedures and practices*
- *Where potential hazards are outside own authority to rectify, timely and accurate information is passed to the appropriate person*
- *Instructions relating to exposure to substances and equipment hazardous to health are complied with*
- *Protective clothing and items appropriate to the situation are worn when relevant*
- *Instructions relating to the lifting and handling of materials are followed*

Employers have a duty to protect their employees and keep them informed about health and safety, in the same way as the employees have a responsibility to look after themselves and others. If you identify a problem this should be discussed with the employer or safety representative if there is one. It is possible for you to contact the Health and Safety Executive, your local authority or perhaps the local fire brigade direct if you feel your employer is putting people's health or lives at risk.

▶ *What are all employees expected to know about their workplace?*

All employers, employees and trainees in the workplace or training centre should know:

1 how to contact 'first-aiders'
2 where to locate the first-aid box
3 what to do in the event of a fire
4 where to locate fire equipment
5 how to select/operate fire equipment
6 where to locate the accident book
7 who to report hazards to
8 how to lift/handle materials correctly
9 when/where to use protective clothing.

This information should be covered in the safety policy, rules and emergency procedures of the organisation during induction training. If you do not know the answers to the 9 points above, now is a good time to ask your supervisor for advice.

▶ *What are the possible hazards?*

There is a wide range of possible hazards in an office and it is the responsibility of everyone to ensure that potential accidents are prevented before they happen. Examples are drawers left open, cabinets placed in front of fire extinguishers, open scissors or sharp objects left on desk tops, chairs left in gangways and overloaded electric sockets. Are you guilty of throwing items such as sticky tape or correction fluid across the room to a colleague? Many people do this and it is only after an accident has occurred that they think twice before doing it again!

It is imperative that staff appreciate the dangers that can occur from hazards such as:

- slippery or poorly maintained floors
- lifting heavy items without bending properly
- staircases and fire exits used as storage facilities
- poorly maintained or frayed carpets
- standing on chairs to reach high shelving
- removing safety guards on machines
- trailing electric or telephone leads

Fig 2.1 Some safety hazards in the office

- obstacles in gangways
- using faulty electrical equipment
- faulty storage/stacking of business items
- improper treatment of hazardous substances
- unsuitable positioning and use of furniture.

The above list is by no means exhaustive as the potential hazards are many and changeable. All you need to do at any one time is to look around your own working area and spot any potential hazards – pay particular attention to items in the list above but always be on the look-out for other, less obvious, hazards. It is very important that we all understand and try to reduce risks by ensuring that we are fully aware of safe working practices.

■ DIY 2.1.1

You should now be aware of some of the possible risks in an office. In order to ensure that your own work area is kept free from hazards, copy out the list

SAFE AND TIDY CHECKLIST			
Question?	**Answer**		**Comments**
	Yes	**No**	
Filing cabinets 1 Are drawers left open? 2 Can more than one drawer be opened at once? 3 Are drawers overcrowded?			
Telephone 1 Is it easy to reach? 2 Are wires kept out of the way? 3 Is mouthpiece clean?			
Computer 1 Is brightness suitable? 2 Are screen and keyboard positioned correctly? 3 Do you have enough light without glare?			
Desk 1 Is it tidy? 2 Is it an obstruction? 3 Is it the right height? 4 Is all equipment stored safely?			
Chair 1 Is it comfortable? 2 Does it support your back? 3 Do you leave it in gangways?			
Electrical equipment 1 Do you have trailing wires? 2 Do you know how to treat faulty equipment? 3 Do you know how to check the mains supply? 4 Do you know how to recognise faulty equipment?			
Hazards 1 Do you know to whom you would report a hazard? 2 Would you complete a written report? 3 Would you tell them verbally? 4 Do you recognise the hazards that are outside your authority to rectify?			

Fig 2.2

shown in Fig 2.2 (you may type this if you wish and present it to others as a useful health and safety questionnaire), and complete it with regard to your own working area.

Look back at the safety hazards picture on page 26 and then write in your own words details of the hazards you can see.

▶ *What health and safety laws should you be aware of?*

There are legal minimum health and safety requirements that have to be followed in both the office and other working areas. Health and safety legislation covers lighting, heating, space, cleanliness, ventilation and so on to ensure people are offered a safe and comfortable place in which to work. It is in the company's interests that standards and procedures are followed in order to reduce absenteeism through poor working conditions, illness or accident.

Legal action against an employer failing to provide a healthy and safe place of work include fines, closure of premises and even imprisonment for persistent offenders. However, health and safety at work is such an important aspect of the welfare of employees that most employers do not need the threat of legal punishment to provide good working conditions.

There are about 30 Acts of Parliament governing the working environment. Some of the more important ones are discussed below.

Health and Safety at Work Act 1974 (HASAWA)

This is an enabling Act, which means that it is designed to bring together all the previous legislation and make sense out of it. However, at the moment many of these earlier Acts exist side by side with the HASAWA. The basic idea of the Act is that there should be a joint effort by employers and employees to provide a safe and healthy working environment.

The employer has to provide safe:

● equipment and systems of work
● working conditions and adequate arrangements and facilities for welfare

- use, storage, transport and handling of substances and articles
- means of access to and from work.

If an accident should occur the employer must investigate this fully and all staff should be fully informed, supervised and trained in accordance with their work role.

Employees are responsible for:

- taking care of their own safety
- the safety of other people affected by their actions
- co-operating with employers and any other persons involved in carrying out duties under this law.

The HASAWA includes the Electricity at Work Regulations 1989 and The Reporting of Injuries, Diseases and Dangerous Occurrences Regulations 1985 (RIDDOR).

The Electricity at Work Regulations 1989 have been made under the Health and Safety at Work Act of 1974 and cover establishments

Fig 2.3 Employees are responsible for taking care of their own safety . . .

such as colleges, hospitals and commercial premises. The purpose of these regulations is to require precautions to be taken against the risk of death or injury from electricity at work. Injury or death caused by electric shock, electric burn, fires of electrical origin, electric arcing or explosions initiated or caused by electricity are covered by these regulations.

There are maintenance guidelines for all electrical equipment – even the office kettle, word processor and electric fan have to be inspected and maintained on a regular basis. Employers are required to label their electrical equipment with details of when it was last checked and the date of the next inspection. Green labels are used for equipment that has passed its test and red labels used for equipment that is not satisfactory. If a piece of equipment is found to be dangerous it must be removed.

Fig 2.4 An example of a completed green label

The **Reporting of Injuries, Diseases and Dangerous Occurrences Regulations 1985 (RIDDOR)** state that an accident book must be kept by anyone who employs workers. In the event of an accident the employer must maintain a written account of what happened, which must be made available for inspection by the relevant authority. If an employee is off work, due to an accident, for more than 3 days the employer must inform the local authority environmental health department or an inspector from the Health and Safety Executive, depending on who has legal responsibility for the particular premises. The relevant authority must be informed verbally within 24 hours of the accident occurring, and in writing using form F2508 within 7 days. This information is used to identify accident trends and unsafe working practices.

The type of accident report required is not stated by RIDDOR – it is left to the responsible person to use a form or record that best suits the purpose. A photocopy of form F2508 kept in a file would be acceptable.

Accident Report Form (To be completed by Line Manager)		
Accident Details:	Location:	
	Department:	
	Date: Time:	
	Name & Address:	
	Sex: Age:	
Details of Injuries: Signature _____ (Line Manager)	Occupation:	
	Witnesses:	
Distribution: Copy 1 to Human Resources Copy 2 to Facilities Manager Copy 3 to Health & Safety Representative Copy 4 to Facilities Manager Central Services Notification of Unsafe/Unhealthy Conditions form completed. YES/NO* (Only complete where necessary) *Delete as applicable		

Fig 2.5 An accident report form

Section 2(3) of the Health and Safety at Work Act 1974 states that if 5 or more people are employed then, by law, the company has to have a written statement detailing its health and safety policy. The statement should be specific to the company and set out the general policy for protecting the health and safety of employees at work and the arrangements for putting that policy into practice. This statement must be brought to the attention of all employees and others who may be affected by the employer's business and it should be updated when working conditions change.

The Office, Shops and Railways Premises Act 1963

This Act is much more specific than the HASAWA which has a general approach to health and safety in the workplace. The Office, Shops and Railways Premises Act stipulates working requirements and informs employees of their rights.

This Act states specific requirements, such as:

● adequate floor space for each employee
● temperature above 16°C and a thermometer displayed

- adequate ventilation without draught
- adequate, separate toilets
- washing facilities with hot and cold water
- soap and clean drying facilities
- fresh drinking water
- facilities to hang and dry clothes
- isolation of noisy machinery
- safe and clear floors and stairways
- machinery or correct procedures to lift heavy weights
- chairs provided for employees who stand to do their work
- availability of trained first-aid staff
- adequately stocked first-aid boxes
- machine guards where necessary
- clear gangways and fire exits
- fire drills/assembly points brought to notice of all staff
- adequate fire extinguishers in working order.

Under this Act the **Information for Employees Regulations 1989** provide employers with a large poster that has to be displayed clearly in all offices. The poster informs employees of their rights and gives local information detailing the employees' local enforcing authority and the address of the local employment medical service.

■ DIY 2.1.2

Do you know where your Information for Employees Regulations poster is? If not, find out. On a piece of A4 paper write out the name and address of your local enforcing authority and the address of the local employment medical service.

There are other Acts in operation such as:

- The Fire Precautions Act 1971
- The Employers' Liability (Compulsory Insurance) Act 1969
- The Employers' Liability (Defective Equipment) Act 1969
- The Occupiers Liability Act 1957.

■ DIY 2.1.3

In order to revise your knowledge of the most important health and safety laws, complete the following sentences with the missing words. It is advisable to write out the whole sentence so that it can be used as evidence of understanding.

1 The Health and Safety at Work Act (_ _ _ _ _ _) is designed to bring together all the previous legislation and make _ _ _ _ _ out of it.

2 The basic idea of the Act is that there should be a joint effort by _ _ _ _ _ _ _ _ _ and _ _ _ _ _ _ _ _ _ to provide a safe and healthy _ _ _ _ _ _ _ environment.

3 The employer has to provide safe:
   a _ _ _ _ _ _ _ _ _ and _ _ _ _ _ _ _ of work
   b working conditions and _ _ _ _ _ _ _ _ arrangements and facilities for welfare
   c use, _ _ _ _ _ _ _ _, transport and _ _ _ _ _ _ _ _ of substances and articles
   d means of access _ _ and _ _ _ _ work.

4 Employees are responsible for:
   a taking care of their _ _ _ safety
   b the safety of other _ _ _ _ _ _ affected by their actions
   c co-operating with _ _ _ _ _ _ _ _ _ _ and any other persons involved in carrying out _ _ _ _ _ _ under this law.

5 The HASAWA includes the _ _ _ _ _ _ _ _ _ _ _ at Work Regulations 1989 and the Reporting of Injuries, Diseases and _ _ _ _ _ _ _ _ _ Occurrences Regulations 1985 (RIDDOR).

6 The _ _ _ _ _ _ _, Shops and Railways Premises Act stipulates working requirements and informs employees of their _ _ _ _ _ _.

7 This Act states specific requirements, such as:
   a adequate floor _ _ _ _ _ for each employee
   b temperature _ _ _ _ _ 16°C and a thermometer displayed
   c adequate _ _ _ _ _ _ _ _ _ _ _ _ without draught
   d adequate, separate _ _ _ _ _ _ _
   e washing facilities with _ _ _ and cold _ _ _ _ _
   f soap and clean _ _ _ _ _ _ facilities
   g fresh _ _ _ _ _ _ _ _ water
   h facilities to _ _ _ _ and _ _ _ clothes
   i isolation of _ _ _ _ _ machinery
   j safe and _ _ _ _ _ floors and _ _ _ _ _ _ _ _ _
   k machinery or correct procedures to _ _ _ _ heavy weights
   l chairs provided for _ _ _ _ _ _ _ _ _ who _ _ _ _ _ to do their work
   m availability of _ _ _ _ _ _ _ first-aid staff
   n adequately stocked _ _ _ _ _ _-_ _ _ boxes
   o machine _ _ _ _ _ _ where necessary
   p clear _ _ _ _ _ _ _ _ _ and fire _ _ _ _ _

    q fire drills/assembly _ _ _ _ _ _ brought to notice of all _ _ _ _ _
    r adequate fire _ _ _ _ _ _ _ _ _ _ _ _ _ in working order.

8 Under this Act the Information for _ _ _ _ _ _ _ _ _ Regulations 1989
    provide employers with a _ _ _ _ _ _ that has to be displayed _ _ _ _ _ _ _ in
    all offices.

9 The poster informs employees of their _ _ _ _ _ _ and gives information
    detailing the employees' _ _ _ _ _ enforcing authority and the address of
    the local employment _ _ _ _ _ _ _ service.

Control of Substances Hazardous to Health (COSHH)

A wide range of substances, from chemicals used in industrial
processes to cleaning preparations or even natural substances like
fungus, are capable of damaging health. In all types of business –
factories, farms, leisure activities, offices, shops, to name but a few –
workers' health can be at risk from the hazardous substances staff
encounter from day to day if the right precautions are not taken. There
are essential requirements for controlling exposure to hazardous
substances and employers are responsible for protecting people who
might be affected by these substances.

The basic principles of occupational hygiene are listed below.
Employers must:

1 Assess both the risk to health arising from workplace exposure to
   hazardous substances and decide upon what precautions are
   needed.
2 Introduce appropriate, effective measures to prevent, or adequately
   control, the exposure.
3 Ensure that control measures are used, that equipment is properly
   maintained and procedures observed.
4 In some cases monitor workers' exposure and carry out appropriate
   health checks.
5 Inform, instruct and train employees about the risks and
   precautions to be taken.

Substances that are hazardous to health include substances labelled as
dangerous, for example very toxic, toxic, harmful, irritant or corrosive
substances. Agricultural pesticides and other chemicals used on farms
and substances with occupational exposure limits are also classified as
hazardous to health. These substances may also include harmful micro-

organisms and substantial quantities of dust – indeed any material, mixture or compound used at work, or arising from work activities, which can harm people's health.

Figure 2.6 shows some signs you may have already seen indicating a warning about hazardous substances.

Employers have to ensure that the exposure of employees to hazardous substances is prevented or adequately controlled. The employer has to decide which control measures are required for the employees' workplace in order to deal effectively with any hazardous substances that may be present. This may mean preventing exposure by:

1 removing the hazardous substance by changing the process;
2 substituting with a safe or safer substance, or using it in a safer form.

Where this is not possible then they must control exposure by, for example:

1 totally enclosing the process;
2 using partial enclosure and extraction equipment;
3 general ventilation;
4 using safe systems of work and handling procedures.

It is the employer's responsibility to choose the method of controlling exposure. The use of personal protective equipment – for example,

Fig 2.6 Hazardous substance symbols

respirators, dust masks and protective clothing – can be used as a means of protection in those situations only when other measures cannot control exposure.

The employer has an obligation to ensure that all control measures are kept in efficient working order and good repair. Controls should be examined and tested regularly and respirators and breathing apparatus also have to be examined frequently. The employer should monitor the exposure of workers in certain cases, for example:

1 Where there could be serious risks to health if control measures were to fail or deteriorate.
2 If they cannot be sure that exposure limits are not being exceeded.
3 Where they cannot be sure that particular control measures are working properly.

It may be the case that medical examinations have to be carried out. The services of a doctor, trained nurse or trained supervisor could be used to check employees for effects such as severe dermatitis, or for asking questions about breathing difficulties if the work involves substances known to cause asthma. A simple record must be kept of any examinations carried out.

It is the employer's responsibility to keep their employees informed about:

1 the risks arising from their work
2 the precautions to be taken

and, if carried out:

1 the results of monitoring
2 the results of health surveillance.

■ DIY 2.1.4

Make a list of any hazardous substances you use whilst at work. Discuss this list with other members of your group also including the precautions you have to take to prevent injury or accidents. Write a short summary of your discussion. Take a photocopy of the illustration on page 37 showing types of protective clothing. On a separate sheet of paper write out why each of these items may be required.

▶ *What type of protective clothing might be used?*

Depending upon the type of materials you, or other members of staff, deal with it may be a requirement to wear protective clothing. This may be a simple apron or overall to prevent you from getting dirty or it may be a hard helmet, protective footwear or perhaps goggles to prevent injury if an accident occurred. It is important that you know where protective clothing is kept and how to use it properly. The clothing must be maintained and cleaned according to instructions and always replaced in the correct location.

It may be the case that it is your job to give out protective clothing to members of staff or people visiting your company. This may be carried out on a booking in and out basis or the clothing may be available for them to help themselves. However, it is important that this clothing is worn at all times and that visitors are informed of the rules and regulations regarding protective clothing operated by your employer for the visitor's safety.

▶ *Are the health and safety requirements likely to change?*

The answer to this is most certainly 'yes'. Our surroundings continually change and therefore the guidelines and legislation set out by the government, and more recently the European Union, will also be adapted to take into account the changes in our working environment.

Eye protection must be worn Wear hard hat Wear ear protectors

Respirators must be worn in this area Protective footwear must be worn Hand protection must be worn

Fig 2.7 Requirements for safety clothing

It is useful to note the most recently implemented EU directives that now act as part of the UK health and safety legislation and regulations:

1 Introduction of measures to encourage improvements in the safety and health of workers at work – 89/391/EEC.

2 Minimum health and safety requirements for the use by workers of personal protective equipment at the workplace (third individual Directive within the meaning of Article 16(1) of Directive 89/391/EEC) – 89/656/EEC.

3 Minimum health and safety requirements for the use of work equipment by workers at work (second individual Directive within the meaning of Article 16(1) of Directive 89/391/EEC) – 89/655/EEC.

4 Minimum health and safety requirements for work with display screen equipment (fifth individual Directive within the meaning of Article 16(1) 87/391/EEC) – 90/270/EEC.

5 Minimum health and safety requirements for the manual handling of loads where there is a risk particularly of back injury to workers (fourth individual Directive within the meaning of Article 16(1) of Directive 89/656/EEC) – 90/269/EEC.

▶ *How should you lift and handle materials?*

Lifting and handling everyday working materials will cause no concern and can be dealt with on an everyday basis. However, it is important that when dealing with materials that are heavy or awkward to move that you use the correct procedure for this. Firstly, you may need help and this may come in the shape of a trolley or another person. If an item is far too heavy to lift then it may be the case that arrangements can be made with the caretakers to move the item for you. A written request for this may have to be made.

When lifting heavy items yourself you must take care to follow the correct procedures.

1 Bend your knees and take the strain on your legs not your back.
2 Lift smoothly and do not jerk.
3 Keep the weight close to your body.

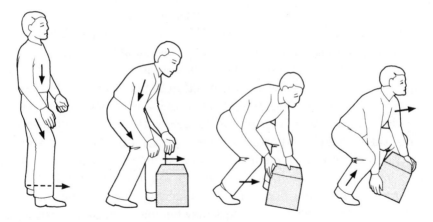

Fig 2.8 Correct method for lifting heavy items

4 Stand upright and do not lean sideways.
5 Keep your spine straight.
6 Use trolleys and other aids if available.
7 If in doubt GET HELP, or use mechanical aid.
8 Realise your limitations and do not risk your health.

The majority of back injuries are caused by people lifting heavy items incorrectly. Follow these procedures and you will use the strength of your legs to lift the item and not the weakness of your back.

▶ *What is correct handling?*

The type of handling and storage will depend upon the kind of stock and the size of the business or training centre. Large organisations will have a stockroom with specialist staff employed purely to take charge of the stock. A small organisation may only have a stock cupboard with one person in charge of the key.

Every item of stock must be stored neatly and be easily accessible when required. Shelves should be labelled so that it is easy to find what is needed, and the stockroom or cupboard should always be locked. It is important that the storage area is kept dry at all times to prevent paper-based items from becoming damp and going mouldy. Large or heavy items should be kept low so that lifting is not required and when new stock arrives it should be placed at the back or at the bottom so that the older stock is used first.

It is important that you treat hazardous stock with care. Any liquids that are toxic, inflammable or give off fumes, for example thinners, glue or duplicating fluid, must be kept in a separate area and you must never smoke in this area or in the stockroom itself. It is also very important that you are aware of the action to take to prevent accidents and to be able to carry out remedial action if an accident does occur. If you identify any hazards, or problems arise with storing certain stock items, this should be reported to your supervisor or the health and safety representative immediately. Likewise if damage occurs to any stock while it is being stored, this should be reported – it may still be under guarantee and the supplier could arrange for exchange or repair, or alternatively the business may be able to make an insurance claim.

■ DIY 2.1.5

You have been asked to set up a small area for stationery items. You have to decide whether you are going to place the items listed below on a shelf at the top, middle or bottom of the cupboard. Make three lists under the headings of top, middle and bottom, and identify the items you would place in each position by using their stock number.

ITEMS

10 reams A4 typing paper (white) – PA4W

1 gallon duplicating fluid – DF1

20 reams A4 typing paper (headed) – PA4H

4 staplers – ST10

10 boxes staples – ST5

2 boxes A4 carbon paper – CP06

1 ream A3 red poster paper – PA3PR

1 large box photocopier toner – PCT041

2 small boxes elastic bands – EBS2

1 ream A3 white card – PA3CW

10 red pens – RP1

5 reams A4 typing paper (yellow) PA4Y

20 typewriter cartridges – TWCB1

5 small boxes paperclips – PCS1

1 typewriter – TWE1065

45 blue pens – BP1

1 ink duplicator – IDE1066

1 litre glue – 1LG

Completing Element 2.1

To complete this element on contributing to the prevention of hazards in the workplace you will need to put all DIY tasks in your folder and carry out a final assessment.

Competence must be proven dealing with:

- faults in mains supplies
- faults in equipment
- obstructions to safe passageways
- hazardous substances
- faulty storage
- hazardous equipment
- unsuitable positioning and use of furniture

This must follow instructions provided by the organisation to ensure compliance with manufacturers' recommendations, legal requirements and good working practices.

Claiming credit

Once you have completed your final assessment, you will need to write in your record book or folder how, when, where and what you have done to prove that you are competent.

The following is an example of how one trainee completed this claim:

While on work placement at Coopers & Co for 3 weeks I worked in the Personnel Department, where I kept my work area tidy and stored away equipment I had used safely. My supervisor showed me how to use the photocopier, franking machine, guillotine and other office equipment properly and I followed these instructions at all times. I did not recognise any hazards at

41

Cooper and Co, but did complete a task where I had to make recommendations for the prevention of accidents in the workplace (see work folder). If I had identified a hazard I would have reported this verbally to my supervisor immediately.

I always follow the correct procedures for lifting heavy items and know how to stack/store business items safely. These were kept in a walk-in cupboard on labelled shelves with heavy items kept at the bottom. I never used equipment at work or at the training centre that I was not authorised to use and I am aware of the HASAWA and other legislation regarding employers and employees (see work folder for evidence). When I was at Coopers I told my supervisor that it was unsafe to keep white spirit in the store room and explained that it was flammable, it was removed immediately and placed in a separate area where it could not cause a hazard. Also, in my part-time job at a newsagent I am aware that I am not, by law, allowed to sell solvents or adhesives to people under the age of 18 years.

■ Element 2.2
CONTRIBUTE TO THE LIMITATION OF DAMAGE TO PERSONS OR PROPERTY IN THE EVENT OF AN ACCIDENT OR EMERGENCY

Performance criteria

- *Established procedures for dealing with identified fires and emergencies are promptly and correctly followed*
- *Dangerous occurrences are reported promptly and accurately to an authorised person*
- *Injuries involving individuals are reported promptly and accurately to competent first-aider or authorised person and appropriate interim support maintained when necessary to minimise further injury*
- *Relevant reporting procedures are implemented promptly and accurately*

Common forms of accident or health emergency include fire, flood, risk of explosion, toxic fumes and accidents. In any of these events it is important that you know the correct procedure to follow to minimise the emergency and act efficiently. The procedures you may need to follow in any of these incidents include evacuation, activating alarms, detaching equipment from mains supplies and reporting accidents correctly. It is vital that you understand your own limitations when dealing with emergencies and that you know when and how to contact help if necessary.

▶ *What are the relevant procedures to follow in an emergency?*

A busy organisation is likely to be crowded with staff, visitors and customers and it is important that in order to protect these people and the organisation's property much thought is given to fire and accident procedures. If the organisation stores inflammable, toxic or perhaps corrosive materials then even more attention should be paid to emergency procedures and every member of staff should know exactly what to do in the event of an emergency. Staff will be expected to escort visitors or customers who are unfamiliar with the evacuation procedure from the building.

When you join an organisation as a new member of staff you should undergo induction training which will show you what to do in the event of an emergency, how to recognise or sound the alarm and how to follow the evacuation procedure. It is important for you to know how to raise the alarm, who to contact in the event of an emergency and how to evacuate yourself and possibly others from the building as quickly and safely as possible. You must know the quickest route to follow out of the building and at which point outside you should assemble for a name call.

■ DIY 2.2.1

On a piece of A3 paper draw a plan of the area in which you work. This may be a large office, training room, library or one floor of a small organisation. On your plan show the following:

- doors
- fire extinguishers
- furniture
- sand buckets or water buckets
- fire escapes
- sprinklers
- fire alarms
- smoke detectors.

Keep this plan as you will need it for the next DIY task.

▶ *Fire precautions*

Fire precautions must always be strictly followed. There must be an effective means of giving a fire warning – for example, a loud ringing bell or hooter that all staff recognise as being a fire alarm. Fire-fighting equipment must also be available and must be maintained properly so it is always ready for use. Familiarise yourself with the type of fire-fighting equipment available, in particular the different coloured fire extinguishers that can be used for different types of fire.

All fire exits and fire doors must be **marked**. A fire door must **never be left open** – as the purpose of this door is to hold the fire back to give you more time to escape, it will be of little use if it is left open. Fire exits must be clearly marked as members of staff, visitors and customers will need to find them in order to get out of the building in an emergency. Fire exits must **never be locked** and must be **kept clear at all times**; they should never be blocked by items such as boxes or office equipment that is not in use.

All fire procedures should be displayed on a noticeboard and brought to the attention of all members of staff regularly. Most organisations have details of fire procedures in each separate room giving details of the assembly point and the quickest route out of the building from that particular room. Remember that you should never smoke in a non-smoking area and you should never put lighted cigarette ends in to a waste-paper basket. If you work in a non-smoking area it means just that, and do not be tempted to smoke in toilets or quiet areas as this is likely to offend other members of staff and could be dangerous.

▶ *What types of fire extinguishers are there?*

It is important that you understand the use of each of these fire extinguishers and the fires for which they are designed. There are six commonly used fire extinguishers, as detailed in Fig 2.9. In the future some of these will change due to the Montreal protocol on environmental issues.

There are other types of fire-fighting equipment that may be available for use in an emergency. Equipment such as **fire blankets, sand buckets, sprinklers, smoke detectors, hosepipes** and **fire alarms** are there to protect you in the event of a fire and to give you an

FIRE EXTINGUISHERS		
Colour	**Contents**	**Use for fires**
GREEN	Halon, BCF	Paper, wood, fabric, liquids, fat, paint, spirits, oils, gases (such as oxygen, butane and propane), and electrical fires.
CHROME	Gas	As above.
CREAM	Foam	As above, but not electrical fires.
BLACK	CO_2	Liquids, fat, paint, spirits, oil, gases and electrical fires.
BLUE	Powder	Metals, such as magnesium, on fire.
RED	Water	Paper, wood and fabric fires.

Fig 2.9 Types of fire extinguisher

opportunity to prevent a large fire breaking out. However, never under any circumstances risk your own life by trying to tackle a fire without giving the alarm signal first.

DIY 2.2.2

You have already drawn a plan of the area where you work. Check that you have put on it all the fire-fighting equipment including sand buckets and so on. On your plan colour in each extinguisher according to its colour. Now add an A4 sheet to your plan giving details of the type(s) of fire for which each different coloured extinguisher in your work area could be used.

You will also note that each extinguisher carries details on how to operate it in an emergency. Add these details to your A4 sheet including diagrams to clarify the information.

▶ *Why have an evacuation procedure?*

Remember that an organisation may have to be evacuated not only in case of fire. It may be that there has been an explosion, accident, flood or bomb alert, or perhaps a suspicious package has been found. Fire, police or ambulance may have to be called, but do not do this yourself unless you are the person who is responsible – it is likely to be your supervisor's or switchboard operator's responsibility to call the emergency services.

In the event of an evacuation customers and visitors and possibly other members of staff will need help evacuating the building as quickly and safely as possible. It is important for you to act quickly, but to keep calm and never panic. There will be a set procedure to follow in order to evacuate each office, department, floor and so on, and this will include making sure that no one is left behind.

Every person in the work area should be encouraged to leave the building quickly but not to panic and run. In the event of a fire never use the lift when evacuating as heat, smoke and fire is likely to be sucked upwards through the lift shaft, also the lift may break down and leave you stranded. It will be your supervisor's responsibility to ensure that all members of staff have left the building and it is likely that they will do this by carrying out a name call. In order to help your supervisor, make sure that you report to them as soon as you have left the building so that they know you are out of the building and safe. Never re-enter the building until you have been told it is safe to do so and be on the lookout for other members of staff who have not reported in.

It is very important for you to understand that fire exits, fire doors and fire-fighting equipment are there to help you in the event of fire. They must never be hidden or obstructed in any way and if access is blocked this should be reported to your supervisor immediately. It is too late once someone has been injured or possibly killed.

In the event of a fire it is useful for you to know how to use the fire-fighting equipment, but if it is a real emergency never risk your own life by trying to tackle the fire. It is more important that you sound the alarm and evacuate the building along with other members of staff and leave the fire-fighting to the experts.

■ DIY 2.2.3

Do you know the evacuation procedures for your organisation? Write a brief report explaining the emergency evacuation procedures in use. If you do not know what these are now is a good time for you to find out. Also include information regarding the emergency services, who takes the responsibility for calling them and how you would go about reporting an emergency yourself.

▶ What is 'first aid'?

In the event of a customer, visitor or another member of staff being injured or taken ill it is important to have access to a first-aid box so that treatment may be given, perhaps whilst waiting for an ambulance to arrive. If a first-aid box is not required it is still important to know how to make the person comfortable and safe whilst awaiting help.

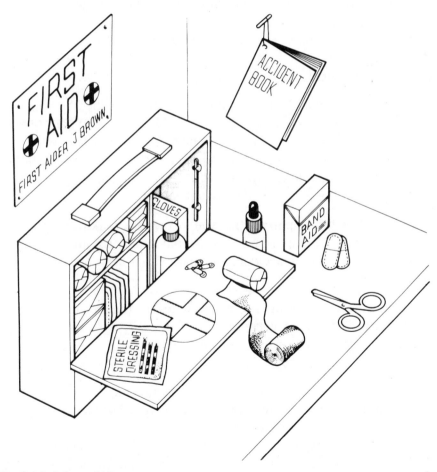

Fig 2.10 A first-aid box

There should be qualified first-aid staff available who will be able to use the contents of an adequately stocked first-aid box. In a large organisation it is likely that first-aid staff will carry pagers so that they may be contacted quickly and given details of the incident.

The first-aid box should contain:

1 Individually wrapped sterile dressings of assorted sizes.
2 Sterile eye pads with attachment.
3 Individually wrapped triangular bandages.
4 Safety pins.
5 Medium/large/extra large size sterile, individually wrapped, unmedicated wound dressings.
6 Cleaning tissues, cotton wool, antiseptic, disposable gloves.
7 Disposable wipes.
8 Guidance notes on the use of the first-aid box.
9 Reorder forms.
10 List of contents.

The first-aid box should only contain items that a qualified first-aid person has been trained to use. They should not contain medication, for example aspirin, of any kind as the first-aider is not a trained doctor. The first-aid box should be kept in a central place for all staff to use and it is reasonable to expect that at least one member of staff in your organisation will have had first-aid training.

As an employee it is important that you follow safe working practices. If you see a potential hazard report it to your supervisor immediately before somebody has an accident and make sure that you are aware of the following:

1 who has had first-aid training in your office or training centre
2 where the first-aid box is kept
3 who to contact in the event of an emergency
4 how to record/report accidents.

Unless you have been trained to use the first-aid box yourself do not try to treat an injured person. Summon someone who is trained as quickly as possible. If the accident has been caused as a result of a broken fixture or fitting, or something which has been spilled on the floor, make sure that you clean up or clear up so that the accident spot is removed as soon as possible.

It is important that you do not panic – you must remain calm and clear headed. This will reassure anyone who has been injured and give them confidence that help is on hand and you know what you are doing.

▶ *What should you do if someone has an electric shock?*

To help a person suffering from electric shock:

1 Shout for help.
2 Switch off power.
3 If power cannot be switched off immediately pull or push casualty clear with a broom or wooden chair.
4 Unless wearing thick, rubber-soled boots, stand on lino, rubber or wood.
5 Do not touch casualty with bare hands unless power is switched off.
6 If casualty is breathing place them in the recovery position.
7 If casualty is not breathing apply rescue breathing, check pulse, and if absent, apply heart compression.

What are 'rescue breathing', 'heart compression' and the 'recovery position'?

Immediate and proper examination and treatment of injuries may save life – and are essential to reduce pain and help injured people make a quick recovery. All organisations must have an appropriate level of first-aid treatment available by law. An appointed person should take charge in an emergency, call the ambulance and look after the first-aid equipment. The first-aid box should contain guidance on the treatment of injured people, in particular how to keep someone alive by artificial respiration (rescue breathing), how to control bleeding and how to deal with an unconscious person.

There are government guidelines that cover 4 main areas of resuscitation:

1 **Recognise a lack of oxygen.**
   This may arise from electric shock, drowning, poisoning, head injury, gassing, etc, and can cause unconsciousness, noisy or heavy breathing, or abnormal skin colour.

2 **Act at once.**
   Switch off electricity, gas, etc, remove casualty from danger and send someone for help. Get a clear airway and remove any

1 **RECOGNISE A LACK OF OXYGEN**

Arising from

ELECTRIC SHOCK
DROWNING
POISONING
HEAD INJURY
GASSING etc

May be causing

UNCONSCIOUSNESS
NOISY OR
NO BREATHING
ABNORMAL COLOUR

2 **ACT AT ONCE**

SWITCH OFF ELECTRICITY, GAS, etc.,
REMOVE CASUALTY FROM DANGER
SEND SOMEBODY FOR HELP

GET A CLEAR AIRWAY ...
REMOVE ANY OBSTRUCTION ... then

LIFT JAW

TILT HEAD BACK

BREATHING MAY RESTART ... IF NOT ...

3 **APPLY RESCUE BREATHING**

START WITH FOUR
QUICK DEEP BREATHS

SEAL NOSE AND
BLOW INTO MOUTH

or

SEAL MOUTH AND
BLOW INTO NOSE

KEEP FINGERS ON JAW
BUT CLEAR OF THROAT

MAINTAIN HEAD
POSITION

AFTER BLOWING INTO
MOUTH or NOSE,
WATCH CASUALTY'S
CHEST FALL AS
YOU BREATHE IN

REPEAT EVERY 5 SECS

**AFTER FIRST FOUR
BREATHS TEST FOR
RECOVERY SIGNS**

1. PULSE PRESENT?
2. PUPILS LESS LARGE?
3. COLOUR IMPROVED?

PULSE POINTS

4 **IF NONE, COMBINE RESCUE BREATHING & HEART COMPRESSION**

PLACE CASUALTY
ON A FIRM SURFACE

COMMENCE
HEART COMPRESSION

HEEL OF HAND ONLY
ON LOWER HALF OF
BREASTBONE
OTHER HAND ON TOP,
FINGERS OFF CHEST

BREASTBONE

HEART

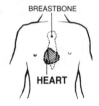

KEEP ARMS STRAIGHT
AND ROCK FORWARD
TO DEPRESS CHEST
1½ INCHES (4 cm)

APPLY 15 COMPRESSIONS
ONE PER SECOND ... then
GIVE TWO BREATHS

RE-CHECK PULSE ...
IF STILL ABSENT
CONTINUE WITH
15 COMPRESSIONS
TO TWO BREATHS

IF PULSE RETURNS
CEASE COMPRESSIONS
BUT CONTINUE
RESCUE BREATHING

Fig 2.11 'Emergency Aid' poster (Reproduced courtesy of RoSPA)

obstruction. Tilt the casualty's head back and lift their jaw. Breathing may now restart.

3 **Apply rescue breathing.**
   Start with four quick, deep breaths, seal nose and blow into mouth. Keep fingers on jaw but clear of throat. Maintain head position. After blowing into mouth or nose watch casualty's chest fall as you breathe in. Repeat every 5 seconds.

   After first four breaths test for recovery signs such as: pulse present; pupils less large; colour improved. The pulse points can be checked by feeling the wrist or neck.

4 **If none, combine rescue breathing and heart compression.**
   Place casualty on a firm surface and place heel of hand only on lower half of breastbone with other hand on top keeping fingers off the chest. Keep arms straight and rock forward to depress chest 4 cm. Apply 15 compressions, 1 per second, then give 2 breaths. Recheck pulse and if still absent continue with 15 compressions to 2 breaths. If pulse returns cease compressions but continue rescue breathing.

A member of staff who has had training in first aid will know how to carry out rescue breathing and heart compression if this is necessary. However, such action will only be required in extreme cases such as those listed above. In the case of fainting, unconsciousness, epileptic fit and so on, where the casualty requires time to come round, the recovery position (Fig 2.12) should be used so that they may recover in a comfortable position where they cannot cause harm to themselves.

If the casualty is lying on their back:

1 Place their right arm slightly under their body, lean over them and pull them towards you so that they roll on to their front.

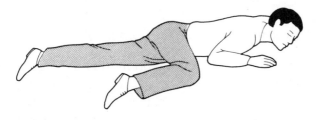

Fig 2.12 The recovery position

2 Move the casualty's head so it is on its side facing you and bend their left arm upwards so that the hand is placed flat on the floor by their face.

3 Bend the casualty's nearest leg upward at the knee so that the body is turned slightly and is supported by the leg.

4 Cover the casualty with a blanket if in a cold place and stay with them until they recover or further help arrives.

▶ *How could you prevent machine accidents?*

There are special rules for machines used in offices. Some are classed as dangerous machines, which people can use only after full instruction and sufficient training under close supervision. Examples include packaging equipment, guillotines and other cutting equipment.

Before you use such a machine make sure:

1 You know how to switch it off before you switch it on.

2 All guards are fitted and working.

3 All materials are clear of working parts of the machine.

4 Area around machine is clean, tidy and free from obstruction.

5 Your supervisor is told at once if you think a machine is faulty.

6 You are wearing appropriate protective clothing.

Never:

1 Use a machine unless you are authorised and trained to do so.

2 Try to clean a machine when plugged in or switched on.

3 Use a machine with a danger sign or tag attached.

4 Wear dangling chains, loose clothing, gloves, rings or long hair that could get caught in moving parts.

5 Distract people who are using machines.

▶ *How should accidents be reported?*

If an accident has occurred it is important this is reported. An accident report form can be used to give details of the accident. It is vital that this form is completed after an accident, so that if the same accident occurs again and again the trend will be identified and can be put right. If, for example, a number of staff had all injured themselves falling over a broken drawer in the filing cabinet then it would be the employer's responsibility to have the drawer repaired before another accident occurred. There is an example of an accident report form on page 31.

All accidents at work should be reported to your supervisor and recorded in writing using an accident report form. The reasons for this are:

1 The information can be used to investigate the cause of the accident and help to reduce hazards in the future.

2 A written record of the accident may be required by law.

3 The injury, no matter how small, should be given attention. It may happen that what seems to be a small injury may give rise to serious problems later.

DIY 2.2.4

Copy a page from an accident report book or ask your supervisor for an accident report form. Complete this form with the following details:

At 10.00 am today the accounts secretary, Zoe Thorner, who was celebrating her 18th birthday, tripped over a lead in the secretarial section of the Personnel Department. The lead was trailing across the floor from the word processor to the electric socket. Charlotte Vandy was with her at the time and was able to administer first aid to Zoe's twisted ankle. Charlotte also had to unplug the word processor quickly as the electric lead was ripped partly from the plug and the socket was making a strange noise. Zoe was taken home to 198 Tremlow Road, Wolverhampton, and is expected to have the next 4–5 days off work.

On a separate piece of paper explain:

● Who you think caused this accident.
● Why Charlotte unplugged the word processor.

Completing Element 2.2

To complete this element on contributing to the limitation of damage to persons or property in the event of an accident or emergency you will need to put all DIY tasks in your folder and carry out a final assessment.

Competence must be proven in dealing with: emergencies such as fire, flood, risk of explosion, toxic fumes and accidents. Procedures such as evacuation, activating alarm systems, detaching equipment from mains supplies and reporting accidents must be covered.

Claiming credit

Once you have completed your final assessment, you will need to write in your record book or folder how, when, where and what you have done to prove that you are competent.

The following is an example of how one trainee completed this claim:

When I first attended the training centre I was given an induction training for 2 days and I was taken through the procedures for dealing with fires and emergencies. This included how to raise the alarm and who to report dangerous occurrences to. I was told to contact the centre's switchboard operator to summon a first-aider and was shown how to put a casualty into the recovery position and carry out rescue breathing. I was able to practise this on another trainee and used a dummy to practise rescue breathing.

During induction training I was also shown the different fire extinguishers and how to use one of them, the location of fire-fighting equipment and alarms. I have completed tasks where I have drawn a plan of my working area including all safety equipment, doors, furniture, fire extinguishers, etc., which included details of the centre's evacuation procedures and a completed accident report form.

■ Element 2.3
CONTRIBUTE TO MAINTAINING THE SECURITY OF THE WORKPLACE AND ITS CONTENTS

Performance criteria

- *Security procedures are correctly followed*
- *Actions taken to deal with security risks are within limits of own authority*
- *Potential security risks outside own authority are reported to the appropriate person*

Whether you work for a large or small organisation, the way in which you deal with visitors is very important. A visitor is anyone that comes to see you or your colleagues and does not work in your department or organisation on an everyday basis.

This could be someone from:

- another department or section
- another branch
- another company or other organisation
- a customer or client
- people attending a meeting
- people delivering or collecting items
- people attending an interview or asking about vacancies.

Some of these visitors will be expected and others will be unexpected. The way in which these visitors are greeted and your attitude towards them is very important. However, whilst creating the correct company image you must be constantly aware of security and ensure that information is not given out to the wrong person in the name of politeness. Security relating to people, equipment and information should always be treated as a priority.

▶ *In terms of security, how should visitors be treated?*

When receiving visitors you should always try to be:

- polite
- courteous
- positive
- friendly
- helpful
- patient.

However, to protect the security of your organisation you must also be prepared to be:

- tactful
- diplomatic
- firm
- direct
- assertive.

Above all, you should always be on the lookout for anything suspicious or out of place, and be prepared to act on your suspicions by telling an appropriate authority, such as your supervisor, as quickly as possible.

Unless a caller is authorised, no confidential information should be given (verbally or written) to them. Confidential information includes personal details of staff, their exact whereabouts and appointments schedule, financial details about the organisation and its customers, details of future projects or contracts, etc. If you are unsure whether information may be passed on or not, always check with your supervisor.

■ DIY 2.3.1

Make a list of the types of visitors that come to your workplace or training centre. What is the purpose of their visit?

Many companies now have strict rules about the security of the building. Callers and visitors may not be allowed to walk round the offices without a member of staff accompanying them. Usually a member of staff will collect the visitor from reception and accompany them to the meeting office. A receptionist should not leave reception unattended in case another visitor arrives and is left to wander round the building unsupervised.

In the majority of organisations visitors are still allowed to find their own way to the office they require, but care must be taken to ensure the visitor is given clear directions so that they do not get lost. When the business is complete and the visitor wishes to leave, the member of staff with them should make sure that they know how to get out of the building. There may be a quicker route from the building than the one by which they entered or the visitor may be required to leave the building through reception so that their name can be logged out of the visitors' register.

Some organisations rely solely on the visitors' register as a means to record visitors' details and the nature of their business. In some cases, such as government offices or high-risk areas, the visitor may need to have their bag, briefcase or belongings searched before being allowed to enter the building. The visitor may even be required to leave items at reception, and these should be labelled with the visitor's name and kept in a safe and secure place until their return. In some extreme cases a body search may be carried out. Any company carrying out such procedures is likely to employ specialist staff such as security guards to attend to these duties.

VISITORS' REGISTER						
DATE						
Identity Badge No.	Time in	Time out	Name	Company	Appointment with	Action Taken

Fig 2.13 Visitors' register

Some organisations issue visitors with a badge or pass at reception to show that they have been authorised to visit the building. The badge or pass should be returned when the visitor leaves the building. Plastic badges bearing the name of the organisation and the word 'visitor' are often used, and may be numbered for extra security. Badges with a blank space for the visitor's name to be inserted are also popular and provide a more personal touch. Special reception registers are available that allow visitors to enter details of their business alongside their name, a copy of the name portion of the register is then torn out and inserted into a small plastic holder, to be used as a badge.

■ DIY 2.3.2

What security measures are taken when people visit your workplace or training centre? If there are none, do you think there should be? How would you be expected to deal with an unauthorised person? Explain your answers fully.

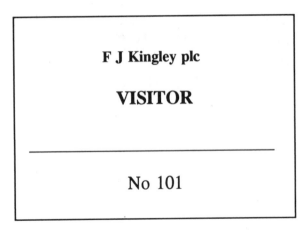

Fig 2.14 Visitor's badge

▶ *How can equipment be made secure?*

A busy office is likely to be filled with expensive equipment such as computers, word processors, printers, photocopiers, fax machines, telephones, and so on. It is unlikely that a thief would try to steal large equipment such as photocopiers or mainframe computers. However, smaller equipment such as word processors that can be dismantled into a number of smaller, separate parts may be the target for a thief. It is usual practice to lock an office that is to be left unattended, not only to secure equipment but perhaps personal items such as coats and handbags.

Equipment should be labelled with an indelible ink pen stating the name or initials of the organisation together with the postcode. If the equipment is stolen but later found by the police it can be easily traced back to its rightful owner using this information. Small, valuable equipment such as a desk-top franking machine must always be locked away in a secure place unless it is being used. Most office equipment will carry a serial number and this should be noted when the equipment is first installed; by doing this the equipment can be identified if it is stolen.

▶ *How can information be made secure?*

All company files could be classed as confidential. Personal information, company reports, financial accounts or minutes from a business meeting should never be discussed with people outside the company. It is important to recognise that information dealt with on a daily, routine basis may be of interest to a rival company. A member of staff may be interested in a colleague's salary or perhaps their home address and telephone number. Therefore, it is important that you do not leave paperwork lying round the office, however innocent you may think it is.

To secure paper-based information make sure all files are kept in one place under lock and key. Folders containing sensitive information should be marked 'CONFIDENTIAL' and must not be left on a desk or lent out to unauthorised personnel, however nice and friendly they may seem. Dead files should never be put in a bin or skip – they should be shredded or incinerated so they are unreadable.

Confidential information held in a computer must also be protected. Passwords or keywords should be used to restrict access and protect information, and only authorised staff should know the password or keyword which should be changed regularly and never written down. Printouts should be kept in a folder marked confidential and disks should be kept locked away in a cupboard, not just locked in their disk box. Information stored on a computer database will also be covered by the Data Protection Act (*see* page 131 for more information).

■ DIY 2.3.3

Look around your working area and identify 3 potential security risks. These might include direct access to computer information, unlocked filing cabinets, doors left open, and so on. Write to your tutor or office supervisor and explain the risks you have identified together with details of how you think the risks could be prevented. Your work should cover at least one side of a piece of A4 paper.

▶ *How would you deal with a breach in security?*

A situation such as a member of staff being threatened, equipment being stolen or information about the company being leaked would all be treated as a breach in security. In any of these cases it is important that you know the correct procedure to follow. You may need to get assistance quickly if you have an aggressive, suspicious or unauthorised visitor – in this case you may need to contact your supervisor quickly, dial an internal emergency number to summon a security guard, or contact the police.

If you are suspicious of a person, or even another member of staff, who you think is, or has, been stealing from the organisation you must report this to your supervisor immediately. It is only by your quick action that further theft can be prevented. Also, remember that if you identify a potential security risk you must report this immediately so that something can be done about it. Make sure that you follow all security procedures properly and that potential security risks outside your own authority are reported to the appropriate person. Never under any circumstances risk injury to yourself and recognise your own scope for dealing with security risks.

Completing Element 2.3

To complete this element on contributing to maintaining the security of the workplace and its contents you will need to put all DIY tasks in your folder and carry out a final assessment.

Competence must be proven in dealing with the security for:

- people
- equipment
- information.

You must know how to deal with unauthorised persons and show that you are able to identify potential security risks. You must be familiar with your organisation's security and reporting procedures, and recognise your own scope and limitations for dealing with security risks.

Claiming credit

Once you have completed your final assessment, you will need to write in your record book or folder how, when, where and what you have done to prove that you are competent.

The following is an example of how one trainee completed this claim:

When I completed 3 weeks' work experience at Coopers & Co reception, I was told to issue all callers to the Company with a visitor's badge. The visitor's badge had a number on it and this was entered in the visitors' register alongside the name, company name and type of business. The visitor had to book out of the company and return the badge when they had finished. All visitors had to report to reception and no one was allowed in to the building unless they had an appointment; if they did not have one I would contact the relevant person and ask if they could see the visitor, or I would offer to make them an appointment. If an unauthorised person tried to enter the building I would call security on Extension 123 and tell them. I recognise that I could request a person not to enter the building but under no circumstances should I try to stop someone physically myself. I did not identify any potential security risks at Coopers and Co but if I had I would have reported these verbally to my supervisor. I have carried out a task in my training centre where I identified risks and wrote a report to my tutor with details of how they could be put right (see work folder).

I did not give unauthorised information to visitors or staff. At the end of each day the equipment was locked away or switched off and left secure.

UNIT 3

Operate and take care of equipment

■ **Element 3.1**
FOLLOW INSTRUCTIONS AND OPERATE EQUIPMENT

Performance criteria

- *Instructions are understood before operating equipment*
- *Operating procedures and techniques follow operating instructions*
- *Procedures for dealing with problems in operating equipment are followed correctly*

▶ *What type of equipment are you likely to operate?*

There will be many different types of machinery and equipment that you will be expected to operate whilst working in an organisation. It is important that you know exactly how to operate the equipment properly before trying to use it. In most companies you will get an induction programme which will probably include how to use the necessary equipment. If you do not, always ask your supervisor for a demonstration on how to use the machine and make sure you read all the instructions available, from the company and the manufacturer.

▶ *Photocopier*

If you have completed Unit 7, Element 7.2 you will already know what facilities are available on photocopiers. You should be able to cross-reference the work carried out for Unit 7 with this unit, but you will need to discuss this with your tutor.

The facilities available may include A4 and A3 copies, back-to-back copying, enlarging and reducing, collating and stapling, copying on to acetate for overhead projectors and many more. When working you will probably have access to a photocopier, the facilities available on it will depend on the size of your organisation and the uses of the machine.

■ DIY 3.1.1

You have a new junior starting in the office who will be working with you for the first 2 weeks. Write out a checklist for him to follow on how to use the photocopier. Make sure that you include any special instructions that your organisation has and check the manufacturer's instructions, if available. Include any health and safety points that he should be aware of.

▶ Computers and typewriters

Whenever you work in an office one of the most frequent tasks is to produce documents.

You will probably be required to use a machine to produce documents of your own and for others. Computers vary enormously in size and the facilities that they offer. There are two main parts to any computer system, the hardware and the software.

▶ What is hardware?

The hardware is the actual computer machinery: the screen (or VDU – visual display unit); keyboard; processor (or CPU – central processing unit); disk drives and the printer.

The CPU is the part of the machine which reads the information (data) and the disks in the disk drives store the information. The CPU will contain a hard disk (also called a fixed disk) which cannot be removed from the machine. It will also have one or two slots in the casing to insert floppy disks to store the information externally. The drives that contain the disks are usually called C for the hard drive, and A and B for the floppy disk drives. Other drives may be created but this is not important for this unit. You would only need to know about making extra drives if you intended becoming a computer technician or programmer.

Fig 3.1 Computer hardware with two boxes containing disks for software

▶ *What is software?*

Software is the program that makes the hardware work. The programs are supplied on floppy disks, which are usually 3.5" or 5.25" in diameter and are protected by a cover of either hard or soft plastic. The disk itself is visible and looks like a dark brown, smooth, circular piece of plastic – it should not be touched or it will be damaged. Programs are written in languages that the CPUs can understand. The most common of these computer languages are BASIC (Beginner's All-purpose Symbolic Instruction Code) and COBOL (COmmon Business Orientated Language). You will not need to understand these languages unless you intend to become a computer programmer. Most of the people who use computers do not understand how they work, only how to operate the programs which they use.

■ DIY 3.1.2

Look at the machinery that you use in your work or training centre. Make a list of all the hardware and software that you use. Do you know how to use all the hardware properly? Write out instructions on how to switch on and off your equipment. Number the points and make them short and easy to follow.

Most of the programs used in a business or college are loaded from the floppy disks to the hard drive. This is called installing a program. The program can then easily be used on a daily basis without having to reload it every time. Each time a program is loaded on to the hard drive it uses up space, and a hard drive will have a limited amount of space. Therefore it can only hold so many programs at one time. The number of programs held depends on the size of the program and the size of the hard drive.

▶ Looking after the equipment

On page 78 we discuss how to clean the parts of the computer. You should also check that the screen is placed at a comfortable distance from the keyboard, to make sure you do not suffer from eyestrain. Also make sure you alter the brightness of the screen to suit you, using the brightness control and the contrast control. The screen should be facing away from windows, or direct artificial light, to reduce the glare. If this is not possible, an anti-glare screen may be attached. There should be sufficient space around your keyboard to place your work and to use a mouse or joystick.

■ DIY 3.1.3

Make a health and safety checklist for equipment, including your computer (all parts), and your chair and desk. Type the list and check your own equipment and that of a friend. Does it meet all the requirements? An example is shown in Fig 3.2.

Equipment	Check	Yes	No	Suggested Alteration
desk	correct height			
	adjustable			
	enough space			
	correct light			

Fig 3.2 Health and safety checklist

▶ How should you look after your disks?

Floppy disks are fragile. They can easily be damaged and damage may result in losing all the information you have stored on them. The

65

information is stored on the disks in tracks, which are similar to the grooves on a record, each track having a circle which can hold a certain amount of information. Disks may be single-sided or double-sided. Double-sided disks can store information on both sides, therefore storing more information than single-sided disks. Disks can also be single or double density, the density of the disk referring to the amount of information that can be stored, if the disk is double density, twice as much information can be stored on it as on a single density disk. The speed at which the CPU runs will depend on which type of disk you can use. It is similar to a video recorder where if you halve the speed at which the tape runs through the machine, you can store twice as much.

The 5.25" disk covers are flexible plastic, but should never be bent. As mentioned earlier, all disks are protected by a plastic cover. The top of the disk is smooth and has no edges, while underneath three edges have been folded over and electronically 'stapled' in place. The exposed parts of the disk should be in the middle and an oval slot on one side. This oval slot is on the side which should be pushed first into the disk slot in the casing of the CPU.

The 3.5" disk is protected by a hard plastic cover which has an arrow printed on the front to indicate which way it should be inserted into

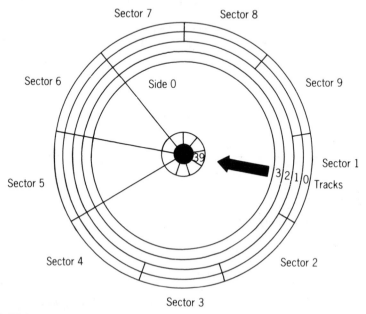

Fig 3.3 Disk track diagram

Fig 3.4 A 3.5" disk

the CPU disk drive. It also has a metal protection cover over the exposed part of the disk – slide it back carefully to see the disk.

Both these disks may also be called diskettes. Before any disk can be used for storing information it will need to be formatted (sometimes called initialising). Formatting a disk prepares it to accept information from the system you are running on your computer. It is usually done by using the 'format' command, but you will need to check with your supervisor or tutor before you carry out a format on equipment with which you are unfamiliar. If you format an existing disk all the information already stored on it will be lost, as formatting cleans the disk completely.

▶ *Protecting the information on your disk*

On the 5.25" disk you will see a small rectangular cut in the left-hand side. This is the write protection notch. If you do not want to put any further information on the disk or you want to make sure you do not delete any of the information you have on the disk, you can stick a label over the notch. This will then stop you from storing or deleting any further information, as the CPU will not accept changes to that disk.

On the 3.5" disk at the bottom right-hand corner at the back of the disk you will see a small plastic square that will slide up and down. In the up position, the disk would be write protected. (It is rather like breaking off the plastic square from the video tape cassette to stop anyone from recording over it.)

Another way of protecting information stored on a disk is by saving the file with a password or keyword. Before the CPU will allow you to look at the information stored or to delete the file it will be necessary to type in the password. If you use passwords, make sure you remember them. If you write them down, make sure it is somewhere that is not easily found by everyone else in the office. Check before starting your own system that your organisation does not have regulations regarding the use of passwords.

▶ *Labelling your disks*

To protect the exposed areas of the 5.25" disk you should place it in a paper cover and store all disks in a disk box. This may be a small box which can store 5–10 disks, or a desk-top box which can store many more. Each of the disks should be labelled, and it is useful to put the label in the corner which you hold when placing the disk into the CPU. When placed in the disk box the labels should be in the top left-hand corner.

Always write on the label *before* you stick it on to the disk. If you need to change the writing on the label of a 5.25" disk at a future date, you can use a fibre tipped pen, but do not use biro or pencil as the pressure of writing on the label may damage the disk.

▶ *Using your disks in the CPU*

To insert a 5.25" disk into the CPU, hold the label and insert the disk into the slot before pushing the lever down into position. To insert a 3.5" disk into the CPU, hold the disk in the right-hand corner and push it into the slot until it clicks down into place.

▶ *Protecting your disks from damage*

The disk box should be kept in a dry place which does not become too hot or cold and should not be exposed to extensive light. The disks should also be kept away from the top of the CPU, from telephones, electrical equipment, steel or any magnetic surface as these may corrupt your disk (even a steel knife and fork could corrupt a disk). A corrupted disk may mean that you will be unable to get your data back, but you should check with a computer technician as they will have access to special programs that can retrieve data or repair damaged disks. Data could also be lost through accidentally deleting a file, overloading or handling the disk.

■ DIY 3.1.4

Complete the following sentences as fully as possible to show that you understand computer equipment and terms.

1 The CPU is ....
2 Formatting is ....
3 A corrupted disk is one that ....
4 Disks should be protected by ....
5 Disk drives are usually called drive .... for the hard disk, and .... for the floppy disk drive. A second floppy disk drive would be called ....

Back-up copies. To reduce the chance of losing your data through a corrupted disk, it is usual to make 'back-up' copies. This means that you keep a copy of the data on a second disk. In some businesses there is a set procedure for making back-up copies, so check with your supervisor at work or ask your tutor how frequently you should make back-ups. Even hard disks may get corrupted so do not rely on keeping all your data on hard disk only. For this reason some businesses change their hard disks and have back-up copies of them, especially if they are dealing with a vast number of pieces of information every day.

■ DIY 3.1.5

Design a leaflet for two juniors, who will be working with you on work experience for three weeks, informing them of how to look after disks. Include handling, storage and protection, labelling, write protecting and backing-up. If possible type your leaflet, but otherwise make sure that it is suitable for use in the office, ie it should be formally presented. If you wish, use labelled diagrams to help explain the points made, or cut out pictures from a supplies catalogue to illustrate your leaflet.

▶ *Saving your data*

It is important to save your data regularly. If you are working all day on the same document, you may save it every half an hour or so. This is just to make sure that you do not lose all the work for example through someone accidentally switching off your computer or through an electrical power cut. Some programs remind you to save your work by flashing a message at you while you are working, and also by slowing the system down, so you save quickly to enable you to get on! Some programs will create a back-up for you and save automatically every 20 minutes or so.

To save a file it is necessary to give it a filename, which is used to recall the file when you wish to edit or change the information. The names you choose for files may depend on the organisation's policy or they may be entirely up to you. However, if the choice is yours try to have a system that is logical and easy to remember.

The filename will usually indicate the content of the file, and should contain no more than eight characters (preferably only letters as in some programs numbers and other characters have special meanings to the computer). Some databases are also particular about whether small letters or capital letters are typed. Therefore, if you decide to call your file JUMPERS, when you want to call the file back by entering the file name as jumpers it may not be able to find it. This is called 'case specific', because the computer is looking for a particular 'case', ie lower case instead of upper case letters.

The second part of the filename is called an extension. Your computer will automatically issue an extension to your file. Those that may appear in your computer file listings will probably include:

.COM command files that inform the computer how to run the program

.EXE executable files which are similar to command files and contain instructions to the CPU

.BAT batch files that contain lists of commands

.SYS system files that contain information about your hardware

.DOC document files that contain the information you have put in

.DBF database files

The last two extensions will be the ones with which you have most contact. You do not need to worry about remembering the extension filenames, but you should keep a record of the filenames you allocate to your data.

▶ *What type of programs are you likely to use?*

The type of programs you are likely to use in an office will be accounts packages, word processing, diary planners and databases. In a specialised department they may also use spreadsheets and statistical packages for processing figures, financial packages for forecasting and running a business, or computer aided design (CAD) packages. These CAD packages assist in drawing and estimating and are commonly used in the drawing offices of engineers and designers. You will probably already have used a word processing package and be familiar with some of the functions.

▶ *What precautions should you take with computer equipment in the office?*

- Switch off all machinery at the end of the day. (The only exception may be the telephone answering machine, which will take telephone calls in your absence, and the fax machine, which may send and receive messages during the night.)
- Make sure that any connecting wires are not trailing across the floor. They should be taped under the desk or placed along the walls of the room.
- Do not overload sockets. Multi-extension leads should be used when several items need to be plugged in at the same time. Alternatively, extra sockets should be installed. Check the leads regularly for fraying or broken connections.

New regulations under the Health and Safety at Work Act 1974 (HASAWA) and the Electricity at Work Act (*see* page 28) state that all electrical equipment must be regularly checked to confirm it is safe to use. Consult your tutor or health and safety representative if you are not sure about the state of any of the equipment you use.

■ DIY 3.1.6

Look at the posture used by your colleagues when using keyboard equipment. Note those that are incorrect and why they are incorrect (Figure 7.2 on page 186 in Unit 7 will help you). The reasons may include:

- chair not adjusted correctly;
- chair does not have adjustable backrest;
- footrest required but not available;
- desk incorrect height (normal height desk used);
- head not upright, document holder not used.

Some typewriters may have limited facilities similar to a computer. For example, some have memories and automatic correction facilities. Manuals are usually available for new staff to read, to find out what the facilities of the equipment are. Quite often equipment is not used to its full potential. This is because a person will use it for what they need, and no more.

▶ *Telephone, fax and answer machines*

You may have a combined telephone, fax and answering machine, or they could be separate items of equipment. If you have completed Unit 5, Element 5.1 you should be able to cross-reference the work carried out but you will need to discuss this with your tutor.

Telephones are one of the most frequently used pieces of equipment. There are so many different models available now that it would be impossible to cover all the operating instructions in this unit. There are also many different facilities and types of equipment that become available as the telecommunications companies improve their services. The telephone may be the way in which your organisation keeps in touch with all of its customers and clients. It is therefore essential that you know exactly how to use the equipment available properly, otherwise you may end up disconnecting and losing a valuable customer.

All office equipment should be secured at the end of each day. Some machinery will need to be left on (for example, the fax to receive incoming messages), other equipment should be turned off for safety. Under the Health and Safety at Work Act (*see* page 28) you are responsible for ensuring that any faults or hazards identified in equipment are reported immediately to the supervisor. If you are able to put the fault right then do so, but do not endanger yourself. A common fault is to find that leads to equipment start to trail and may become a hazard to those walking around the office. Secure the leads if possible with cable ties. All electrical equipment must be tested on a regular basis under the Electricity at Work Regulations (*see* page 29).

Completing Element 3.1

To complete this element on following instructions and operating equipment you will need to put all DIY tasks in your folder and carry out a final assessment. Competence must be proven in dealing with reprographics, data and text processing and text transmission. The instructions used must include those provided by the organisations and by the manufacturers. You should also be aware of good working practices and legal requirements. Your evidence may include log books that you have kept of the machinery used, observation notes made by your supervisor, fax sheets, computer printouts, recordings from telephone answering machines, and photocopies. Additionally you may make a personal statement about the tasks you have undertaken.

Claiming credit

Once you have completed your final assessment, you will need to write in your record book or folder how, when, where and what you have done to prove that you are competent.

The following is an example of how one trainee completed this claim:

I have worked for the last month at Cold Service and have used the following equipment: photocopier (Xerox 5034), fax/answerphone (BT CF90), computer PCIV 286 Opus and printer Epson EPL7100. I made sure that I used the equipment safely and as instructed by my supervisor. When faults occurred I referred to the manuals supplied by the manufacturer. I have kept log books and records of the occasions I used the machines.

Element 3.2
KEEP EQUIPMENT IN A CLEAN AND WORKING CONDITION

Performance criteria

- *Cleaning of equipment and replacement of consumable items follow instructions*
- *Safeguards taken are appropriate to the cleaning or replacement activity*
- *Discarded items are disposed of safely and appropriately*

- *The equipment and nearby work area are left in a clean and tidy condition*
- *Identified equipment faults and risks are promptly and accurately reported to the appropriate person*

You may be asked to clean a particular piece of equipment and will probably be responsible for cleaning your own equipment on a regular basis. It is important that you know how and what you are able to do, without causing accidents or damage to the equipment. Water and liquids should never be placed on or near electrical equipment. Whenever cleaning machinery it should be disconnected from the mains if possible.

▶ *What can you clean on a photocopier?*

Quite often the glass on a copier will get smeared and this may cause poor copies. Marks can be made from hot or greasy hands, wet correcting fluid, marker and felt-tip pens, wet ink and dust. Nearly all of these marks can be removed by using a clean soft cloth. However make sure that the cloth does not leave pieces of fluff or threads on the glass. If some of the marks are more stubborn, then a cloth slightly dampened with spirit may be used. Manufacturers of photocopiers will provide a spirit which is recommended for use on glass and this should be used whenever possible. Alternatively a surgical spirit or correcting fluid thinners may be used. *Never* have the cloth wet or you could cause a serious accident or damage to the machine.

Sometimes the casing of the machine will become grubby, and although this will not affect the efficiency of the machine, cleaning it will improve the appearance of the office and increase the image of your organisation.

When a photocopier stops working, there could be a simple reason. The majority of machines have an indicator panel showing the fault. The most common are 'add paper', 'toner low' and 'jam'. Replacing the paper is usually quite straightforward, but replacing toner could be the responsibility of a technician or a particular member of staff. Toner cartridges are very expensive and if handled incorrectly can be hazardous. The toner is usually a dry powder ink which can stain if in contact with skin, clothes or carpets. The cartridges should always be replaced according to the manufacturer's instructions and usually protective gloves are recommended. When removing the old cartridge this should be properly wrapped before throwing it away, in order to protect the cleaners and those removing the rubbish. It is a good idea to put the old cartridge back in the box that the new cartridge arrived in.

■ DIY 3.2.1

Make a list of the faults that you have experienced when using a photocopier. Next to each fault write down the action you took. It is a good idea to keep an ongoing record (like the one below) of the problems as this would be acceptable evidence for this unit.

Name and address of organisation where the machine is located: .... Type of machine used: Model.. Manufacturer		
Date	**Type of fault found**	**Action taken**
I confirm that the above details are correct and are a true record of the work carried out by .... Signed ....(Supervisor) Date..		

Fig 3.5 Photocopier fault checklist

▶ *Looking after your keyboarding equipment*

Your machine is like any other piece of equipment in that it needs looking after if you want it to work properly. The biggest problem in the office, as far as electrical equipment is concerned, is the amount of dust which they attract. Machines that are not regularly cleaned will collect dust and you will find that this will start to clog the machine – in the end it may stop. To avoid this happening, make sure that you cover the equipment at the end of each day with a dust cover.

You will find that the machines will gather dust on the outer casing, keyboard and screen (if there is one), and once a week these should be cleaned. *Remember – never clean a machine while it is connected to the mains electricity.*

Your college or organisation may have a special contract for machine cleaning, in which case they may not wish you to get involved with cleaning at all. Alternatively, someone in the organisation may be responsible for machine maintenance and cleaning. However, you should be aware of which parts may be cleaned and how to look after a machine of your own. The purpose of looking after the machine is to ensure that you reduce the chances of breakdown. All machines are supplied with manuals, and you should refer to these for precise instructions on how to look after your particular machine.

A special cleanser can be used to clean the outer casing (you will find some recommended brands in office equipment catalogues) but do not spray any electrical parts. Brushes or small vacuum cleaners can be used to clean away dust that has gathered in the keyboard or inside the case of typewriters. *Never* remove the case of a word processor or computer as there are parts in the machine which contain high voltage electricity.

▶ *Which parts can be cleaned on manual typewriters?*

These machines have mechanical parts and do not use electricity. When you press the key, it moves a bar, which makes the key come up from its place in the 'basket' of keys and hit the roller (the platen). As the key returns to its place, the carriage moves along one space. The front cover can be taken off the machine and a brush used to clear away the dust that has gathered. You may also find that there is a collection of rubber dust or correction paper dust that has collected under the typing point – all this can be brushed out.

If the machine is using a nylon ribbon, the keys may become blocked with ink. A small, hard-headed brush, like a toothbrush, needs to be used to remove the ink from the keys, especially keys such as o, a, e and p, as the ink collects in the letters. A special type of cleaning paper (which is rough like a sandpaper) can be purchased to put in the machine. If you type all the letters of the alphabet – (capitals and small letters, numbers and punctuation), the paper will automatically clean the keys. You may find that keys for o, a, e, p, etc need to be pressed more than once.

When you have finished cleaning the keys, always put some scrap paper in the machine and use all the keys again. This will make sure that any loose bits of ink and dirt are cleared away and do not make a mess on the next piece of typing you produce. If there is any dried correcting fluid on the machine, this should be carefully removed using a small piece of cotton wool and surgical spirit or thinners, or similar liquid. Make sure you replace the lid of the spirit after use, and store it safely in the storage cupboard.

Ribbons should be changed when required, but when cleaning the machine it is a good idea just to check that any nylon ribbon is still in order and that no holes are appearing near either of the spools.

The roller, or platen, on the machine is the large black roller that the paper feeds around. This must be kept smooth; otherwise when the keys strike the paper, the letters will not form properly and will appear to be twisted. To help in preventing a platen from becoming damaged, always use a backing sheet with single sheets of paper. *Never* type without paper in the machine, or the keys will dig into the roller and cause permanent damage.

If you need to move the machine, make sure first that you lock the two margins together to stop the carriage from slipping while the machine is being lifted. The heaviest part of the machine, the back, should be nearest to you. If you are lifting from the floor, remember to bend your knees and keep your back straight – don't bend over. A trolley should be used whenever possible to move machinery.

▶ *Which parts of an electric or electronic machine can be cleaned?*

The difference between an electric and electronic machine is that the electronic machine contains microchips. Both machines do the same kind of work, but the electronic machine normally has more functions than the electric.

Unplug the machine from the mains electricity and then it can be cleaned on the outside, in the same way as a manual machine. Use a soft cloth and a recommended cleanser to remove the dirt, dust and correction fluid. *Do not* get any cleanser on the inner parts of the machine. On removing the front cover, the dust can be removed carefully from the inside. Use a soft brush to sweep the dust through the holes in the bottom of the machine's frame, or use a small hand-held vacuum cleaner.

If the printing head is a daisywheel or golf ball, and a nylon ribbon has been used, careful cleaning is necessary to remove bits of ink. Special fluid is available to soak the daisywheel and a brush can be used on the golf ball. Alternatively, both can be cleaned by using the correction sheet described in the section on cleaning manual machines.

All food and liquids should be kept well away from electrical equipment and, if an accident should occur, unplug the machine quickly to disconnect the equipment immediately from the electricity supply. Wet keyboards should be drained as quickly as possible and placed in a warm position to dry. Consult an expert before reconnecting the machine to the electricity supply, to make sure it is safe to do so. Any sticky liquids need to be cleaned off immediately.

Some machines have lights that flash or a beep that sounds when a fault occurs or a ribbon needs replacing. Look at the manual and ensure you are familiar with your machine so that you can identify faults when they occur.

▶ *Which parts of a word processor or computer can be cleaned?*

Very few parts can be cleaned without unplugging from the electricity supply. You should clean the screen regularly with an anti-static spray (recommended by the suppliers or local stationers). The casing can also be wiped clear of dirty fingermarks and dust. You will need to use a brush or small vacuum to remove dust from between the keys. *Never* remove the casing from computers or word processors. The screen of the monitor is sensitive and should not be left on when not in use, and static from the screen will also attract dust. If the machine is not going to be used for a while, turn the screen brightness down or turn the monitor off.

Keep food and liquids away from all word processors and computer equipment. If an accident should occur, remove any disks, unplug immediately to disconnect the equipment from the mains electricity supply, and call your supervisor.

▶ *Printers*

If you have a word processor, it will be connected to a printer. There are two different types of printer, one called impact (where contact is made with the paper) and the other called non-impact (where contact is not made with the paper). Examples of impact printers are dot matrix printers or daisywheel printers.

A dot matrix printer creates the letters and other characters by printing dots in the shapes of the character. The more dots, the better the quality of the printing, as there is less space between the dots. The printer head is rectangular in shape and is made up of pin heads, the pins being pushed forward to form the shape of the character. Dot matrix printers can print 100–200 characters per second and can also produce diagrams and graphics.

A daisywheel printer works in a similar way to the daisywheel on a typewriter. The spokes of the printing wheel have characters on the

Fig 3.6 **A computer system with printer**

Fig 3.7 A daisywheel

end and the wheel turns to allow the correct character to touch the paper. A daisywheel can print up to 70 characters per second, but cannot produce diagrams and graphics.

Both of these types of printer are widely used, and if you have a computer at home with a printer, it is likely to be one of these. They are fairly inexpensive to buy but are quite noisy and because of this they tend not to be used very much in large offices. To reduce the noise, some companies cover the printer with an acoustic hood or screen, or when possible the printer may be located in a separate room.

Examples of non-impact printers are ink jet or laser printers.

An ink jet printer squirts tiny jets of ink on to the paper to form the characters, and the quality is very good. An ink jet printer can print up to five pages a minute. It is also able to form pictures and graphics.

A laser printer uses laser beams to transfer the characters from the screen on to a drum, which turns and transfers the characters on to the paper. Lasers can produce a page of A4 typing in about six seconds. They can also produce excellent graphics (graphs, diagrams and pictures).

Ink jet and laser printers are quiet to run but are more expensive than the impact printers to buy. The maintenance of the laser printers can also be quite expensive as they require toner and parts to be changed when high numbers of copies are made. Colour printing is possible but the print quality obtained may not be good enough for business letters.

You will probably be required to replace items on the printers, such as refilling with paper or placing memo or letter-headed paper in the paper tray when required. On occasions you may be required to replace the ink cartridge or ribbon. You should know what the procedure is to obtain replacement parts in your organisation. Do not wait until your printer is too low in toner or ink before you get some more. Normally the printer will stop altogether or the quality of the documents becomes too poor to use.

■ DIY 3.2.2

Keep a record of the cleaning and replacement of items that you carry out over the next few weeks. Use a record sheet, as shown in Fig 3.8

Date	Type and make of machine	Action taken

Fig 3.8

Completing Element 3.2

To complete this element on keeping equipment in a clean and working condition you will need to put all DIY tasks in your folder and carry out a final assessment. Competence must be proven in dealing with cleaning equipment such as keyboards, screens, etc. In addition you must replace items such as ribbons, cartridges, staples, stationery (paper in printers or copiers). These are some examples – discuss with your tutor any others you may think of. You must also demonstrate that you are able to dispose of waste items safely and keep a clean and tidy work area. Your evidence may include log books that you have kept of the equipment cleaned, observation notes made by your supervisor, stock records, reports of faults, etc. Additionally you may make a personal statement about the tasks you have undertaken.

Claiming credit

Once you have completed your final assessment, you will need to write in your record book or folder how, when, where and what you have done to prove that you are competent.

The following is an example of how one trainee completed this claim:

I have worked for the last month at Cold Service and have cleaned and maintained the following equipment: photocopier (Xerox 5034), fax/answerphone (BT CF90), computer PCIV286 Opus, keyboard and printer Epson EPL7100. I made sure that I carried out the cleaning in a safe way and followed the instructions of my supervisor and the manufacturer. I replaced staples in the stapler, paper in the copier and printer, ribbon in the typewriter and fax roll in the fax machine, and ensured that a good supply of consumables was available in the office. I made sure that the waste materials were disposed of correctly, eg the empty toner cartridges were wrapped in paper before placing them in the bin. Waste paper was placed in the recycling bin. I have kept log books and records of the occasions on which I used the machines.

UNIT 4
Develop effective working relationships

Element 4.1
CREATE AND MAINTAIN EFFECTIVE WORKING RELATIONSHIPS WITH OTHER MEMBERS OF STAFF

Performance criteria

- *Requests from colleagues that can be met within own responsibility are acted upon promptly and co-operatively*
- *Essential information is passed on to colleagues promptly and accurately*
- *Assistance, when required, is requested politely*
- *Difficulties which affect working relationships are discussed, resolved or reported accurately and promptly to the appropriate person*
- *Methods of communication and support are suited to the needs of colleagues*

▶ *How can you maintain business relationships with other members of staff?*

We have already seen how important it is to deal with callers in a polite and courteous manner. Just as important is how you deal with colleagues – the people you work with.

A business will always have a better image if the staff are cheerful and content with their work. For staff to be happy they also need to be able to get on with each other. It is highly unlikely that all of the staff will like each other all of the time, as arguments and upsets will happen sometimes. However, if everybody tries to get along with each other, the number of arguments occurring should be reduced. It is also important to settle any difficulties as quickly as possible and let normal routine return.

When selecting new staff, the managers will try to appoint someone who can do the job but who will also 'fit in' with the existing staff. This is because they want a team of staff who will be willing to assist each other and work together for the good of the business. It is not always possible to decide at interview whether a person has exactly the right type of personality, qualities and skills to fit into the existing staff team, but with experience a good manager will identify whether a person is likely to have most of the necessary qualities.

When a person is first appointed to a new section or department, it is up to the existing staff to make sure that their new colleague settles in as quickly as possible. The first few days can be quite uncomfortable for new members of staff if the rest of the staff do not make them feel welcome. They will not work to the best of their ability and will be unlikely to want to stay.

■ DIY 4.1.1

Make a copy of the chart in Fig 4.1 on A4 paper and complete the details over the next few weeks. Obtain a signature from your colleague(s)/supervisor/line manager, once the information has been obtained and passed on to them. The completed chart should be kept in your portfolio as evidence of having passed information to colleagues promptly and accurately.

Date	Information requested	Person requiring information	Information obtained from	Confirmed as received promptly and accurately
20/7	Next order number	J Harper	Order file	

Fig 4.1

▶ *How can you make a team work more effectively?*

A good team is one that can work together well when members are very busy or when there are quiet periods. During the busy times you will probably have plenty to keep you occupied, but it is important that you still assist your colleagues when they need help. It could be that they have an important deadline to meet for the manager and need assistance with some of the more routine tasks. At this time you need to be able to sort out your own work into a priority order, so that the most important work gets completed first. The work that is not so urgent may be left for a day or so. You may find that, when a very urgent job comes into the office, everyone is working on it at the same time, to meet the deadline. This could mean working through the normal lunch break and later than the normal finishing time.

When your colleagues ask you to assist it is important to show that you are willing to help whenever you can. In this way a team spirit is developed and the working atmosphere is good.

You should also make sure that you are reliable and honest. If you tell a colleague that you will do something, make sure you do it. Your colleague will rely on you to keep your word and, if you do not, you will be letting your team down. You should also do the job to the best of your ability, and not hurry it to such an extent that you make mistakes. The job will only have to be done again, by someone responsible. Do not get yourself a reputation for being unreliable.

Find out what your colleagues' responsibilities are. You should be totally familiar with their work area, so that if additional work comes into the department, you know who is likely to be responsible for it. Some departments, such as sales and purchasing, may be responsible for customers according to their name, ie alphabetically. For example, one member of staff would deal with customers whose name begins with A–F, another with G–P and a third with Q–Z. If the first person becomes extremely busy, one of the others should be prepared to help out for a while, or if the situation continues perhaps some of the customers need to be reallocated.

◾ DIY 4.1.2

You have a problem at home and need to leave work early. However, your supervisor told you off last week for arriving late and you have recently had a week off with a cold. You do not think that the supervisor is going to give you permission to leave. Make a list of the ways in which you could approach your supervisor and how you would deal with the problem. Discuss your results with your tutor or a colleague. If they make more suggestions, add them to your list.

When you receive instructions from colleagues, make sure you understand them fully before completing the job. The instructions may be given to you verbally or in writing. If verbal, repeat to your colleague what is wanted, just to check you have understood correctly. Write down a list of the jobs you have been given, if there is more than one. If jobs are written down for you, read through these instructions carefully and check any words that you cannot read or understand. Always check if you are unsure, as you may waste time and materials doing the job incorrectly.

▶ What if you are unable to help when asked?

Quite often you may find yourself with too much work on your hands. This may make it difficult for you to stop what you are doing and give your colleagues a hand. All you need to do is explain to them what you are doing and how important it is.

If a colleague disagrees with you and feels that his or her work is more important, discuss it between you. If both of you are unable to agree, then you will need to see the supervisor or manager and let them decide which work has priority. It is always best for colleagues to settle disagreements between them if possible, otherwise an unfriendly working atmosphere may occur. It is sometimes difficult to tell a superior such as your manager that you are too busy to help. Once again, you should explain why you cannot help. If the decision is made that your work can wait, you should carry out the superior's work willingly.

Do not be frightened to tell your colleagues or manager when you are not getting work completed to the deadlines. It could be that you have far too much to do and need help.

▶ What difficulties may you face in working relationships?

You may find that you work with someone whom you dislike or who dislikes you – a personality clash. This difficulty should not be allowed to interfere with the work carried out in the office. Try to be polite and courteous at all times and do not gossip to others about the person. If you hear rumours about someone in the office, do not repeat them. Gossip can cause many problems – whether it is true or not.

Quite often problems that cause difficulties in working relationships are personal problems, for example: body odour; too strong a perfume or cologne; unsuitable clothes or unclean clothes/hair/nails; habits such as smoking, sniffing, eating strong-smelling foods and talking whilst eating; chewing gum; biting nails; jangling jewellery; etc.

■ DIY 4.1.3

List the things that would most annoy you, if someone constantly did them in an office. Which of these things could you put up with, and which would you have to do something about? What would you do?

Things likely to annoy me	I could put up with	I could not put up with	Action I would take

Other problems may occur if a personal relationship develops between two people in the same office. There is nothing wrong with going out with someone from the same office, as long as the relationship develops outside the office and not during work time. It is difficult for other staff to work with colleagues who are constantly discussing their social plans, disappearing to be with each other, or making suggestive comments to each other.

Perhaps more difficult to cope with is someone who is constantly trying to 'chat-up' other members of staff. Quite often the attention received from this person is not wanted and can become a real nuisance. Tell the person concerned in a firm but polite manner that you are not interested, and do not do anything to encourage the comments. Do not embarrass the person in front of other colleagues as this may be humiliating and could lead to an attempt to do the same to you later. If the situation becomes too difficult to cope with, discuss it with your supervisor. If the person concerned is your supervisor, then you should discuss it with the personnel officer or someone who is responsible and in whom you can confide. If the situation develops into a serious problem, then you may wish to see a solicitor or advice bureau who can advise you on sexual harassment matters.

▶ *How can you best give support to colleagues with special needs?*

Many businesses and offices have people working in them who need special consideration from their colleagues. These may include those who are mentally and/or physically disabled, those who lack confidence, those of a different nationality, and those whose religion or beliefs are different to that of the majority. In many cases these people can become isolated and may be made to feel different to others. It is the responsibility of all colleagues, supervisors and managers to ensure that anyone with special needs receives the support needed.

A colleague with special needs may not receive all the information that is passed around the office. Quite often information may be passed verbally as well as in writing, through electronic systems, on noticeboards or even through body language. It is important that information is relayed to colleagues with special needs in the most effective way. For instance someone who is blind will need to be verbally told of written circulated information. A person unable to use computers would need to see a printout of information. You will probably be able to think of other examples. Colleagues with special needs requiring special consideration and support need to be treated by all the staff fairly and on an equal basis as other staff. If you are unsure of how best you can help a special needs colleague, ask them. For instance, some wheelchair-bound staff are quite happy to let others help manoeuvre their chair around the office, though others may resent it.

■ DIY 4.1.4

Find out if your organisation has an equal opportunities policy. If it does, place a copy of it in your portfolio and write down as many examples as you can find of how the policy is being carried out in your organisation. What are your responsibilities within the equal opportunities policy?

Quite often a disagreement may occur between colleagues and/or supervisors. In most cases it can be resolved by talking about the problem and agreeing a course of action. If the disagreement cannot be resolved in this way, a member of staff may wish to take the matter further. Most organisations have an agreed disciplinary and grievance procedure. This is the procedure that is followed if the management need to discipline a member of staff or if a member of staff disagrees with action taken by a colleague or supervisor.

■ DIY 4.1.5

Find out what your organisation's disciplinary and grievance procedure is. If there is a union within your organisation they may be able to help as may the person responsible for personnel and staff matters. Make a summary of the procedure to be followed by **1** the employer and **2** the employee.

Completing Element 4.1

To complete this element on creating and maintaining effective working relationships with other members of staff you will need to put all DIY tasks in your folder and carry out a final assessment.

Competence must be proven in dealing with staff relationships which must include your line manager, supervisor and colleagues.

Claiming credit

Once you have completed your final assessment, you will need to write in your record book or folder how, when, where and what you have done to prove that you are competent.

The following is an example of how one trainee completed this claim:

While working at D & G in my part-time job I make sure that I pass on important information to my colleagues and supervisor as quickly as possible. When requested to find information I find the right piece, (for example, this may be in the files, on the computer, by making a phone call or by asking a colleague in another section) and pass the information back to the person wanting it as quickly as possible. If the information needed is a lot, then I write or type it before passing it on. This reduces the chance of mistakes happening. I always try to be polite, even when I am busy myself.

There have not been many occasions when I have disagreed with people at work, but when no one would change shift with me I asked the supervisor if the rotas could be rearranged.

I have not worked with many people with special needs, although one of my colleagues is deaf and I must always make sure that I am in front of her when I speak, or I tap her on the shoulder to let her know I wish to talk to her. I told her when the fire bell was ringing and we left the building together.

■ Element 4.2
GREET AND ASSIST VISITORS

Performance criteria

- *Visitors are greeted promptly and courteously and their needs identified*
- *Visitors are given only disclosable information*
- *Visitors are directed or escorted to destination, as required*
- *Reasons for delay or non-availability of assistance are explained politely*
- *Situations outside own responsibility are referred to the appropriate person*
- *Methods of communication and support are suited to the needs of the visitors*

▶ Receiving and assisting visitors

Whether you work for a large or small organisation, the way in which you deal with callers is very important. A caller is anyone who comes to see you or your colleagues and does not work in your department on an everyday basis. This could be someone from:

- another department or section
- another branch
- another company or other organisation
- a customer or client
- people attending a meeting
- people delivering or collecting items
- people attending an interview or asking about vacancies

Some of these callers will be expected and others will be unexpected.

All of these people are classed as 'visitors' when they call on you for information or for your help. The way in which these visitors are greeted and your attitude to them is very important.

If you do not look presentable (neat and tidy clothes and hair), they may already be forming a poor impression of you before you even speak. If, when you speak, your language is poor or unclear they may not be convinced that you are able to help them and may doubt your ability, and this may lead to doubts about the organisation's products or services.

Businesses such as building societies and airlines have special uniforms for staff that deal with customers and clients. This makes sure that the staff are always neatly presented and do not wear clothes that may be considered 'unsuitable' for the office. It also gives the organisation an 'image' which the customers can associate with it – the staff are easily recognised. Staff do not have to buy suitable clothing to wear to work and have a feeling of 'belonging' to the organisation. Some organisations may also have rules about footwear, make-up and jewellery, for men and women.

DIY 4.2.1

Make a copy of Fig 4.2 on to A4 paper. Complete it over the next 3 weeks, listing the visitors you receive and state whether they were expected or unexpected. Tick if they are internal or external to the company and list the action you took. The action may include: directed them to the sales department, gave them information from the accounts file, found the file for them, found the right telephone number, etc.

Date	Visitor	Internal	External	Action taken

Fig 4.2 Action checklist for visitors

The way in which you greet your visitors may depend on the organisation's policy and who the visitor is. If they are staff from another department you may be familiar with them and use their first names. For example, you may say 'Hello John. What can I do for you?' This is informal but polite and friendly. Normally the managers, directors and most senior members of staff would not be called by their first names, but may be greeted in a similar way.

External visitors to the business are usually greeted by saying 'Good morning (or 'Good afternoon'). How may I help you?' If you know their name, it is polite to use it: 'Good afternoon, Mrs James. How may I help you?' sounds more friendly and helpful. For regular external visitors, such as representatives from other companies, delivery and post staff, cleaners, etc you will probably get to know their first names and greet them on an informal basis.

If you need to pass on an external visitor to another member of staff, always find out the visitor's name before explaining to your colleague how he/she can help. This will allow your colleague to use the person's name, which will leave the visitor with a good impression.

Fig 4.3 A reception area

▶ *What skills will you need?*

As soon as visitors enter the room you should show that you have noticed them, by looking at them and smiling. If you are busy on the telephone, indicate that you will not be long. One of the most important skills is listening.

Listening. Very few people listen properly when someone is speaking to them. You should show visitors that they have your full attention by looking at them and keeping eye contact, and stop doing whatever you were doing when they came in. Wait until the visitor has finished speaking before you reply (even if you know the answer when visitors are half-way through speaking, it is polite to let them finish). If you are unsure of what the visitor wants, ask questions and, if you are still unsure, call your supervisor or a colleague to assist.

■ DIY 4.2.2

Organisations have different ways of greeting their visitors. Write down the approved method in your organisation for:

1 greeting visitors who are external to the company and
2 greeting visitors who are internal to the company and who are:
   (a) a senior manager
   (b) a supervisor from another section
   (c) a friend from another section.

Non-verbal signs. Not only will visitors be getting an impression about you when they see you, but you will also have a first impression about them when they enter your office. Those visitors who feel confident and know what they want will probably walk straight into the office and go up to a member of staff. Those visitors who are unsure of what or who they want, may enter the office and hover by the door, looking round to see whether they can see anything or anyone familiar. Quite often these people are waiting for someone to approach them and offer help. You will need to try to *read the non-verbal signs of communication* (gestures, movements, facial expressions, eye contact): another skill to develop to help you deal with visitors effectively. Reading body language can be very important when receiving visitors , and it can assist you in identifying possible difficulties, such as aggressive or suspicious visitors.

◼ DIY 4.2.3

Draw up a sheet with the two column headings shown below. Look at the next 10 people that walk into your room or go past you and try to think of a word that describes their body language.

Person   **Body language**
1   confident   ⎫ some examples:
2   shy   ⎪ you may
3   angry   ⎬ think of
4   unsure   ⎭ others
5
6
7
8
9
10

Speaking. Once you have listened to your visitors, you will need to tell them how you can help and what will be done. Your *oral skills* are extremely important and are the most frequently used method of communication. When you speak, use a friendly manner, speak reasonably slowly and in a clear voice. Always keep eye contact and speak directly to the visitors. Avoid looking away from visitors , even when giving directions, as they may not be able to hear what you say. If you need to interrupt a colleague, always apologise first 'Sorry to interrupt you but, ...'. This helps to create a pleasant working atmosphere and relationship between staff members.

▶ *What else can you do to create a good impression?*

A clean and tidy reception area will always impress visitors, both in the main reception area and in your own office. Make sure that any deliveries are not placed in the way of visitors and are moved as soon as possible. Visitors who arrive irate, angry or anxious should be calmed down as quickly as possible. Listen to any complaints, but never agree that the complaint is justified; find someone who can deal with the problem as quickly as possible. If there is a delay, always keep the visitors informed of what is going on. Offer tea/coffee to those visitors that need to wait for a while or offer them an alternative appointment if they are unable to wait.

▶ *What if the visitor asks for confidential information?*

Unless a visitor is authorised, no confidential information should ever be given (verbal or written). Confidential information includes personal details of staff, their exact whereabouts and appointment schedule; financial details of the organisation and its customers; details of future projects or contracts etc. If you are unsure whether information may be passed on or not, always check with your supervisor.

Many organisations now have strict rules about the security of the building. Visitors may not be allowed to walk round the offices without a member of staff with them. Usually a member of staff will collect the visitor from reception and accompany them to the meeting office. A receptionist should not leave reception unattended in case another visitor arrives and is left to wander round the building unsupervised. In the majority of organisations visitors are still allowed to find their own way to the office they require. You must ensure that the directions given are clear and precise, otherwise the visitor may get lost.

When the visit has finished the member of staff with the visitor should make sure that he/she knows how to get out of the building. There may be a quicker exit door than the door by which they entered.

If you are escorting a visitor, make sure you keep to a steady pace. Make conversation about simple things such as the weather, if it is their first visit to the company, if they had problems finding the company, etc. Do not try to discuss their business with them. You may have to escort elderly or disabled visitors. Always walk at a pace that is comfortable for them and, if the visitor is blind, offer your arm and tell them when steps or corners are nearing. Foreign visitors or those with speech difficulties may find it hard to explain who or what they want. Have patience and do not finish off their sentences for them, or they may become anxious and flustered.

Some companies issue visitors with a badge or pass card to show that they have been approved to visit the building. Others may have a reception book to write down the details of all visitors. In some cases, such as government offices, the visitor may need to have their bag, briefcase or belongings searched before being allowed to enter the offices. In some extreme cases a body search may be carried out. Any organisation carrying out such procedures is likely to employ special staff such as security guards to attend to these duties.

■ DIY 4.2.4

Make a list of at least 10 qualities that a member of staff who is responsible for receiving external visitors should have, for example: politeness, well dressed. How many of these qualities do you have? Could you improve any of them?

▶ *What information should you be able to access?*

Regardless of which office you are working in, you should always be able to put your hand on a copy of the internal telephone directory or telephone list and a copy of the organisation chart (the family tree of the company). This will tell you who works in which department, where they are located and perhaps their duties. It will help you to

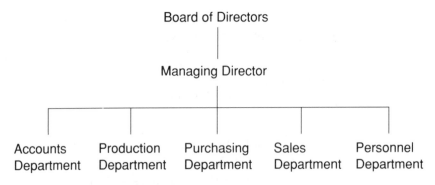

Board of Directors

Managing Director

| Accounts | Production | Purchasing | Sales | Personnel |
| Department | Department | Department | Department | Department |

Fig 4.4 An organisation chart for a company

identify the person to whom you wish to refer a visitor, if you are
unable to help the visitor yourself.

■ DIY 4.2.5

You have a school pupil who is coming to work with you on reception for 2
weeks' work experience. Write down some instructions on how to deal with the
following:

1 receiving visitors from within the organisation
2 receiving visitors from outside the organisation
3 receiving visitors with special needs (give examples)
4 receiving casual callers such as post, delivery services, window cleaners,
milk, etc
5 finding out the reason for the visit
6 what to do if they are unable to answer a question.

Draw a map of the location of the offices on one floor of your organisation.
Design a record sheet that could be used by the work experience pupil to
record the visitors received (see Fig 4.5).

Telephone. You should also be familiar with your telephone system.
You may need to obtain information from another department or obtain
an external number to get information for your caller. This means you
should know how to:

● obtain an internal number
● obtain an external number
● transfer an internal number (if possible)
● transfer an external number to another extension.

Date	Name of caller	Reason for calling	Action taken

Fig 4.5 Log sheet

You may need to get assistance quickly if you have an aggressive or suspicious visitor, in which case you may need to call an emergency number:

● be aware of any emergency number or security number within the company
● know how to call the external emergency services.

Completing Element 4.2

To complete this element on greeting and assisting callers you will need to put all DIY tasks in your folder.

Competence must be proven in dealing with expected and unexpected visitors. Records of visitors received must be part of the evidence in your folder.

Claiming credit

Once you have completed your final assessment, you will need to write in your record book or folder how, when, where and what you have done to prove that you are competent.

The following is an example of how one trainee completed this claim:

NVQ Administration Level 1

When I was on the reception in the NVQ office in College I received visitors who were from other groups as well as teachers from other departments. As they approached the reception desk I said 'Good morning/afternoon, how may I help you?' Once I knew what or who they wanted, I asked for their name (and wrote it on my log sheet). I then found them the information they required or told them where they could find the person they wanted. Sometimes I was asked to make a photocopy or send a fax. If I was asked something I did not know, I asked my tutor. I would not give out confidential information. Most of the visitors received were unexpected.

I worked for 3 weeks in a building society, and although I was not allowed to greet the visitors on my own, I worked with one of the clerks who allowed me to greet the visitor and find out what they wanted. He then dealt with the request, although if it was a form that was required I got it from the cabinet.

I also receive a lot of visitors in my part-time job at the newsagents. The requests made by them are usually about what they want to buy, or they want to know how much their bill is. If I am unable to help I call Mr Mac, the owner. I have several customers who have special needs, such as not being able to reach the goods they want, and some who are not able to speak English very well. I always make sure that I am as helpful as possible and I am patient.

UNIT 5
Process information

■ **Element 5.1**
**PROCESS INCOMING AND OUTGOING
TELECOMMUNICATIONS**

Performance criteria

- *Communications are responded to promptly and clearly using approved organisation manner*
- *Callers are correctly identified and requirements established accurately*
- *Queries are answered within own area of authority or referred to the appropriate person*
- *Outgoing calls, for self or on behalf of others, are correctly obtained*
- *Relevant information is courteously obtained and checked*
- *Relevant information is communicated promptly and accurately to the appropriate person*
- *Faults are promptly reported to the appropriate person*
- *Recording of communications, when required, is in accordance with organisational procedures*

Modern telephone systems have been designed to meet the needs of an organisation of any size. A switchboard that allows a number of incoming calls to be connected and then transferred to the relevant person or department may be used. Internal telephones allow members of staff to contact each other direct using an internal telephone extension number. They also allow contact with the main switchboard, which may have to be used to request an outside line in order to make an external telephone call.

You will find that all organisations, whatever their size, depend upon telephone contact. Some conduct a major part of their business over the telephone, for example, orders for goods from a mail-order catalogue. They rely on well-trained members of staff to answer and

99

record information quickly, efficiently and accurately. Mistakes cost time and money and will not be tolerated by a business organisation. In an emergency situation, mistakes might even cost lives.

When members of staff answer the telephone, they act as representatives of that organisation and therefore must create the right impression. Staff have a responsibility to communicate information accurately and clearly, using an appropriate style, tone and vocabulary. Good communication skills are essential if this is to be achieved. A member of staff who sounds competent, efficient and gives a good impression of the organisation over the telephone is a valuable addition.

▶ *What equipment are you likely to use?*

There is a wide range of telecommunications equipment available to suit the demands of each organisation. This depends on the size of the organisation and the department in which you work. You may find

Fig 5.1 An office telephone

yourself using a telephone switchboard with up to 10 incoming lines and numerous internal extensions; or you may be responsible for using an office telephone using a single, direct line out or one linked to a main switchboard.

Telephone

Modern telephones offer numerous additional facilities, such as last number redial, memory, selective call-barring, secrecy. They also offer diversion services, such as no-reply diversion or engaged diversion, 3-way service and call waiting. There are other facilities and services available, some of which are free although others will be charged for. It is important that you understand the facilities available on the telephones you use at work (and at home) and appreciate how these might be used to improve your efficiency when at work.

■ DIY 5.1.1

No-reply diversion and engaged diversion are services that can improve the efficiency of your office. Why might an organisation use these services and what advantages do they offer? If you already use a diversion service on your telephone, give details of how to operate the service.

Switchboard

A switchboard is used to accept incoming calls, allow them to be answered and then transferred to the appropriate person or department. Calls can be held or 'parked' while the switchboard operator deals with other calls, locates a particular person or finds out information. Switchboards can be used to monitor all outgoing external calls made by members of staff. They will need to request an outside line from the switchboard operator before they can dial out. Some switchboards require the operator to dial the number and then transfer the call to the member of staff once it is connected. Other switchboards can be set up to allow extensions to have direct access to an outside line by dialling a number, eg 9.

Switchboards can be programmed to prevent long-distance calls being made. BT national standard rate calls can be made between 0800–1800 hours, although calls made using BT chargecard and mobile telephones are charged peak rate between 0800–1300 hours. Cheap

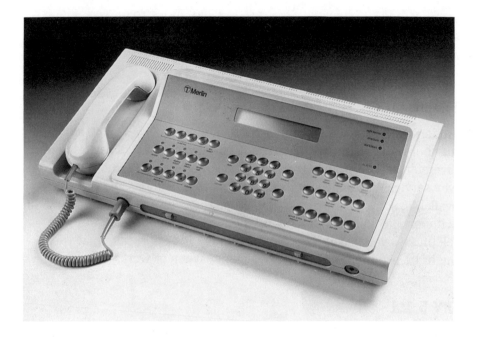

Fig 5.2 An electronic switchboard

rate calls can be made from 1800–0800 hours. Saturday and Sunday are also charged at cheap rate. Internal calls made within an organisation are free of charge as they are operated through the organisation's own switchboard.

Answering machines

These machines are used to answer the telephone when no one is available, ensuring that no calls or messages are missed. An announcement is recorded which invites the caller to leave a message after the 'bleep'. Answering machines allow the office to be unattended whilst orders and messages are left, recorded on the machine, during any time of the day or night.

If you are answered by an answering machine, do not be frightened. Speak slowly and clearly, stating your business and remembering to leave your name and telephone number. It is also wise to state the date and time of day that you are calling. If you do find yourself surprised by an answering machine, replace your receiver, write down your message and call back when you have prepared yourself.

Fig 5.3 An answerphone

The first person in the office in the morning should play the recorded messages to find out if there is anything important that needs attention straight away. When the tape is played back it is wise to have a pen and paper ready to jot down all information and telephone numbers.

▶ *How should a telephone be answered?*

1 A ringing telephone should be answered as quickly as possible (some organisations guarantee that your call will be answered in no more than 4 rings!).

2 Identify the organisation and yourself clearly (organisations will have an approved method of doing this).

3 Use a pen and paper to note all information.

4 Identify the caller and either deal with the call yourself or transfer the caller to someone who can help. (Announce the name of the caller before transferring the call to the other person.)

5 Always remain courteous, polite and – above all – helpful.

6 Keep the caller informed of your actions so they are aware of any delay and never tell a caller to 'hang on'.

7 If the call is for someone who is not available, ask if anyone else can help; if not, take a message.

8 Do not give confidential information – pass the call to your supervisor.

9 If you do not have requested information at hand, offer to ring the caller back.

10 Before ringing off, make sure you have recorded all the information required, including the caller's telephone number. (You may also have to complete a log book of all incoming calls.)

■ DIY 5.1.2

Design a log sheet on a piece of A4 paper that can be used to record all incoming calls received and dealt with by you. The log sheet will need headings such as date and time, name of caller (together with company name if relevant), brief details of request and action taken. If you have taken a message for someone, keep a copy of the message and attach this to the back of your log sheet.

▶ *How would you deal with a wrong number?*

First try to help the caller. Give your own organisation's number again to clarify where the mistake has been made. If your number is different to that required, the caller can ring off and dial the correct number. If the caller has been given your organisation's number by mistake, ask for more details about the enquiry and see if you can find the correct number.

If you find that you regularly receive calls for another organisation, keep a note of their number so that it can be passed on to the caller quickly and efficiently. Never be off-hand with a caller who has the wrong number, but be polite and helpful as this will create a good impression of your own organisation. You may find that you receive a lot of wrong number calls because your number is similar to that of another organisation, or above or below their number in the directory. If you greet callers correctly and give a good impression you may attract additional business.

▶ *How would you ensure a message is taken accurately?*

Firstly, remember to keep pen or pencil, scrap paper and telephone message pad next to the telephone. You will need to pass on the following information:

1 Name of caller and organisation/department.
2 Caller's telephone and extension number.
3 Details of message.
4 Name/department/room number of person for whom the message is intended.
5 Date and time of call.
6 Your name as the receiver of the call.

You may prefer to write information received over the telephone on to scrap paper and then transfer this neatly to the message pad. If you are busy, however, it may be safer to write directly on to the message pad so that you do not forget the call. It is vitally important that messages are passed on promptly to the correct person so that the call can be returned. Do not leave messages lying around your desk. A lost message to return a call could mean a lost order for business and a very angry colleague.

When you have taken a message, you should always confirm the details back to the caller. Repeat the name and contact number to ensure that mistakes have not been made. One wrong digit in a telephone number will cause confusion and create a bad impression of your organisation if the call cannot be returned. Messages must give full information. It is not acceptable to write that 'a man called ...', or, 'I think her name was ...'. If you are ever unsure of what a caller has said, do not be afraid to ask him/her to repeat details or spell out words you do not understand.

Page 121 gives details of the telephone alphabet which can be used to clarify information over the telephone.

■ DIY 5.1.3

Read through the following telephone conversation.

You   Good morning, Coopers and Co, how may I help you?
Caller Yes, my name is Harper and I would like to speak with your Purchasing Manager.
You   I'm afraid she is out of the office this morning. Would you like to speak with her assistant?
Caller No, I have already left messages with her assistant and have not received a return call.

MESSAGE FOR

M _____

WHILE YOU WERE OUT

M _____

Of _____

Telephone No _____

Telephoned		Please ring	
Called to see you		Will call again	
Wants to see you		Urgent	

Message: _____

_____

_____

_____

_____

_____

_____

_____

Date _____ Time _____

Received by _____

Fig 5.4 A telephone message form

You   I'm terribly sorry, would you like to leave details of your message with me and I will ensure that our Purchasing Manager, Miss Bowyer, gets it as soon as she arrives back in the office?

Caller Well, if I must, it really is quite urgent. My name is Clive Harvey from Office Supplies Limited and I would like to arrange a suitable time to call in and discuss our products with Miss Bowyer. My telephone number is 345274 extension 2674.

You   That's fine Mr Harvey, I'll pass the message to Miss Bowyer as soon as she arrives back in her office after lunch. Can I just confirm the number as 345274 extension 2674?

Caller Yes, that's correct. Oh, that's a thought, where does Miss Bowyer usually have lunch? I could try to catch her before she returns to the office as I am local.

You   I'm sorry Mr Harvey but I'm afraid I cannot give that information out over the telephone, but I will make sure that Miss Bowyer gets your urgent message and returns your call.

Caller Well, I suppose that will have to do for now, but you will make sure you mark the message as urgent?

You   Of course, Mr Harvey.

Caller Thank you and goodbye.

You   Goodbye Mr Harvey.

1 Complete a message slip detailing all relevant information – use today's date and the current time.

2 You have just been informed that Miss Bowyer will not be returning to the office for the next 3 days. What should you do with the message?

▶ *What information can be given over the telephone?*

The amount of information you are able to give over the telephone will increase as you get to know the organisation for which you work. It is important, however, that you recognise occasions when information should or should not be given out. You have already been told that you must be polite and helpful at all times, but this does not mean giving out any information you can lay your hands on in the name of helpfulness.

If you are ever unsure, tell the caller that you do not have the information and that you will transfer them to your supervisor. Alternatively, offer to call them back later to give you time to check. It is important for you to realise that limitations governing disclosable information are there to protect the organisation, its business and its employees.

You will learn from the organisation's literature, such as house journals, organisation charts, internal telephone directories, catalogues and price lists. You will also learn by talking to members of staff about their role and duties in the organisation. With experience, you will know about the products or services offered by the organisation, which departments deal with different areas of work and who to contact if a person is not available.

■ DIY 5.1.4

In order to provide relevant and correct information to callers it is necessary for you to understand how the organisation works and the responsibilities of its staff.

1 Name 3 members of staff and their work titles.
2 Briefly explain the duties of each member of staff.
3 For each member of staff, give an example of the type of information you would request from them.
4 Give brief details of the structure, products and services offered by your organisation.

▶ *How do you make an outgoing call?*

We all think we know how to use the telephone, but it is surprising how easily mistakes can be made. By following a few simple rules, you can avoid making mistakes and help build your confidence.

1 Write down the number and dialling code (check these are correct) and the name or department you require.
2 Make a list of questions or notes needed for the call.
3 Lift the receiver and listen for the dial tone. (You may have a hands-free button that allows you to talk into a small speaker and keep both hands free.)
4 Key in the full number carefully at a steady rate (a beep will be heard each time a number is accepted).
5 If you make a mistake, replace the receiver, wait a couple of seconds and try again.

6 When the call is answered, ask for the person or department required, and/or the extension number, if known; give your own name and/or the name of your organisation, and say on whose behalf you are calling, if relevant.

7 When you are connected, be prepared to repeat the same information again.

8 Talk clearly and concisely, using your notes as a reminder to ensure that you do not forget anything.

9 If the call is for your boss, explain this to the person and then transfer the call, making sure you first announce their name to your boss.

10 If you are cut off, as the caller it is your responsibility to call again.

Costs in time and money can be reduced if calls are kept to the point.

■ DIY 5.1.5

Design a log sheet on a piece of A4 paper that can be used to record all outgoing calls dealt with by you. The sheet will need details such as date and time, name of the person you are calling (together with company name if relevant), telephone number, and brief details of the purpose of the call.

▶ *What sources of information are available?*

You will inevitably use a BT *Phone Book* for your local area, together with *Yellow Pages* and *The Thomson Local Directory*. Use these books to find local telephone numbers, area codes, addresses and even postcodes for business and private users.

Business Pages (similar to *Yellow Pages*) are used by business suppliers and covers a wider area, but not retail outlets and services.

Your organisation should also have an internal directory giving details of all personnel, departments and extension numbers. This should, in addition, also give details of frequently-used external numbers, eg branch offices, so that staff do not use BT's Directory Enquiries, which would incur charges.

The only free BT information service still available is the speaking clock sponsored by Accurist. All other services are offered by private companies, who make a charge for the service. These services are usually advertised in newspapers and often start with the prefix 0891. The Freefone service does not provide information but does encourage potential customers to ring free of charge either through the operator or by using an 0800 or similar number.

Remember that there are other companies, such as Mercury, that supply telecommunications equipment and services in competition with BT.

■ DIY 5.1.6

Use the BT local *Phone Book* to find numbers for:

1 The operator
2 Directory Enquiries
3 Your local railway station
4 Your local bus station
5 The code number for:
   - London
   - Cardiff
   - Bristol
   - Edinburgh
6 The international code number for:
   - Paris
   - New York
   - Sydney
   - Berlin

Use the *Phone Book* to calculate the time difference between:

1 Moscow and Sydney
2 Moscow and New York
3 Sydney and New York

▶ *What about international calls?*

Most international calls can be made using IDD (International Direct Dialling), but if problems are encountered the International Operator can be contacted on 155 for assistance. The International Operator will not only help with international calls but can also give you a demonstration of the tones to expect to hear when calling internationally.

Remember that international calls are charged at a higher rate than domestic calls and, therefore, it is important that you choose carefully the time of day when you make your call. You can use the *Phone Book*, International Time Zones page, to calculate the time difference between Britain and the country you wish to contact.

▶ *How do you establish goodwill and rapport with callers?*

Some organisations will have an informal atmosphere with all personnel on first name terms, others will require a more formal approach where superiors are referred to as Mr... or Mrs... and so on. You may find that whilst you are on first name terms with members of staff they may still require you to be more formal when dealing with an outside visitor.

Customers and clients of an organisation should always be greeted and attended to politely and only be referred to by their first name if they are known by you very well. Do not fall into the trap of calling someone by their first name because they have introduced themselves as, for example John Brown. Members of staff who are happy to be called by their first names in conversation may still require you to refer to them formally when in the presence of customers or whilst dealing with telephone enquiries.

When you are new to an organisation you may be unsure of how to address staff, customers and callers. Never be over-familiar – it is better to be over-polite until such time as you are told to use first names. When dealing with people try to follow a few simple rules, such as:

- sound business-like – do not use slang;
- if someone has helped you, say thank you (they will be more likely to help again if you have been polite);
- when requesting anything, say please (people are more likely to respond);
- get involved and show interest in what you and others are doing;
- be helpful – if you have nothing to do ask if you can help someone else;

111

- use a person's name during conversation and ensure you introduce yourself;
- do not be afraid to ask for help or clarification if you are unsure of anything;
- listen to what is being said (do not be over-familiar and join in with conversations you know nothing about – listen and learn);
- never discuss anything you have heard with other people (as a newcomer, you never know who you may be talking to).

▶ *How do you maintain security?*

The first thing to remember is to use your discretion – if you are ever unsure, ask your supervisor. You will find that during your working duties you will have access to many types of information. It may just be part of a day's work to you but the information you deal with could be very sensitive and of use to other people or organisations. Be helpful, but never disclose information to others that may be considered confidential by your organisation.

Personnel and wages records, financial and medical reports, and information such as sales and profit reports, are examples of records that contain information that should not be given to callers. Think how you would feel if your name, address and personal details were given to 'someone' over the telephone. Would you like to think that other people were given information about your bank account or medical details?

▶ *What about emergencies?*

In the event of an emergency, using the telephone could save someone's life. In order to be effective in an emergency you must know the correct procedure to follow. Do you contact your supervisor or main switchboard operator first? Will you be able to call the emergency services yourself if it is a matter of life or death?

Remember that some telephones will not have access to an outside line and you may have to go through the organisation's switchboard, who will call the emergency services on your behalf. Some organisations have their own internal emergency number, eg 222, which will be answered immediately by the switchboard operator.

If you do have to call the emergency services yourself, be prepared with the relevant information:

- Dial 999.
- Which service do you require – Fire, Police, Ambulance? (You might even need Coast Guard, Mountain or Cave Rescue.)
- Give the name and address of your organisation.
- Give your own name and position in the organisation.
- Give brief details of the emergency.
- Do not hang up until told to do so.

It is vital that you know what to do in an emergency – if you are unsure, now is the time to ask your supervisor.

▶ *What about safety?*

Using the telephone should not be a dangerous activity, but safety rules still apply.

1 Do not trail wires across the floor or walkway.
2 Keep the earpiece and mouthpiece of your telephone clean.
3 Do not eat or drink over telecommunications equipment.
4 Keep the telephone in an accessible place.
5 Do not sit on desk tops whilst using the telephone.
6 Use sufficient extensions for the number of people in the office.

▶ *What other telecommunications equipment is available?*

This unit can be assessed using telephone equipment but you must also prove that you have knowledge and understanding of the different types and uses of other telecommunications equipment. The telephone network can be used to communicate verbally (voice); to communicate data, using modem equipment to download data from one computer to another many miles away; to communicate text using facsimile equipment and electronic mail software to transfer information from one computer screen to another using services such as Telecom Gold. All of these methods of telecommunications use the telephone network to communicate information.

▶ *What is Prestel?*

Prestel links television screens or personal computers to large computers via BT lines. Information is updated every 24 hours and includes:

- company information
- directories
- market research
- business news/services
- share prices
- government statistics
- travel information
- weather information
- sport and entertainment
- banking and investment
- mailbox
- customer guide.

This service allows the user to actually make bookings using their keyboard, for example, for theatre tickets and air tickets. The user is charged according to how long they have used the line, in the same way as with a telephone.

Note: The Prestel service as delivered by BT will soon cease to exist. There are other companies who may offer the same service, eg British Rail is currently working on setting up its own database service. In competition, Ceefax and Teletext are now offering downloading equipment that will enable users to access the Ceefax and Teletext services using computer terminals. This will enable both systems to offer an interactive service rather than just information that can be read from a TV screen. It is also wise to remember that specialist databases exit for information such as holiday bookings.

▶ *What is facsimile?*

Commonly known as 'fax', this machine will transmit an exact copy of a page from one place to another – much like a photocopier, but with the copy emerging from another fax machine at a different location. To send a fax you will need to know the fax number of the company you wish to receive the copy – the number can be found on the company's

Fig 5.5 A fax machine

stationery. If the company is a BT registered customer its fax number can be found by dialling 192 (this information is now in the *Phone Book*).

The original sheet is fed into the machine which scans and then translates the information into a code that can be transmitted via the telephone network – some machines are able to print a confirmation slip once transmission is complete to confirm transmission time, number of pages and number dialled. Fax is particularly useful for sending pictures, graphics, written or printed material accurately and at great speed – the average speed is 48 seconds per A4 page.

The cost of sending a fax is exactly the same as if you had made a telephone call to the same destination, except that to convey the same information verbally would take much longer and would therefore cost more. Extra costs are also incurred if a telephone call, for example an order, needs to be confirmed in writing – one fax would accurately satisfy both of these needs. The company receiving the fax incurs no charges other than the initial cost or rental of the fax itself plus the cost of the paper and toner required for the message. Some fax machines allow messages to be set to a timer so that they can be automatically transmitted during cheap rate times to save money.

▶ *What is electronic mail?*

The terms 'electronic mail' 'Elmail' or 'Email' are used to describe the process of sending and receiving messages electronically either internally in an organisation or externally using telephone lines. With electronic mail, a central computer becomes the equivalent of a postal sorting office, sorting incoming messages into the correct mailbox ready for collection by the mailbox holder. Each holder is identified by their own mailbox number and can be given a unique password to enable them, and only them, to retrieve their messages.

Messages can be transmitted internally within an organisation, perhaps spread over different sites, by using specialised software linked to a central computer – the transfer of messages would be free of charge. Messages transmitted externally would need to pass through a system such as Telecom Gold which incurs a registration fee together with a charge for each A4 page sent. The organisation would also have to provide a computer with built-in modem, or a separate modem.

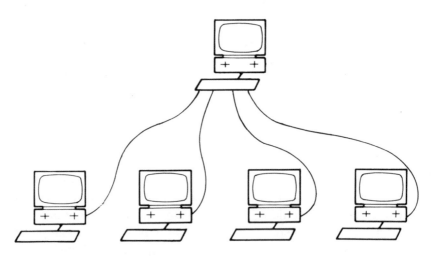

Fig 5.6 A networked computer system

When using Email the message is read from the screen, therefore, paper is not required unless a printout of the message is needed. Some companies use Email for sending internal memos as it saves time in terms of delivery, saves paper and often postage if the company has computers in different areas networked together – this is called a LAN or 'Local Area Network'. Users are notified of a waiting message either by a flashing light on their screen, often with a number to show how many messages are waiting, or a picture such as an envelope appearing on screen.

DIY 5.1.7

What telecommunications equipment is used in your organisation? Write a brief report giving details of each piece of equipment and how and where it is used. Also include details of the reporting procedures you must follow if the equipment develops a fault.

Completing Element 5.1

To complete this element on processing incoming and outgoing telecom-munications you will need to put all DIY tasks in your folder and carry out a final assessment.

Competence must be proven in dealing with internal and external communications. These must be responded to quickly and using your organisation's approved manner. Callers must be correctly identified and their requirements or queries established and answered. If this is not possible they must be referred to the appropriate authority. Outgoing calls must be correctly obtained, relevant information courteously obtained and checked, and relevant information communicated promptly and accurately to the appropriate person. Faults should be reported and recording of communications carried out in accordance with organisational procedures. You must prove knowledge and understanding of the different types and uses of other telecommunications equipment.

Claiming credit

Once you have completed your final assessment, you will need to write in your record book or folder how, when, where and what you have done to prove that you are competent.

The following is an example of how one trainee completed this claim:

When I was on Reception in the college training office for 2 days I answered the switchboard (BT 2+8) promptly. I said, 'Good Morning/Afternoon, Training Office. How may I help you?' I asked who was calling and how I could help them. I would take a message if a person was not available (see folder for evidence) and I was always polite and courteous. If I could not help I would transfer the caller to someone who could, eg my supervisor (see log in folder). I was never asked to give confidential information, but if I had been asked to do so, I would have told my supervisor immediately.

I used the Phone Book and Yellow Pages to find external numbers. I had to call these from the switchboard and then transfer to an extension when connected. I announced the call before transferring it. I asked the purpose of all outgoing calls, and the number required. I kept a log (see folder). I did not have any faults, but if I had I would have reported these to my supervisor and then contacted BT on 154 to report the fault, if told to do so. While in the college training office I also used the fax machine to send text (see evidence folder) and Teletext to find out travel and weather data.

■ Element 5.2
SUPPLY INFORMATION TO MEET SPECIFIED REQUESTS

Performance criteria

- *Relevant sources of information are correctly identified*
- *Appropriate information is obtained and collated*
- *Information is supplied to the appropriate person within required deadlines*
- *Information is supplied in a form appropriate to the urgency and requirement of the request*
- *Help is sought from the appropriate person when difficulties occur in obtaining information*
- *Difficulties in achieving targets are promptly reported and politely explained*

Whichever type of work you do, you will at some time be asked for information. It is unlikely that you will be able to remember everything and it is important that you know where to find the information required. Your boss may ask 'What is Joanne's room number?' or, 'What is the phone number for International Directory Enquiries?'

The type of question will vary – some will be easy to answer and others may take some time to research. The answers may need to be written down in a letter or memorandum, or you may write down the information in note form and report it back verbally.

▶ What sources of information are there?

There are hundreds of sources of information. The ones you may use could include:

- people, including friends and work colleagues
- newspapers and magazines
- telephone directories: internal (lists all the people in the company along with their room number, location and extension number), and external (such as local directories, *Yellow Pages*, *Thomson* directories)
- fax and telex directories
- filing systems – paper-based and computerised, microfiche
- reference books and libraries
- organisations, eg AA, RAC, BT, Tourist Information Office, local council
- specialist organisations connected with your business
- company literature, eg organisation chart, price lists, sales leaflets, stock lists, staff handbooks
- viewdata, eg Teletext and Ceefax
- dictionary, thesaurus and glossary.

■ DIY 5.2.1

Select 5 sources of information from the above list and find out exactly what information is supplied by them. List the types of information in the form of a chart, using the headings provided in Fig 5.7. Some examples have been completed for you.

The communication skills you need to develop in order to collect and supply information are: listening, verbal, writing, visual – and common sense!

▶ How should you use these skills?

Listening skills. It is important to listen carefully to other people when they are passing information to you. The person may be speaking to you face to face, over the telephone (directly or from a recorded message), over an intercom or loudspeaker. Always have a pen and

Information source	Information available	How it is accessed	How it is presented
Dictionary	• spellings and and meanings of words and abbreviations • weights and measurements • countries of the world and so on	visual, reading	written in a book
Directory enquiries	telephone numbers and codes	telephone, verbal	verbal, operator and tape recording
Teletext	pages of information on holidays, goods for sale, TV programmes, weather, etc	TV	written on screen

Fig 5.7

notepad ready in case you need to jot down information. Do not rely on remembering it correctly – especially if numbers are involved. If you are unsure of anything, and you are in direct contact with the other person, ask for it to be repeated and you may be able to ask further questions in order to get more explanation. Read back to the other person the notes you have made to check that you have the correct information, especially any numbers involved. (These could be telephone numbers, prices, quantities, measurements, code numbers, etc.) If the person has requested information from you make sure you fully understand what is needed before you answer. Do not give out false information or information you are unsure of – check it first.

■ DIY 5.2.2

Your manager, Mr Sager, has asked you to plan a route for him to travel by car from North London to Macclesfield. List the roads you would expect him to use and work out the mileage. He will be able to claim 30p for every mile travelled and will be going there and back in the same day. Supply him with the information in the form of a memo (see page 191 if you are unsure of how to lay out a memo) and include the name(s) of the information sources you have used.

Verbal. How you request or pass on information is extremely important. If you are asking someone to help, or you are dealing with a customer or colleague, you should do this politely. Speak slowly so that the person can understand exactly what you are saying and does not get confused. If you have unusual words or names to pass on, spell them out, using a telephone alphabet (see below) if necessary. Some letters and numbers sound similar over the telephone, such as T, B, P, E, G, and 5 and 9. If there is a lot of information it may be better to confirm it in writing later.

A – Alfred	J – Jack	S – Samuel
B – Benjamin	K – King	T – Tommy
C – Charlie	L – Lucy	U – Uncle
D – David	M – Mary	V – Victor
E – Edward	N – Nellie	W – William
F – Frederick	O – Oliver	X – X-ray
G – George	P – Peter	Y – Yellow
H – Harry	Q – Queen	Z – Zebra
I – Isaac	R – Robert	

If you wanted to spell the words *'mot juste'* using the telephone alphabet, you would say M for Mary, O for Oliver, T for Tommy, new word J for Jack, U for Uncle, S for Samuel, T for Tommy and E for Edward.

■ DIY 5.2.3

Telephone or visit your local cinema and ask them for details of the times and prices for 2 films showing this week. Write down your information in the form of a note including a brief description of each film.

Writing. You may be asked to supply or request information in writing. This may be in the form of a letter, memo, message form, report, notice, quotation, enquiry form etc. If your writing is poor, you should try to print or type your documents. Ensure you check your spelling and grammar, especially when sending documents outside your organisation. The image you wish to present is of a well-organised, efficient person which will reflect well on your organisation. Do not write down any unnecessary information, or it may lead to confusion. Make sure you select a suitable method of presenting the information. For instance, you should not send a memo to a customer or client as memos are only used internally, within the organisation. Some types of information are better displayed as a chart or diagram.

■ DIY 5.2.4

The United Kingdom is part of the European Union (EU). Find out the names of the other member countries. Draw a map of Europe indicating the countries that are in the EU. Your map should be on A3 size paper.

Visual. You should try to be observant and notice things, as well as being able to find things. It can be embarrassing if someone asks you to collect an item from a particular place and you cannot see it! It may be that the item is not exactly where the person said it would be, but on the next shelf or in the next drawer. Look carefully and make sure you do not miss anything. Only when you have looked in all the possible places should you return and report that you cannot find the item. If you are able to notice things that need doing, you may be able to predict some of the requests from your customers or colleagues. This will make you a more efficient and valuable employee, and people will appreciate the work that you do, especially if it saves them time.

■ DIY 5.2.5

Look around your office or training centre and identify visual information. This could be in the form of written instructions, advertisements and diagrams. List 5 pieces of visual information and write next to each one the type of information being supplied.

Common sense. A person with common sense is worth a great deal to any company or organisation. Having common sense in dealing with everyday matters is very important. You should not act in an immature way, be careless or unwise. If you show that you can act in a responsible fashion and respond to requests correctly, you are likely to be given more responsibility with less supervision. In this way you will be able to make your job more interesting and look for promotion or a better job, once you are experienced. Those people who need constant supervision and are unable to work by using their initiative become a burden to the organisation. Try to see how you can help, inform, receive and pass on information, and anticipate the needs of others, without having to be asked every time.

▶ *How do you compose notes, letters and memoranda?*

Note-taking

You may take notes from a verbal conversation or from written material. When taking notes from verbal information it is important not to 'switch off' but remain interested and concentrate. Listen actively to what is being said and try to note logically the information that is being given. If points are repeated or information is given that is not relevant, edit this and only record the important points. Never be afraid to ask a person to repeat themselves if you have missed something or do not understand what has been said. Always go through your notes as soon as possible and get back to the person who gave the request/information to clarify points you do not understand.

You may also use note-taking skills to extract information from books, text, viewdata and so on. You may not have time to read each page thoroughly and write down the information page for page. Therefore, it is more likely that you will scan the information, looking for key words or phrases that are relevant to the information you require. When this information is identified it should be read through thoroughly to ensure it is what you are looking for. Write notes in your own words, but make sure you copy factual details such as dates, times, places, names and so on, word for word. Always make sure your notes make sense and that you will understand them at a future date.

Composing letters

The layout of a business letter is covered in Unit 7. However, for this element you will need to prove that you can compose the content of business letters. It is wise to draft your letter first so that you can read through it and check your spelling, grammar, content and detail.

Your opening paragraph should put the letter into context by:

- giving the reason for the letter being written;
- giving details of names, dates, locations or other information to set the scene;
- acknowledging date, receipt and subject of received correspondence.

The middle paragraph(s) give further information in a logical, brief and clearly set down manner, for example the nature of a complaint, details of payments made, information about goods. Some information may be displayed as a table, particularly if it is numerical.

The closing paragraph is used to clarify the main points and state the action requested by the writer from the recipient, for example action to put right a complaint, payment of a bill, placing an order for goods. This paragraph states the reason for the letter and should be followed by a courteous closing statement.

Composing memoranda

The memo is used to communicate information internally throughout an organisation. It can be used to pass on short, one-point messages or may run to a number of continuous A4 pages. It is usual practice to condense the content of information so that only essentials and matters requiring action are communicated to the recipient. The content of a standard memo is as follows:

- Heading: MEMORANDUM
- Name of recipient: TO
- Name of sender: FROM
- DATE
- SUBJECT HEADING

The paragraph content should be kept brief, a salutation and complimentary close are not required. Whilst all communication should be polite, a memo is often used purely to provide a written record for future reference of perhaps a telephone conversation, meeting, or a chat in the corridor. Therefore, it is usual to keep content to a minimum and state only the important facts.

■ DIY 5.2.6

You are the Sports Secretary for Poole Sports Association. Draft a suitable letter to one of the local politicians, Mr G McKerrell, to ask him to present the prizes at your annual presentation evening on 20 May. The heading for the letter should be Presentation Evening. Ask Mr McKerrell if he will be able to present the prizes again this year and make a short speech. The evening is due to begin at 7.30 pm and you would like Mr McKerrell to arrive at 7.00 pm if that is convenient to him. Use the designation of Sports Secretary.

You will also have to draft a short memo to all committee members informing them that you will be writing to Mr McKerrell in the very near future. You think it would be a good idea to ask them for other suggestions just in case Mr McKerrell cannot attend.

▶ *What about confidentiality?*

You must be sure that the information you are supplying is not confidential or, if it is, that you are supplying it to someone who is allowed to have it. You should check with your supervisor if you are unsure about a person's authority. For example, if you are requested by a telephone caller to supply the home address and telephone number of the sales manager, you should politely refuse and, if the caller insists, refer the caller to your supervisor. Confidential information may also include the financial and accounts details of the organisation, staff location and detailed timetables, security arrangements, and customers' records and requirements. In every situation you need to find out who is requesting the information and whether they are entitled to have it. *Never* disclose to competitors information about your organisation which can be used to benefit them or be used against your organisation. This could include customer details, financial position or future plans.

▶ *Presenting information pictorially, graphically and in text*

There are a number of ways in which information can be presented. If you have spent time searching for information it is important that when passing on your findings you do not confuse the person who asked for the information. You should choose a method of presentation that displays the information in an easy-to-understand format.

You must always remember to give a heading to your information and if necessary provide a key. A key is used to explain colour codes or small indicators on a plan or graph. Look at the key used for the London Underground – this identifies each line by using different colours.

Methods of presenting information that you may choose are:

- diagrams
- graphs
- tables

- pie charts
- pictograms.

Diagrams

Diagrams are useful for showing a layout or how something works. You could use a diagram to show the directions of how to get from A to B, or to show what something, such as a piece of equipment, looks like. A map is an example of a diagram.

Graphs

Line graphs are used to show a set of figures. Different lines indicate different figures that can be compared against each other if plotted on the same graph. A line could be used to show sales figures and another to show staff wages in comparison.

Fig 5.8 A map – an example of a diagram

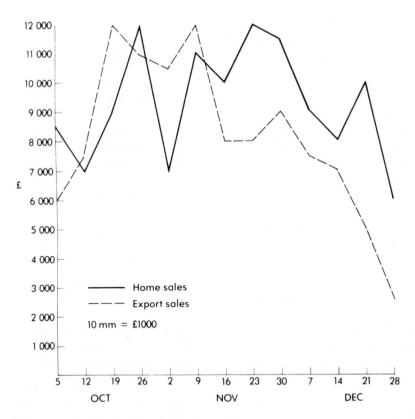

Fig 5.9 An example of a line graph

Tables

A table can be used to present information in a logical sequence by using appropriate headings, columns and lines. The information can be boxed in so that separate pieces of information can be picked out easily. Information that seems complicated when written as text can be presented in a simple format by transferring it into a tabulated form (*see* Fig 5.10).

■ DIY 5.2.7

Look at the following information. Read it through and then present it using both a line graph and a table. You can do this either by hand or using a computer.

The amount of A4 paper being used in the training centre is getting out of hand. In 1991 we only used 40 reams in each of the first 2 months of the year, 45 in March, 40 again in April and down to 37 in each of the last 2 months of the half

FIRST NAME	SURNAME	PASSPORT?	LANGUAGES SPOKEN	AGE
Amanda	White	Y	German	19
Sally	Gower	N	French	20
David	Talbot	N	French	24
Mark	Harris	Y	Italian	23
Rachel	Markham	Y	Spanish	19
Jade	Hamell	Y	German	28
Perri	Franc	Y	French	24
Leila	Scott	N	Hindustani	19
Crystal	Maze	Y	French	30
John	Patel	N	Hindustani	23
Lynne	Christanou	Y	Greek	19
Shervin	Sepanje	N	Spanish	18

Fig 5.10 An example of a table

year. In 1992 the first month was totally over the top with 52 reams used, although the following 3 months dropped to 48, 45 and 40 respectively. The last 2 months remained at 40 reams each. Last year the college introduced a new method of ordering stationery and this seems to have solved the problem. The first 3 months of the half year saw further decreases to 38, 36 and 34 reams respectively and the last 3 months levelled out at 33 reams each. The figures for 1994 are not yet available.

Pie charts

Pie charts are used to show figures as a percentage of the whole. The circle (pie) measures 360 degrees and is divided up into segments to

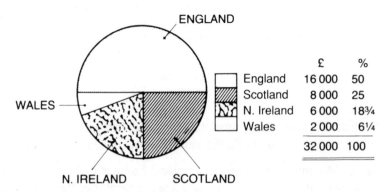

	£	%
England	16 000	50
Scotland	8 000	25
N. Ireland	6 000	18¾
Wales	2 000	6¼
	32 000	100

Fig 5.11 An example of a pie chart

show the different percentages, like the slices of a pie. The larger the slice, the larger the percentage in relation to the whole (*see* Fig 5.11).

Pictogram

Pictograms use symbols or pictures to represent approximate figures. If the symbol or picture is cut in half, so is the amount it represents (*see* Fig 5.12).

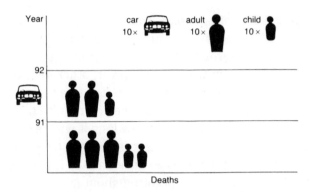

Fig 5.12 An example of a pictogram

■ DIY 5.2.8

Make out a log sheet like that in Fig 5.13 for your evidence folder. When you are asked for information by a customer or colleague, write the details in your log. Some examples have already been provided in Fig 5.13 to show you how to complete the log.

Date	Information required	Source used	Information collected and passed on by
10/6/9–	cinema times	local paper	verbally
12/6/9–	train times	telephoned local station	written note
18/6/9–	enrolment dates for College	called in to College	prospectus collected
20/6/9–	file requested	filing system	file passed on

Fig 5.13 Log sheet for passing on information

129

Put the date in the first column, the information you were asked to supply in the second, the source you used to find the information in the third and the way in which you passed the information on to another person in the last column. This chart will become an important part of your evidence – keep it up to date and clean.

▶ *What about deadlines and prioritising?*

When supplying information, apart from deciding on the source to use and the method of presentation, you must also take time into consideration. Some information will be required urgently and you may only have a few minutes in which to supply it; other information will take longer to find and you may need a day or more to find it. You should always be able to estimate the time you require to find the information and let the person know how long it will be before you return with the necessary facts. If there is going to be a delay and it will take longer than you thought, go back and tell the person, so that they do not think that you have forgotten about it.

If you have several requests, put them in a priority order, so that the most urgent and important ones are first. Set your own deadlines if you do not have to meet a particular time or date; otherwise you may find that things get left and forgotten. You may have other duties to carry out, such as dealing with the post, answering the telephone, running errands or sorting out stock. You will need to include these duties in your priority list, especially when some have to be done at a particular time, eg the post or answering the telephone.

▶ *What information are you allowed to copy?*

The copying of documents is controlled by the Copyright, Designs and Patents Act 1988. It is illegal to copy documents that are protected and the symbol © is printed, normally on the first page or on the back of the first page of the document. If you look at the front pages of this book you will find the symbol as well as a statement that copying is not allowed. However, some documents may be copied if it is for educational purposes and others may be copied if the author's permission is obtained first. You should always check before copying that the document you wish to copy is not protected. Obviously if the document has been written by someone in the office it will be all right to copy it. The Act also covers copyright in music and video tapes, records, TV and radio programmes and computer programs.

▶ *What is data protection?*

If you set up or use a database which has personal information on individuals then, under the Data Protection Act 1984, it must be registered with the Data Protection Registrar. The records should not be kept longer than is necessary and proper security procedures should be introduced to make sure only authorised staff have access to the information stored. The information should also be kept up to date, accurate and never be passed to anyone who may use it for other purposes, eg a list of doctors' patients being passed to a mail-order firm to allow them to send sales material. Further information regarding registration can be obtained from the Post Office or direct from the Data Protection Registry.

Completing Element 5.2

Competence must be proven in dealing with internal and external information sources and information from your own notes. Information must be supplied for requests from within the organisation and from approved persons external to the organisation. You must be able to recognise relevant sources for the information which is to be obtained, collated and supplied to the appropriate person in accordance with the urgency of the request. Difficulties should be explained to your supervisor politely and help requested if necessary. You must prove knowledge and understanding of composing notes, letters and memos and show effective use of language. You must be able to interpret instructions, locate and interpret information and choose from a variety of presentation methods such as diagrams, graphs and text. Your organisation's security and confidentiality policies must be followed. Knowledge of a range of reference material, data protection and copyright laws must be evident.

Claiming credit

Once you have completed your final assessment, you will need to write in your record book or folder how, when, where and what you have done to prove that you are competent.

The following is an example of how one trainee completed this claim:

When completing tasks for my boss in the workplace, I had to use the rail timetables, atlas, dictionary, Prestel and library microfiche. I made sure I used the correct source for the information needed. I obtained the information required and made notes before presenting it. I provided the information to the person requesting it as quickly as possible. I set my own deadlines when none were set for me. If I was unable to find the information requested, I told my boss immediately. When I was unable to use the Teletext system I informed my boss that there would be a delay.

I provided evidence in the form of draft memos, letters and notes and information that I have displayed using graphics and tables. I have also provided a list of reference material used in my office and given examples of when I have been unable to supply information due to the Copyright and Data Protection Acts.

■ Element 5.3
CHECK AND PROCESS ROUTINE, NUMERICAL INFORMATION

Performance criteria

- *Numerical information is checked accurately*
- *Inconsistencies are promptly reported to the appropriate person*
- *The recording and processing of checked, numerical information is carried out as instructed*

When working with numerical information it is very easy to make mistakes. Follow these simple rules and they will help to make sure your calculations are correct:

1 When copying numbers only try to remember 3 digits at a time so that you do not transpose them.
2 Use a ruler to mark your place.
3 Always line up numbers so that the same digits, eg units, tens and hundreds, are underneath each other.
4 Always place decimal points underneath each other.
5 Always write in the figure '0' to keep your figures in alignment.
6 When dividing by 10 move the decimal point one place to the left.
7 When multiplying by 10 move the decimal point one place to the right.

8 When multiplying or dividing using 100, 1000, etc, move the decimal point the same number of places as the number of zeros in the number you are dividing by.

9 Round your total to the nearest whole number, eg 1.5 and above should be rounded up to 2, and 1.4 and below should be rounded down to 1 (except when calculating VAT which is always rounded down).

10 When you have finished your calculations always check that they are correct. If you are unsure, ask someone else to check them for you.

When using a calculator the following points may be of help:

1 Take care when inputting figures into a calculator – use a calculator with a printout if possible.

2 Turn up a section of the paper roll before starting a different calculation.

3 Use the CE button to clear the last entry if you make a mistake, and the C button to clear everything.

4 Use the C button at the beginning of each calculation to make sure no figures are left in the memory.

5 Do not enter zeros after the decimal point. If dealing with pence, enter the decimal point first.

6 Round decimal answers up or down to two decimal places.

7 Use your common sense – does the answer look right?

You may need to use the following formulae:

1 When converting imperial to metric measurement, divide the weight by 2.2, eg 20 lb ÷ 2.2 = 9.09 kg.

2 When converting metric to imperial measurement, multiply the weight by 2.2, eg 20 kg × 2.2 = 44 lb.

3 When converting time to the 24-hour clock, add 12 to all pm times and put a '0' in front of am time, adding zeros to make the time up to 4 digits. For example, 8 pm + 12 = 2000 hours, and 8 am = 0800 hours.

4 When converting time from the 24-hour clock, subtract 12 to convert to pm time. If the figure is smaller than 12, remove the '0' if there is one and add am. For example, 2000 hours – 12 = 8 pm, and 0800 hours = 8 am.

5 When converting pounds into foreign currency, multiply the amount of pounds by the exchange rate. For example, £100 × $1.80 = $180.

6 When converting foreign currency back into pounds, divide the amount by the exchange rate. For example, $180 ÷ $1.80 = £100.

7 Averages are calculated by dividing the sum of the values by the number of the values in the set. (This is also called the mean.) For example, 24 + 26 + 20 = 70, ie the sum of the values is 70. The number of the values in the set is 3, because 3 figures were added together. To calculate the average: 70 ÷ 3 = 23.3.

8 To calculate the percentage of a number, multiply the number and the percentage figure together and divide by 100. For example, to find 12% of 340: 12 × 340 ÷ 100 = 40.8.

9 To calculate a quantity as a percentage, divide the smaller number by the larger number and multiply by 100. For example, if asked what is 24 as a percentage of 400: 24 ÷ 400 × 100 = 6%.

10 To calculate how much VAT to add on to a figure, multiply the figure by 17.5 and divide by 100. For example, £30.00 × 17.5 ÷ 100 = £5.25. This means that you would sell the goods for £35.25. When calculating VAT, always round down your answer.

■ DIY 5.3.1

Work through the following calculations to test your numeracy skills. Copy out each sum and show your calculations.

1 952 + 2498 + 903 + 89 =
2 20 + 9398 + 698 + 12 875 =
3 92.8 + 210 + 2332 + 15.82 =
4 435 113 – 869 584 =
5 17 649 – 4783 =
6 298.87 – 114.35 =
7 7583 × 7 =
8 8391 × 12=
9 25 × 24 =
10 65 784 ÷ 26 =
11 478 ÷ 4.5 =
12 895.12 ÷ 10 =
13 Convert 12 kg, 20 kg and 45 kg into imperial weights.
14 Convert 16 lb, 25 lb and 50 lb into metric weights.
15 Convert 8 pm, 10.30 pm and 7.50 pm to the 24-hour clock.
16 Convert 1600, 0950, 1420 and 1158 hours from the 24-hour clock.
17 You are offered $1.65 to the pound. How many dollars will you get for £550.00?

18 After your holiday you have $55 left. How many pounds will you get in exchange if the rate is $1.65 to £1?

19 What is the average of 26, 95, 386, 184, 927?

20 You weigh 10 stone 2 lb, and your 3 friends weigh 9 stone 2 lb, 8 stone 1 lb and 7 stone 13 lb. What is the average weight?

21 How much VAT would you add to the following amounts: £2.98, £78.75, £9787.87?

To prove competence in this unit you must deal with numerical information. The performance criteria do not state what type of information is required as this depends upon the office or training centre in which you work. For the purpose of this unit the most likely tasks that you will deal with, ie petty cash, checking invoices and verifying expenses claims forms, have been used.

▶ *What is petty cash?*

The word 'petty' means 'small' or 'minor', and petty cash means small amounts of cash. In an office small amounts of cash are quite often needed to pay for items such as travel, cleaning materials, string, registered post and stamps, tea/coffee, light bulbs, etc. The amount of cash kept in the office depends on how much is spent in an average week.

The imprest. The person responsible for the book-keeping, usually the chief accountant or chief cashier, will discuss with your supervisor how much cash is used on a regular basis for small items. This amount is called the *Imprest* and it is replaced on a regular basis, either weekly or monthly, depending on how quickly the amount is used.

For example, in a small office the amount used on petty cash weekly is £20. The chief cashier would give £20 to your supervisor at the beginning of the first week. During the week £15 has been actually spent on small items, leaving £5 in the petty cash at the end of the week. The supervisor would go to the cashier and request that £15 be given to the department to replace the money spent and again make up the imprest of £20. The is called 'restoring the imprest'.

The cash book. When the cashier pays an amount to the petty cash officer, an entry will be made in the *cash book*. It will contain the date, the amount and the name of the person to whom the money was paid.

A reference number is given to the petty cash officer, which will usually be the page number of the cash book on which the entry was made, eg CB3 – cash book page 3. This reference is used by the petty cash officer when paying out sums against vouchers. The reference number will usually be written in the Folio number space on the petty cash voucher.

▶ *When are payments made from petty cash?*

It depends on the office whether payments are made on request or at a particular time each week. In a small office it is likely that staff will be repaid immediately for sums paid out. However, nothing should be paid unless the member of staff has an authorised petty cash voucher.

▶ *What is a petty cash voucher?*

A petty cash voucher should have detailed on it the date, the amount requested and a description of the expenditure. It should be signed by the person wanting the repayment and authorised by the supervisor.

Fig 5.14 A petty cash voucher

The voucher should also have any receipts attached to it as proof of the payment made. Unless a request for payment is made with a petty cash voucher, no payment should be made.

If the voucher has been completed correctly, the petty cash officer should enter the folio number and the voucher number (this will be the next number to be allocated) on the petty cash voucher and pay out the amount of cash requested. The numbering system for voucher numbers may start at the beginning of the year, eg 94/1 (year/voucher number) or at the beginning of each month 94/2/1 (year, month, voucher number). The company may already have an approved system in use. Otherwise you should discuss with your supervisor the system you wish to use. The *petty cash analysis sheet* will also have to be completed (this will be discussed later).

◾ DIY 5.3.2

Photocopy the blank voucher given in Fig 5.14 or ask your tutor for a supply of blank vouchers. You will need 6 for the following task. Make out vouchers for the following:

1 Flowers for reception office, bought on 6 Feb, costing £4.65.
2 Tea and coffee for visitors, bought on 7 Feb, costing £3.92.
3 Window cleaning carried out on 7 Feb, he charged £9.00 plus £1.57 VAT totalling £10.57 (show the VAT separately on the voucher).
4 Stamps bought at the Post Office on 8 Feb, totalled £8.00.
5 Bus fare paid when delivering an urgent parcel to Head Office on 9 Feb, £2.40.
6 The post room ran out of string on 9 Feb so you bought some which cost £2.90 plus VAT of 50p which totalled £3.40.

Sign the vouchers yourself and ask your supervisor to authorise them. Calculate the total amount spent from petty cash. Keep the vouchers safe as you will need them later for another task. (The reasons for including VAT (value added tax) in two of your vouchers will be explained later.)

▶ *What if a voucher is not produced?*

Anyone asking you to supply money from the petty cash without an authorised voucher should be referred to your supervisor. It may be that their claim can be approved, such as an office junior that has been asked to get some stamps but does not have the necessary cash. Such an irregularity may be quite usual but the decision to pay the cash must be made by your supervisor and not you. Some members of staff may ask for a 'loan' (perhaps for their lunch) and these requests should be turned down with a polite but firm 'No'. All the money issued needs to be accounted for. If the accountant or auditors were to choose to check your cash tin, you could be in severe trouble if any cash were 'on loan' to a friend. If you find any money missing, this should be reported immediately to your supervisor and the chief cashier. Any irregularities, or anything that is not routine, should be reported promptly to someone in authority.

▶ *What security measures should you take?*

Each payment from the petty cash must be supported by a petty cash voucher and this will ensure that only approved amounts are paid. In addition, regular checks should be made to make sure the correct amount of cash remains in the tin. It is normal to have a lockable petty cash tin which has 2 sections, the bottom section keeping all the notes and the top section being divided into partitions for the different coins, similar to a cash till in a shop. At the end of every week, or daily if several amounts have been paid out, the money should be counted and checked against your vouchers. The locked tin should be kept in a drawer or cupboard that is also kept locked and only authorised persons should have access to the tin. The keys should be kept in a secure place and this should not be known except by authorised persons. It is also advisable to change the place on a regular basis.

When paying out money, count the sum required from the petty cash tin on to your desk. Then close the tin and count the money out in front of the person requesting it. This helps to reduce mistakes and ensures that the person receiving the money does not claim you gave them the wrong amount. If you are giving change to someone who has given you a banknote, keep the note given to you on the desk until the change has been given and accepted. This is in case someone states that they gave you a higher value note than you thought. Make sure that you enter all payments, in and out, on the analysis sheet (*see* Fig 5.15)

PETTY CASH ANALYSIS SHEET

Debit										Credit	
Date	Folio	Amount £ p	Details	V No	Amount £ p	Travel	Stationery	Post	Refresh-ments	Reception	VAT £ p
Jan 2	CB1	20.00	Received cash imprest								
" 3			Magazines for reception	1/1	5.50					5.50	
" 3			Milk	1/2	2.50				2.50		
" 4			Cleaning	1/3	11.75					10.00	1.75
" 5			Total for week		19.75				2.50	15.50	1.75
" 5			Balance carried down (c/d)		0.25						
		20.00			20.00						
" 8		0.25	Balance brought-down (b/d)								
" 8	CB2	19.75	Cash received								

Fig 5.15 Petty cash analysis sheet

▶ *What is an analysis sheet?*

This is a summary of all the payments made, both in and out. It enables you to check whether the amount in the tin is correct and it is also the document that the chief accountant and auditors (those that examine the company's accounting procedures and documents) will want to check. It is vital that you write clearly and are 100 per cent correct, as the analysis sheet is an important document and needs to be read by several people. Look at the example in Fig 5.15. You can see that the imprest agreed is £20 and this has been entered on 2 January. The folio reference is CB1, which means that the cash book entry has been made on page 1. The amount of £20 has been entered on the left-hand side of the analysis sheet (the debit side).

The first voucher to be agreed is voucher number 1 of month 1 (1/1), and it totals £5.50 for magazines that have been bought for the reception area. The amount has been written in the Amount column on the right-hand side of the analysis sheet and also in the Reception column. The second voucher is for Milk that has been purchased for the office. This totals £2.50 and the amount has been written in the Amount column and the Refreshments column.

The third voucher is a little different as it has VAT (value added tax) included. VAT is currently set at 17.5% but this amount is reviewed regularly by the government and may go up or down. The VAT must be shown separately – this is because businesses may be able to get their VAT repaid (if they are registered) and the accountant will wish to know exactly how much VAT you have paid out over the last accounting period. Any amount that includes VAT should be divided by 117.5 and then multiplied by 17.5 to find out what the VAT is, eg:

$£11.75 \div 117.5 = 0.1 \times 17.5 = 1.75$

To find the original cost of the goods, before VAT was added, divide by 117.5 and multiply by 100, eg:

$£11.75 \div 117.5 = 0.1 \times 100 = 10.00$

This means that the original amount of the goods was £10.00 and 17.5% VAT on this is £1.75; add these together and the total amount paid for the goods is £11.75.

You will need to practise these formulae until you can remember them!

PETTY CASH ANALYSIS SHEET

Debit						Credit								
Date	Folio	Amount £ p	Details	V No	Amount £ p									

Fig 5.16

■ DIY 5.3.3

Using a calculator work out the VAT included in the following amount, remembering to round down your answers.

1 £5.00	6 £28.45
2 £15.00	7 £64.92
3 £13.50	8 £111.11
4 £27.50	9 £217.46
5 £32.75	10 £500.00

Check your answers against those given below. They are not in the same order.

£9.66	£2.23	£16.54	£2.01	£74.46
£4.87	£4.23	£32.38	£4.09	74p

Putting the amounts under the separate headings in the analysis sheet also allows you to double check that your arithmetic is correct. The balance paid out for the week (calculated by adding down the amount column) should equal the totals of the itemised columns. Each column should be added up and the total written on the same line as the total for the week. If you now add the totals of the itemised columns across the page, the figure should equal the balance in the amount column (do not include the amount column total when adding across). In Fig 15.5, this would mean adding the Refreshments, Reception and VAT totals together. This is called a self-balancing ledger.

■ DIY 5.3.4

Make a photocopy of the blank analysis sheet (Fig 5.16) on page 141 (or ask your tutor for a blank sheet). You have been asked to run the petty cash whilst someone is on holiday. You are starting a new analysis sheet with an imprest of £25 which has been allocated from the cashier on 1 February. Your folio number is CB6. There is no balance to be brought down from last month. Head the analysis columns with Stationery/Post, Travel, Cleaning, Refreshments, Miscellaneous and VAT. Using the vouchers you prepared in DIY 5.3.2, fill in the folio numbers on your vouchers and allocate voucher numbers which run in order. Enter the details on the analysis sheet. Using a calculator, add up the amount column on the right-hand side and the analysis columns (double check your arithmetic by adding the totals across as well as down). Write in your total amount paid for the week, the balance to carry forward, the total imprest (in both amount columns), and the amount brought forward for the next week (13 February).

How much did you have left in your petty cash tin at the end of the week?

▶ *Why check invoices?*

One of the most important jobs in the company is checking the *invoice* is correct. First the invoice must be checked against the *delivery note*. Whoever received the goods should have checked them against the delivery note and signed to say it was correct, or written on the note what was wrong. If an order is too big to check at the time, or the person receiving the goods is too busy, the delivery note may be signed 'Goods received but not checked'. A copy of the signed delivery note should be available to the Accounts Department to check against the invoice when it arrives. If there are any items on the invoice that were not received, then the supplier needs to be informed. In the same way, if there are any items on the delivery note that have not been included in the invoice, the supplier should be informed.

When checking an invoice, as well as checking it against the delivery note you should also check the calculations. Make sure that you use a calculator for this. If more than one of the same item has been ordered, you may need to check that the total charged is correct. You will also need to check the addition and any VAT charged. VAT is currently charged at 17.5% but this may change when the government reviews its budget. Some items do not have VAT charged on them (some are exempt and others are zero-rated, ie 0 per cent VAT), and you will need to check with your Accounts Department whether an item has VAT or not. Examples of items that do not have VAT included at the moment are most foods, books, children's clothes and children's shoes.

If you carry out these important duties you will probably have a supervisor who can assist you when you have any queries. If you discover any differences on the invoice or delivery note you should report these promptly. Your supervisor will probably then double check the discrepancies before informing the supplier.

■ DIY 5.3.5

Check the delivery notes shown in Figs 5.17 and 5.19 against their invoices shown in Figs 5.18 and 5.20. Make a note of any differences and write a memo to your supervisor setting out your findings. Say whether you have approved the invoice for payment or whether the supplier needs to be contacted. Remember that it is also important for you to check the calculations made on the invoice.

▶ *Verifying expenses claims forms*

Expenses claims are used by employees to claim back money spent on the organisation's behalf or during the course of carrying out their business. Expenses claim forms have to be checked, problems or queries sorted out and finally passed for payment.

The employee will be expected to support their claims with receipts, orders or advice notes; calculations will also have to be checked. The expenses claim will have to be authorised as valid and will need an expenses code before payment can be made.

The type of expenses claimed will depend upon the size and type of business. A company with a large sales team will expect to pay expenses for accommodation, meals, telephone charges, travel tickets and taxis. An employee can also claim for items such as entertaining clients, tips and petrol.

The receipts supplied with the expenses claim form will have to be checked against the entries on the form. The hotel bill will give a breakdown of what was spent and will look something like that in Fig 5.23.

The expense claim form has been completed with details of meals that include drinks at the bar. Money spent over the bar does not count as subsistence (necessary meals) and some organisations would expect Mr James to pay this amount himself as a personal expense. However, some organisations will allow their employees to spend money, usually up to a certain limit, on personal items. This is treated as a gesture of goodwill to compensate the employee for having to spend time away from home.

DELIVERY NOTE

To..D & G Scaffolding................................. Date.26 May....

..Wimborne...

BH2 9JJ

Quantity	Description	Price
2 packs	A4 Yellow Executive Pads	—
10 packs	A4 Typing Paper	—
1 pack	Manilla Envelopes 9" x 4"	—
10	Box Files	—
1	Postal Scales & Adaptor	—

Goods received...Signed

Fig 5.17

INVOICE

To..D & G Scaffolding.................. Invoice No.1029.........

..Wimborne............................... Date.12 June........

BH2 9JJ

Quantity	Description	Price
2 packs	A4 Yellow Executive Pads @ £5·65 each	11-30
10 packs	A4 Typing Paper @ £1·89 each	18-90
1 pack	Manilla Envelopes 9" x 4"	10-95
20	Box Files @ £3·25 each	65-00
1	Postal scales	59-95
		166-10
	+ VAT @ 17·5%	29-07
	TOTAL DUE	195-17

Payment required within 30 days./Cash received*
E&OE
*Delete as appropriate

Fig 5.18

145

DELIVERY NOTE

To...D & G Scaffolding............................ Date..July 7th

.....Wimborne..

.....BH2 9JJ.....................................

Quantity	Description	Price
6 rolls	Fax paper 24G - M - T	—
20 disks	3.5 DD 226/19	—
5	"Tru" Highlighters 223/22	—
2	Four hole punch	—
20	Shorthand notebooks	—

Goods received...Signed

Fig 5.19

INVOICE

To..D & G Scaffolding............................ Invoice No..1925.............

.....Wimborne.................................... Date..August 10th...........

.....BH2 9JJ.....................................

Quantity	Description	Price
6 rolls	Fax paper 24G - 0 - T @£3·29 roll	23-03
20 disks	3.5 HD 226/19 £12·99 box 10	25-98
10	"Tru" Highlighters 222/22 64p each	6-40
2	Four hole punch @£14·99 each	14-99
20	Shorthand Notebooks @ £2·99 each pack 10	7-47
		92-86
	+VAT@17·5%	16-25
	TOTAL DUE	109-11

Payment required within 30 days./Cash received*
E&OE
*Delete as appropriate

Fig 5.20

DIY 5.3.6

Look at the expenses claim form for a typical 3-day sales trip shown in Fig 5.21. Copy out the form and work out the total claim. Using the expenses code table in Fig 5.22, complete the code column with the correct code against each expense.

EXPENSES CLAIM FORM				
NAME	DATE	DATE FROM	DATE TO	LOCATION
T James	5.12	1.12	3.12	Glasgow
DATE	DETAILS		EXPENSE	CODE
1.12	Train ticket		89.90	
	Taxi		3.20	
	Hotel		56.00	
	Dinner		23.89	
	Telephone		5.90	
2.12	Lunch		6.89	
	Newspaper		1.20	
	Taxi		4.60	
	Theatre × 2		52.00	
	Dinner × 2 (Sales Manager – Southern plc)		59.00	
3.12	Newspaper		0.86	
	Taxi		2.30	
	Lunch		5.99	
Signed .... Total amount of claim .... Authorised				

Fig 5.21 Expenses claim form

EXPENSES CLAIM FORM CODE TABLE	
Expense	Code
Telephone	T1a
Accommodation	A1b
Entertaining	E1a
Tips	T2b
Petrol	P1a
Taxi	T3c
Travel tickets	T4d
Food	F1a
Newspapers	N1a
Personal items	P2b
Bar	B

Fig 5.22 Expenses code table

Every organisation will have its own rules and allowances for personal items. The Inland Revenue, however, would see spending money at the bar as a perk of the job which should be taxed. This means that when an expenses claim form is submitted the items that do not attract tax, such as accommodation and travel, are paid back in full. Items such as drinks at the bar will be taxed in the same way as a salary.

It is important for you to understand your own organisation's policy for payment of expenses. Small amounts are probably paid from petty cash, although these still need a receipt to be provided. Expenses that are taxable and non-taxable depend upon whether they are deemed to be necessary as part of the job – your local tax office will be able to give you up-to-date information on this.

■ DIY 5.3.7

You have already totalled Mr James's expenses claim form but now realise he will have to pay tax on some of this. Add together all the taxable items shown on his hotel bill (Fig 5.23) and, assuming he pays a 40% tax rate, work out how much tax he must pay. Deduct this from the balance to arrive at the expenses due back to Mr James. Write this figure at the bottom of the expenses form before asking your supervisor to authorise payment.

THE COUNTY HOTEL
GRAND PARADE
GLASGOW

DATE OF DEPARTURE: 3.12.9-   VAT REG NO: 34526 67548

Name of Guest: Mr James   Room No: 143

Method of Payment: Cheque

Date	Detail	Cost
1.12	Accommodation	56.00
	Meals	15.89
	Bar	8.00
	Telephone	5.90
2.12	Newspaper	1.20
	Meals	48.50
	Bar	10.50
3.12	Newspaper	0.86
	TOTAL	147.74

Fig 5.23 Hotel bill

Completing Element 5.3

To complete this element on checking and processing routine, numerical information you will need to put all DIY tasks in your folder and carry out a final assessment. It is necessary for you to check numerical information. This could include a wide range of tasks such as: checking the postage book and remittances books calculations (Unit 9), comparing the photocopier log book figures against the photocopier counter (Unit 7), monitoring and completing stock records cards (Unit 9), as well as the tasks involved in calculating petty cash, checking invoices and verifying expenses claims forms. Use cross-referencing in this element for any tasks carried out under another element that involved checking numerical information.

Claiming credit

Once you have completed your final assessment, you will need to write in your record book or folder how, when, where and what you have done to prove that you are competent.

The following is an example of how one trainee completed this claim:

In the training office I checked delivery notes against invoices and made a list of all the differences. I used a calculator to check the calculations on the invoices and any errors were reported to my supervisor. If invoices were correct I passed them for payment, if incorrect the errors were identified. I recorded all the vouchers on the analysis sheet after putting the folio number and voucher number on the voucher. When I completed the analysis sheet I made sure the itemised columns added together were the same as the total column. All VAT was checked. While on 3 weeks' work experience in the Accounts Department of Coopers & Co I checked expenses claims forms against receipts and calculated mileage claims. If the forms were correct they were initialled and passed for payment. If not, they were passed over to my supervisor.

I also checked numerical information in Units 7, 8 and 9. Please refer to these units for more evidence of competence.

UNIT 6

Store and retrieve information using an established storage system

■ **Element 6.1**
STORE INFORMATION USING AN ESTABLISHED STORAGE SYSTEM

Performance criteria

- *Information is stored promptly, in correct location and sequence*
- *Stored materials are undamaged, safe and secure*
- *Information is classified correctly*
- *Classification queries are referred to the appropriate person*
- *Systems for locating information are up to date, accurate and in a prescribed form*

It is very important that you understand the need for effective storage of information. In an office you will be surrounded by many types of information storage, including the office filing cabinets or database program on the computer. In order to retrieve the correct information quickly, it is vital that you understand how each system works. Remember that each office will use the filing system that best suits its needs. Therefore, you must be able to use and understand how each particular system operates in practice.

Different offices will use different types of equipment to store information depending upon how confidential the information is, or how long it has to be kept for business or legal requirements. There are a number of filing methods and equipment, and various classifications that may be used to simplify and assist quick retrieval of information. If you and the company you work for wish to be seen as organised and efficient, then you cannot afford to operate a filing system that leaves you scrabbling through piles of paperwork or having to admit that you cannot find a client's file!

Large organisations often use a centralised filing system, which means that all departments keep their files in the same place – the Filing Department. The advantage of this is that, because all files are kept in one place, specialist staff can be employed who are experienced in the storage and retrieval of information. It also saves money in terms of only having to purchase filing equipment for one department instead of for many.

Smaller organisations usually employ a departmental filing system – in other words, each department is responsible for its own storage and retrieval of files. This system allows each department to use methods and classifications that best suit the information being stored and instant access to files can be gained. A departmental system is usually smaller and therefore more manageable. It also allows better storage of confidential material, as only departmental staff with authorisation are allowed access.

Whatever classification is used, it is important that all staff in the office understand how the system works. If files and documents are placed in the correct sequence, this will prevent delays when they need to be retrieved again. Remember that both you and the business for which you work will want to be organised and efficient – you will not achieve this if customers are kept waiting on the telephone, or in person, while you attempt to find their file in a disorganised filing cabinet!

▶ What classifications are there?

Files are 'classified' – sorted into a logical order so that quick retrieval is possible. There are five main classifications used for filing:

1 Alphabetical
2 Numerical
3 Subject
4 Geographical
5 Chronological

Alphabetical filing

Files are arranged in alphabetical order, usually by surname or perhaps by the name of the organisation. Primary guide cards are used to identify

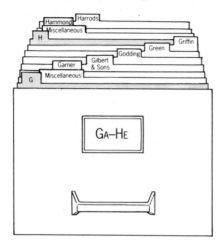

Fig 6.1 An alphabetical filing classification

where files beginning with A, B, C, D, and so on, are placed. These cards help you to go straight to the relevant letter instead of working through the alphabet. Secondary guide cards can also be used to break down each section further. Aa–Ag, Ah–Ap and Aq–Az are three examples of secondary guide cards that allow you to find files more quickly.

The advantages of alphabetical filing are:

1 New files are spread throughout the filing cabinets according to the surname or name of the organisation – new files are often used more frequently and this classification prevents congestion in one part of the filing system.

2 You can gain direct access to the files – this means you do not have to use any other classification. You go straight to the filing cabinet and remove the file or document you require.

3 Staff easily recognise the logical sequence of the alphabet – if you are ever in doubt, just look in the telephone directory to see where the name should fit into the alphabetical sequence.

If you do use an alphabetical classification, there are rules that all staff have to follow if files are not to be placed out of sequence. It is essential that you and all other staff are aware of these rules if files are not to be lost!

Rules for alphabetical filing:

1 Use the first letter of the surname or organisation as your primary guide; then the second; third, and so on. For example:

BARBER, J D
BARRY, K
BINNEY, T
BURNS, D F
BYRNE, L

2 If names are the same, order the files according to the initial. If there
is no initial, this name comes before a name with one initial – which
would come before a name with two initials, and so on. For
example:

COLLINS
COLLINS, S
COLLINS, S J
COLLINS, W
COLLINS, W D

3 Ignore titles, although you will still need to record these for
correspondence. For example:

DERBY, Miss K L
DEVONSHIRE, MR F G
DIXON, Sergeant-Major F J
DORSET, Rev B
DULL, Ms M

4 Hyphenated names are filed under the first letter of the first name.
For example:

EBONY, L K J
EVANS, L K
EVANS-MOORE, P
EWART, O
EWART-HARRIS, S

5 If names begin with 'Mc', 'McC' or 'Mac' they are all classified as if
spelt 'mac': For example:

McBRIDE, A
McCLOUD, M
MACDONALD, K Y
McKINLEY, Y
MACKINLEY, Y T

6 Names beginning 'St' or 'Saint' are both classified as if spelt 'saint'. For example:

ST Peter's College
SAINT Saviour's Rest Home
SAINT Vincent's Food Supplies

7 Ignore 'The', 'A' and 'An' in the name of companies. For example:

The SELECT Food Company Ltd
SEMPLE Associates
SHARPE, K W
A SINGLE Stitch

8 Treat numbers as if they are spelt in full. For example:

FARMER, P L
FERN, D
404 Club
FURNESS, G H

9 Names beginning with a prefix such as 'de', 'du', 'von', 'van', 'O', etc, are treated as part of the main name, although you must remember, however, that 'nothing' comes before 'something' – that is why van Morrissey comes before vandy in this example:

O'GRADY, T
O'MALLY, L
VAN MORRISSEY, J
VANDY, Philippa
VON TRAPP & CO

10 District councils, local authorities and boroughs are filed under the name of the district. For example:

BEXLEY, London Borough of
CROYDON, London Borough of
LAMBETH, London Borough of

◾ DIY 6.1.1

Copy the following list of names, but rearrange them into correct alphabetical order. (Ignore the figures in brackets.)

(1) JULIE HARTOPP   (2) STUART SMITH   (3) JAMIE HIGGS

(4) SARAH FOSTER   (5) JOHN O'MALLY   (6) ABIGAIL SMITH

(7) MARC POWELL   (8) JO WHITE   (9) FAYE DUNN

(10) PAUL RIDER   (11) KAREN KHAN   (12) NOREEN PATEL

(13) RUSSELL WINTER   (14) TYRONE CHAN   (15) RICHARD AHMED

(16) JEREMY ISSACS   (17) IBRAHIM ALI   (18) FAYE O'BRIAN

(19) KAREN DAVIS   (20) JENNA VANDY

Did you remember to do this by surname?

Numerical filing

This requires each person or company to have their own personal identity number, like an employee number or customer account number. Each file is placed in numerical order according to this number. Filing by numbers is normally very simple, because there are no set rules to follow, as in alphabetical filing. However, it is important to file in the correct numerical sequence and not to leave out or mix up figures – this would result in files being very difficult to find again as they would be in a totally illogical place.

When using a numerical classification, new files are simply given the next number along, although this can create congestion because new files are all together in the same place. Remember that we have already said that new files are usually the most active, which could result in all staff wanting the same files from the same place in the same filing cabinet. Numerical filing systems might use employee or

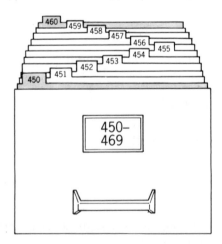

Fig 6.2 A numerical filing classification

payroll numbers, student enrolment numbers or even telephone numbers to sort information into a logical sequence.

However, this classification is an indirect filing system. In other words it is not possible to go directly to the filing cabinet and remove the file. As it is unlikely that you will be able to remember all identity numbers, an alphabetical index is used. For example, this might store customer details, alphabetically by name. When you need a customer's file, you look through the index for the customer's details and make a note of their identity number. You then use this number to find the position of their file in the numerical filing system.

■ DIY 6.1.2

Here are the student enrolment numbers for each of the students already sorted alphabetically in DIY 6.1.1 Sort these into numerical order. (Ignore the figures in brackets.)

(1) 178412	(2) 985453	(3) 472649	(4) 827308
(5) 1042292	(6) 879740	(7) 087736	(8) 199428
(9) 234226	(10) 376747	(11) 0775367	(12) 896752
(13) 762990	(14) 178768	(15) 298176	(16) 344698
(17) 907587	(18) 908465	(19) 124856	(20) 987384

Did you notice that 2 enrolment numbers were longer than the others? Remember that 'nothing' comes before 'something', therefore, you should have put the 2 longest enrolment numbers last.

Subject filing

This is used to keep all information and documents on one subject in the same place. A school teacher or examinations board may use this classification to store their paperwork. Each subject can be subdivided. For example, the English file may be divided into separate divisions under the names of different teachers or examiners. The subject files themselves are kept in alphabetical order, and any subdivisions within them are also kept alphabetically to help easy retrieval.

The main problem with this classification is that regularly-used files can grow too large. This means that retrieval of information may take longer and therefore the efficiency of the system is affected. It is important

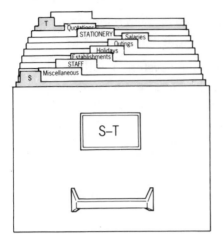

Fig 6.3 A subject filing classification

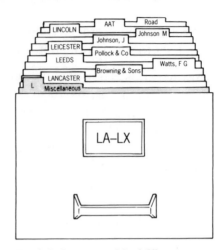

Fig 6.4 A geographical filing classification

that subject areas which are expanding quickly are subdivided to break down the subject into smaller sections. This allows information to be filed in smaller units, which will aid quick and easy retrieval. However, subdividing has to be done by someone who understands the system and subject matter very well in order to ensure that the system is broken down into a logical sequence that all staff understand.

Geographical filing

This arranges names into alphabetical order according to their location. The location can then be subdivided into smaller areas within that region. Primary guide cards can be used to show the name of the main region, and secondary guide cards to indicate each area within that region. This classification is often used by sales or travel companies who need to keep all information on one area in the same place.

Staff who use this system must have a good working knowledge of the areas and subdivisions used. A company may divide the files under country, county and town, for example. Staff would be expected to recognise that correspondence from Poole would be placed under Dorset which is in England.

Chronological filing

This places material into date order, usually with the earliest date being first. This classification is normally combined with other classifications. For example, documents located in an alphabetical or

158

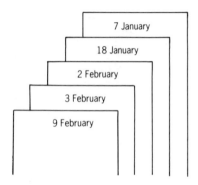

7 January

18 January

2 February

3 February

9 February

Fig 6.5 A chronological filing classification

numerical file would be placed in date order, with the most recent first. Documents such as business letters, memos, price lists and advertising literature are classified in this way so that the most up-to-date material is always at the top of the file.

▶ *How do you sort documents?*

The first thing you must always do is to pre-sort your filing. All this requires is that you go through the filing and sort it into a logical sequence according to the classification used in the office. A concertina folder may be used for pre-sorting, labelled with the same divisions as your filing cabinet (*see* Fig 6.6). This will enable you to sort all the letters and documents, before they leave your desk, into the order in which they will be placed in the filing cabinet.

Advantages. There are many advantages to this:

1 Once you have found a particular file, you can place all the relevant paperwork inside it – this saves time as you do not have to go back to the same file when more paperwork is found further down the pile of filing.
2 Once you have opened a cabinet drawer, you will place all paperwork relevant to that drawer into its files – you will not have to jump from drawer to drawer.
3 The time spent filing and when others are prevented from access to the filing cabinet will be reduced.
4 Pre-sorting can be done in your own time and can be slotted in with other duties – because you can take your time, your filing should be more accurate, and documents will be located in the correct place.

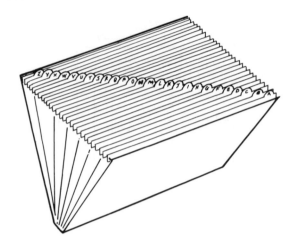

Fig 6.6 A concertina file

5 Paperclips can be removed, documents stapled and damaged paperwork repaired while you are still at your desk.
6 Correspondence for the same file can be sorted into chronological order before you leave your desk.

Once you have pre-sorted the filing, place documents neatly in the file, squarely and not sticking out. Make sure the document is placed into the file and is not allowed to slip between dividers or out of the file itself. If the file is full, divide it into two separate sections, by starting a new file, but make sure you label the new section for easy identification. If there is no file, this may be because the person or business is new and a file will need to be made up, but check with your supervisor first!

▶ *How do you 'open' a new file?*

Most businesses will have new clients, personnel and so on, for whom new files will need to be prepared to hold their forthcoming documentation. In some businesses the job of opening new files is the sole responsibility of the office manager or supervisor, although they may authorise you to do this for them! It is essential, to avoid confusion, that you follow the system already used by the business.

The steps to follow will include some, or all, of the following:

1 Confirm with your supervisor that a new file is required.

2 Confirm the name or number of the new file with the supervisor – also check the required colour coding if this is used.

3 Write or type the name or number of the file directly on to the folder or on to a sticky label – always position this in the same place for each file.

4 Write or type a title strip (if needed) and place this in the correct position in the filing system.

5 Place the folder, complete with contents, in the correct position in the filing cabinet.

6 Write or type an index card, if required.

7 Confirm to your supervisor that the file has been opened and placed into the filing cabinet.

■ DIY 6.1.3

Prepare 20 labels to stick on to folders for the students already sorted in DIY 6.1.1 and DIY 6.1.2 The labels should have the surname in block capitals, followed by a comma and then the first name. Above the name of each student insert their enrolment number – you will be able to identify these by matching the numbers in the brackets. Present these labels in their correct numerical sequence.

Moving files

It may be necessary to move other files in order to allow space for new files to be slotted in. This is a problem if filing space is limited. It may require folders in a drawer to be moved backwards to allow enough room for a new folder to be inserted. If this means moving files from one drawer to another, remember that a new label will be needed for the front of the filing cabinet drawer to identify its files. The best filing systems offer flexibility and allow expansion of the system as the business grows.

■ DIY 6.1.4

The group of students you have now created labels for are called BSIA – ADMINISTRATION. These folders, when completed, will fill the top drawer of your vertical filing cabinet – prepare a label to go on the front of the drawer to identify its contents.

▶ *What should you do if unsure of a file's position?*

All business transactions involve keeping records such as letters, invoices, statements and orders, which have to be grouped in some form of logical sequence to allow staff to locate and retrieve them easily. Documentation is said to be the 'backbone' of most businesses. Without quick and reliable methods of classifying material and then storing it in suitable forms for easy retrieval, businesses are unable to function with any degree of efficiency.

If you are ever unsure where to place a file, the first thing to do is to look for clues – look in and around the area of the name or number to see if there are similar files or names. Always look backwards and forwards through files in the cabinet to see if the file has been misplaced. Also, read through the document or correspondence itself to see if there are any other pointers as to where the file may be – it could be under a business name rather than an individual's name!

Only after a thorough search should you ask your supervisor for help. If you show that you have already looked in the more obvious places, your supervisor will not feel that you are wasting time. Bear in mind that office staff may have a slightly different filing system to the one with which you are familiar. It is up to you to familiarise yourself with their system and to ask for assistance when unsure.

Remember that information filed out of place is very difficult to find again and will affect the efficiency of other members of staff and, ultimately, the business itself. There is nothing more frustrating than trying to find a file that has been misplaced by another member of staff. So make sure that person is not you by always asking for assistance if unsure.

▶ *What is an index?*

An index may be provided in many shapes and forms, but its primary use is to provide information quickly and easily. The index itself may contain all the information required – for example, details of medical treatment received at the doctors. Alternatively it may carry selected information, such as the identity number of a customer file which is kept in a numerical filing system. Indexes are used in libraries to assist

Fig 6.7 Card index boxes

with the exact location of books, which may be classified according to the author, title or reference number of the book.

The index that you are most likely to use in an office is a card index.

Card indexes

These are usually kept in small, square, plastic boxes which contain a number of lined postcard-size cards divided by primary guide cards. A separate card is used for each person or business, detailing their address, telephone number and any other relevant information. A second card may be stapled to the first if more space is required. In a library you are likely to find separate index boxes for author, title and reference number. Each card will give exactly the same information, but in a different order. Different coloured cards may be used to identify other information, such as subject area, and cards may be written or typed.

■ DIY 6.1.5

You are now required to prepare an index card for each of the students in the Administration group (you may use paper cut to postcard size). The index is to be kept in alphabetical order according to surname, therefore the surname will have to go at the top of the card, followed by the student's first name and then their enrolment number. Add the correct address and telephone number to each card. To do this, match the numbers in brackets to your original lists in DIY 6.1.1 and DIY 6.1.2.

(1)	19 Landers Way, Poole	786578
(2)	12 Tring Place, Bournemouth	789567
(3)	23 Urwin Crescent, Bournemouth	767584
(4)	89 Grenville Road, Poole	765356
(5)	98 Shore Road, Poole	789056
(6)	94 Britannia Road, Poole	734867
(7)	3 Glen Road, Poole	—
(8)	34 Wellington Road, Wareham	680745
(9)	16 Saltash Way, Dorchester	563425
(10)	1 Union Street, Weymouth	234156
(11)	9 Union Street, Weymouth	231769
(12)	56 Oxendon Way, Bournemouth	768598
(13)	76 Somerly Close, Parkstone	764983
(14)	89 Connaught Crescent, Poole	761098
(15)	77 Sunnyside Road, Poole	709164
(16)	1 Salisbury Road, Wareham	680356
(17)	143 Binley Road, Weymouth	—
(18)	19 Penn Hill, Poole	—
(19)	76 Rosey Road, Dorchester	563782
(20)	56 King John Ave, Bournemouth	571880

When you have completed your index cards arrange them in alphabetical order by surname.

▶ *What is a cross-reference?*

It is usual practice to use a cross-reference card or sheet to direct staff to another file for further information. It may be the case that a file could be placed in a number of different locations – a cross-reference card in each location can direct the person to where the actual file is held. A company such as Foster's Footwear would be filed under Foster, but a cross-reference card placed under Footwear would help direct a person quickly to the correct file. A company's name may change or a female member of staff may get married and change her name – both situations require a cross-reference card under the old name to direct the person looking for the file to the right place.

Cross-reference cards, similar to the one in Fig 6.8, are filled in by a member of staff as and when necessary. In the case of a business changing its name or a member of staff changing his/her surname, the old name will be written on the dotted line under 'For correspondence for' and the location of the file on the dotted line under 'See'. If you were opening a new file for James Jones & Co, you might decide to place the file under 'Jones' and a cross-reference card under 'James'.

■ DIY 6.1.6

You have just been informed that Karen Davis has recently married and her surname has changed to Fudge. You will need to amend Karen's index card so that the surname reads as 'Fudge', and then file this under 'F'. To prevent any confusion it is also necessary to insert a cross-reference card under 'D' so that

---

CROSS-REFERENCE CARD

For correspondence for:

....

See:

....

Fig 6.8 A cross-reference card

anyone looking for Karen's details under the surname of Davis will be directed to the correct location.

You have also received some paperwork for Ibrahim Ali and there appears to be some confusion over which part of his name is the actual surname. To prevent confusion in your index system place a cross-reference card under 'I' to indicate the correct location of his index card in 'A'.

▶ *What storage equipment are you likely to use?*

There are three main types of storage equipment used in offices for filing information.

1 Vertical filing cabinets

These are normally made from metal and can be bought as one-, two-, three-, or four-drawer systems. They can be arranged in an office to offer extra worktops or as room dividers. Vertical cabinets allow large quantities of material to be stored in a clean, tidy and organised fashion. The metal cabinets protect their contents from fire and vermin, and because they can be locked, from unauthorised eyes.

Fig 6.9 Vertical filing cabinets

166

Nowadays, the majority of these cabinets allow folders to sit in suspended pockets that hang from runners along the sides of each drawer. Each pocket is held clear of the bottom of the drawer and can slide backwards and forwards; additional pockets can be inserted easily; and title strips are fixed on the top of each pocket to identify its contents. Pockets can be linked together to form a concertina effect which prevents paperwork dropping between folders, or they may be left to hang loosely, which allows the complete removal of the pocket if necessary.

Material is not, as a general rule, placed directly into the pocket, but is placed into a labelled folder which can sit in the pocket and be removed easily – care must be taken to label clearly both the folder and the pocket title strip. When a file is needed the appropriate drawer is pulled outwards to the relevant point indicated by the title strip. However, the open drawer can take up a great deal of space and may create problems in a small, busy office.

Care should always be taken not to leave drawers open, as another member of staff may fall over or bump into them, and only one drawer should be opened at a time, to prevent a top-heavy cabinet from falling over. Cabinets may be locked when not in use to protect confidential, private or sensitive information. If you have difficulty in opening a drawer, first check that it has not been locked, and then check to see if one of the other drawers is slightly open. Modern cabinets have an anti-tilt safety device that will prevent you from opening more than one drawer of the cabinet if another drawer is even slightly open!

2 Lateral filing systems

These are used to store material in rows on shelves – like books in a library. This system is space-saving as it requires no extra room to pull out drawers, and can be fitted from floor to ceiling. Shutters or doors that may be locked when the files are not in use and, therefore, protect confidential material, can also be added. Pockets can be hung from runners on the underside of shelves and folders can be slotted into each pocket in an upright position. Title strips are attached to the side of each pocket to identify its contents – in a similar way to the spine on a book. Folders are easily removed and different sizes of hanging space can be arranged to allow the storage of various sizes of paperwork and documents.

The main disadvantage of this system is that files may become dusty if there is no protective door in use, and files kept at ceiling height are

Fig 6.10 A lateral filing system

not easily accessible. Special ladders and/or standing stools are required by staff to reach files that are above normal height, and title strips may be difficult to read, as they are hung vertically alongside the pocket.

3 Horizontal filing systems

These allow documents to be stored flat, on top of each other. This method is used for large documents such as maps, drawings and plans, as it allows them to be stored without creasing. The front of each drawer is labelled to identify its contents and the cabinet itself is usually waist-high so that it can be used as a worktop. In general practice, it is unlikely to find such a system of filing unless you are employed in an office such as an architect's, that uses or produces such large, specialised plans and drawings.

There are also smaller types of storage equipment that can be used to protect and keep documents in a logical sequence.

Box files and lever arch files

These files are often used in offices to keep 'pending paperwork' that is waiting for a decision to be made on it. A box file or lever arch

168

Fig 6.11 A horizontal filing system

file will keep paperwork neat and secure for short or long periods of time.

Concertina files

These files are also referred to as expanding files because they open out into separate compartments, often labelled with numbers or the letters of the alphabet. These files are useful for pre-sorting documents prior to filing and are often used for storing domestic paperwork such as electricity, gas and telephone bills.

Ring binders

These binders require holes to be punched into the paperwork, or require the use of plastic wallets into which paperwork can be inserted. Guide cards can also be used to divide the information into sections. It is likely that you are currently using such a folder for your coursework.

Pocket folders

These folders are often used to carry paperwork that is stored in a filing cabinet. The flap on the folder helps to keep the contents secure, and the folder can be labelled to indicate its contents. These folders

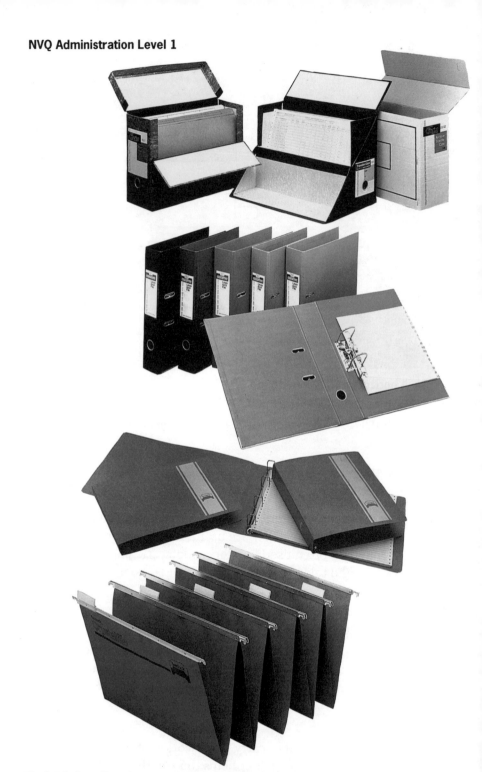

Fig 6.12 Box files, lever arch files, ring binders and suspension files

are particularly useful if storing confidential information, as the folder can be clearly marked with the word 'Confidential' and their design helps to keep the enclosed paperwork secure.

Manilla folders

These folders are brown in colour and consist of once piece of folded card. The folder can be labelled and the contents placed inside. When information is required the whole folder can be removed, or just the paperwork required.

▶ *How should you deal with confidential material?*

All business files will contain information that is confidential to a certain degree, such as personal information, financial accounts, minutes from a business meeting or details about the company's future plans. All these would all be classified as confidential information.

It is important that you recognise that the information you handle on a daily basis may be routine to you but may be of great value to a rival business. A member of staff may be interested in the salary of a colleague, or perhaps their address and home telephone number. Therefore, it is important that you do not leave paperwork lying around the office or leave filing drawers open and/or unlocked when you are out of the office.

Make sure that all confidential files are kept in one place, under lock and key, and that folders are marked clearly with the word 'CONFIDENTIAL'. When a confidential file is no longer required, it should not be placed in the bin: the contents of the file should be shredded or burnt in an incinerator so that they do not fall into the wrong hands.

Confidential information held on a computer database must also be protected. This can be done by using passwords or keywords which restrict access. In other words, only those people who are authorised to look at the information will know the password to get into the system. Passwords should be changed regularly and never written down. They can be used to restrict access to a particular computer file or to prevent the actual computer being used in the first place. Some information held on a computer database will be protected under the Data Protection Act, and this is covered on page 131.

▶ *What is a retention policy?*

Each office will have its own retention policy. This is the span of time that documents will be kept in the filing cabinet before being removed and destroyed, or put into long-term storage. Efficiency is about being able to locate and retrieve files quickly. Therefore, filing cabinets have to be 'pruned' regularly and out-of-date documents removed to free space in the cabinet.

Long-term storage may involve the storing of documents in boxes kept in a storeroom or basement. Each box will have to be marked with details of its contents, and again, kept in a logical sequence to aid retrieval if the files are ever needed again.

General correspondence is usually kept for about two years; tax records for six years; share applications for 12 years; patent licences for 30 years; and some legal documents, such as wills, for a person's lifetime. Files may be transferred into long-term storage, or may be destroyed if they are 'dead'. Alternatively, they may be transferred on to microfilm or on to a computer file.

The retention policy for each business will be different, but it is important to know what it is and never to destroy documents without first gaining permission from a supervisor. If a file is 'dead' – in other words, no longer required – then it should be marked accordingly by the supervisor. If you are ever in doubt, ask; it is too late if you have destroyed the wrong document!

▶ *What are the data protection and copyright laws?*

You will find more information about these laws on pages 130 and 131. However, in basic terms the data protection law protects the information held about you and other people that is kept in a company's computer database. For instance, a large organisation that employs many members of staff would not be able to sell off the names and addresses of their employees to an advertising company that would like to advertise their product.

The copyright law controls the copying of literature, music, video tapes, TV and radio programmes, and computer games. If you can see a 'C' inside a circle on the packaging or cover then this means that the contents cannot, by law, be copied. The copyright law is there to protect the livelihoods of authors.

DIY 6.1.7

In your own words complete the following sentences. Do try to write as much as possible in order to prove that you understand everything that has been covered so far.

1 Characteristics of an effective classification system are ....
2 An indexing system is used for ....
3 Methods of storing information are ....
4 The different classifications in use are ....
5 When dealing with confidential information I would ....
6 The data protection and copyright laws are ....
7 The 2 main methods of classification are ....
8 To ensure that files are undamaged, safe and secure I would ....

Completing Element 6.1

To complete this element on storing information using an established storage system you will need to put all DIY tasks in your folder and carry out a final assessment.

Competence must be proven in dealing with methods of classifying information alphabetically and numerically. Information must be stored promptly and in the correct location in an undamaged, safe and secure state. Information must be classified correctly and any queries referred to the appropriate person. Systems used must be up to date, accurate and in the requested form.

Claiming credit

Once you have completed your final assessment, you will need to write in your record book or folder how, when, where and what you have done to prove that you are competent.

The following is an example of how one trainee completed this claim:

While on work placement at Coopers and Co for 3 weeks I filed all documents in the right place as quickly as possible. I made sure all damaged paperwork was repaired, paperclips removed and I placed paperwork flat and square in the folder. I always closed the cabinet drawer when I had finished. I used an alphabetical system in the personnel department and a numerical system in the accounts. I always made sure documents were put in their right place. If I was ever unsure of where to put a document, I always asked my supervisor for help.

The personnel records were kept in alphabetical order because this was the best classification as the surname could be used. In the accounts department they used numerical filing according to the customer account number. When using the numerical system we had to refer to the alphabetical index if a customer did not know their account number. The index was kept in alphabetical order by company name and each card contained details of the customer account number.

■ Element 6.2
OBTAIN INFORMATION FROM AN ESTABLISHED STORAGE SYSTEM

Performance criteria

- *Required information is promptly located, obtained and passed to correct person or location*
- *Delays in the supply of information are notified and reasons for delay politely explained*
- *Information obtained is correctly recorded, up to date and in the required form*
- *Missing or overdue items are identified and correct procedures followed to locate them*

Do you know where documents such as your birth certificate, medical card or school/work reference are kept? These papers have to be kept because the information they hold will be needed at some future date. Filing, if carried out efficiently, will ensure that, when such documents are required, they will be found quickly and easily. Imagine if you had to keep all the above documents for everyone in your class or office – do you think you would be able to find each document quickly? The answer to this question will only be 'yes' if you have kept these documents in a logical sequence.

Filing means storing information so that it can be found when it is wanted. Organisations keep large quantities of information on file that may be referred to regularly or, possibly, on a one-off basis. However, what is important is that, while all information must be kept secure, it must also be readily and easily available for use, regardless of how 'active' it is. A good filing system will preserve and protect information and at the same time present it in a logical and easily accessible manner. In order to prevent files being mislaid, it is vital that staff understand the procedure in use and follow the office rules for filing.

There are certain filing terms which you must understand.

▶ *Release symbols*

Some offices have trays into which staff place documents that are ready to be filed away. Different trays may be supplied for different departments and subjects, or it may be the case that one tray is used for all filing. Whichever method is used, it is important that trays are emptied regularly and filing kept up to date. If at any point you have a query, place this in a separate tray and deal with it once you have completed the rest of the filing.

Some organisations use special marks or 'release symbols' to show that a document is ready for filing. A line across the page from corner to corner, the word 'FILE' written or stamped on to the document, or a simple 'F' in one corner are all examples of the marks used to show that the document should now be filed. If you are given a document without a release symbol, put it into the query tray so that it may be returned to the relevant department and a release symbol added if required.

It is usual practice for office staff to indicate under what name they want the document to be filed. Staff may circle or underline wording on the document that shows where it should be filed. Alternatively, they will write on the document itself the name under which the document should be filed. If you are ever in doubt, go back to the person who has released the document and ask for assistance. A document placed in the wrong file is very difficult to find and could be lost forever!

▶ *Absent folders*

When a file is removed from the filing cabinet, it is important to keep track of who has the file and to which department or office it has been taken. It is also important for you to know the date of removal, and the

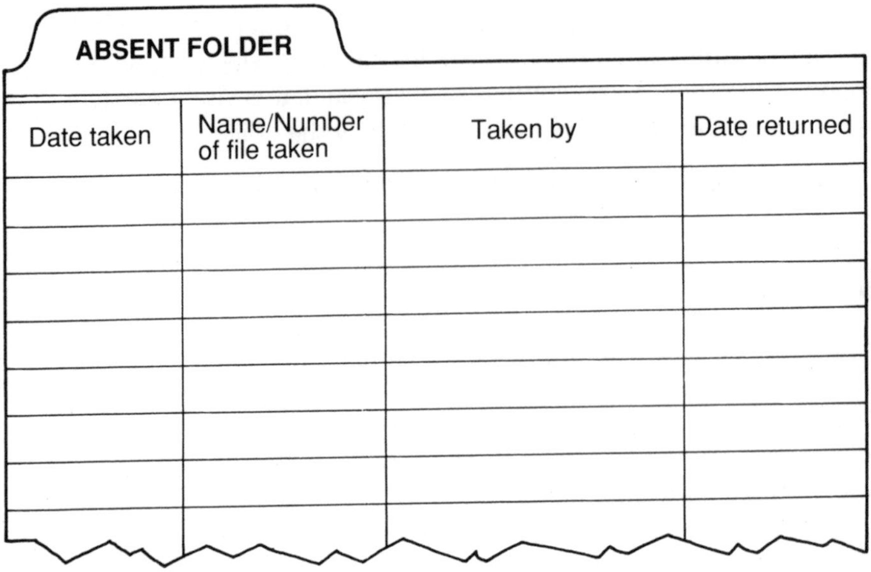

Date taken	Name/Number of file taken	Taken by	Date returned

ABSENT FOLDER

Fig 6.13 An absent folder

date of the file's return to the filing system. An absent folder can be used to detail all this information and this folder is placed in the space left by the missing file. When another member of staff wants the missing file, they are able to see who has it and, therefore, can go straight to that person and ask for its return.

If an absent folder is used, documents for the missing file can be placed in the folder and then moved across when the original file is returned. By looking at the date the file was removed, you will have a good idea of whether the file should have been returned. If the same person keeps the file for a number of weeks and documents are piling up in the absent folder, you should request the file for updating.

Most organisations use a printed form, similar to the one in Fig 6.13, which can be glued on to the front or back of an empty folder. The folder used will normally be the same size and type as those already used in the filing system, although a different colour may be used to show that it is an absent folder. The person taking the original file must complete the details required on the printed form and put the absent folder in place of the original file. When the original folder is returned the absent folder can be removed and used again elsewhere.

OUT CARD				
Document title	Borrower	Department	Date borrowed	Date returned

Fig 6.14 An out card

▶ *Out cards*

If you are responsible for the filing in your office, you will also take on the responsibility for lending out files or individual documents. It is important that you keep track of who has what. If one piece of paperwork or a separate document is removed from a file, this must be replaced with an out card detailing the name of the borrower, department, date borrowed and date returned. It is important to include details of the title of the document or paperwork so that, in the event of it being mislaid, you have a description of what it was.

You will find that some organisations use absent folders and out cards, some will use one or the other and some will not bother with either! If you are responsible for the filing, you will be expected to know where files have gone and who has taken missing paperwork. The efficient way to do this is to complete an absent folder when a complete file is taken and an out card when individual documents or paperwork are removed from a folder. Absent folders and out cards should be kept in a convenient place near to the filing system to encourage their use by all members of staff.

■ **DIY 6.2.1**

Draw up an A4 sheet of paper that can be glued to a folder to make it into an absent folder. Insert the following information:

1 On 19 August Thomas Protheroe from the Accounts Department borrowed the file of Mrs Sylvia Davis. The file was returned on 24 August.
2 On 1 September Miss Natasha Vincent, Sales Coordinator, borrowed the file of D R Carmichael & Co. The file was returned 2 weeks later.
3 On 29 September Spencer Chambers, Head of Personnel, borrowed the file on Hugh Todd Business Systems Ltd. He returned it the next day.
4 On 4 October Danielle Frazer, Managing Director, borrowed the confidential file on Lucy Lockett, which she has not yet returned.
5 It is company policy that all files should be returned to the filing cabinet not more than one week from the date they were removed. Look back at the following information and identify if a member of staff has had a file for longer than one week. If so, write a memo to the member of staff explaining the company policy and requesting that they do not do this again.

▶ *A bring-forward system*

This is also called a reminder system or a tickler file. Many documents have to be followed up, bills paid by a specified date, reminder letters

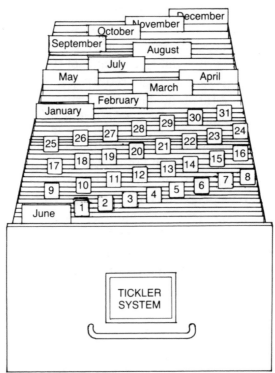

Fig 6.15 A tickler file (bring-forward system)

sent, and so on. These all require action when a particular date is reached, which may be in the near future, or perhaps a year or more away. It is important that some form of reminder system is used to tell staff that a certain task now needs to be completed. A simple way of doing this is to use a desk diary, with entries made for dates in the future to act as reminders.

However, a tickler file or bring-forward system can be used to provide staff with a monthly, day-by-day account of jobs to be done. The system consists of 12 guide cards, one for each month of the year. The current month will have 31 separate cards dividing the month into days. Each of these sections will contain details of jobs to be done on that particular day, reminders of correspondence to be sent out or perhaps information that needs to be 'chased up'.

When letters are received or appointments made that require some future activity, a dated reminder is placed in the appropriate month. When that month is finally reached and becomes the current month, the 31 day cards are moved behind the guide card for that month. All reminders are then sorted into date order and placed into the relevant slot in the file.

Examples of people who would use this system are:

- vets, to remind a pet's owner when annual injections are due;
- doctors, to check when a patient's repeat prescriptions are due;
- accounts staff, to remind them when their clients' annual accounts have to be prepared and VAT returns paid;
- travel agents, to remind them to notify customers that full payment for their holiday is now due.

▶ *How will you work to deadlines?*

Suppose that you are called out of the office to help to complete an urgent project in another office. The task you thought you would complete in five minutes has turned out to be more complicated than you thought. Several files you have been asked to locate have disappeared (the person who has them did not bother to complete the absent folders!). Another member of staff is ill and you find yourself also having to answer their telephone and deal with their visitors. Finally you realise that you will not get the filing completed by the end of the day.

This situation is not unrealistic. The daily requirements of an office can never be anticipated, and a telephone call from a member of staff to say they are ill, a breakdown of machinery, or a job to be completed urgently could all affect your routine for the day.

Efficiency is about working to deadlines and reallocating priorities. Just when you think you have organised your working day to complete all the work in your in-tray, something can happen to throw you off target. You will find you are having to reorganise tasks according to their level of priority – in other words, the most important need to be done first. Tasks that can be left until tomorrow will have to be rescheduled, although it is wise to remember that the longer these tasks take to complete, the more of a priority they become as their deadline moves nearer!

If at any time you feel you will not get your work done as soon as you had planned, it is important that you tell your supervisor. It is always better to offer an alternative – explain why the job has not been done, but that you will be able to complete it first thing tomorrow. If you are totally overwhelmed with work, your supervisor may be able to bring in some extra help to assist you. Do not try to take on more and more work if you find yourself falling behind. Tell your supervisor what is happening as it may have gone unnoticed that you have more work than you can cope with in the time available.

If you give your work colleagues fair warning of any unavoidable delay, they will understand and may even be able to suggest an alternative to help you out. If you do not let colleagues know, they are more likely to be annoyed and blame you for not completing routine tasks.

■ DIY 6.2.2

The main part of your job is to file away records and locate them when requested. However, you are not the only person using the files and you are finding it very frustrating that other members of staff remove files without telling anyone. Last week you spent half an hour looking for a file that was sitting on someone else's desk. You have asked your supervisor, Mrs Broomfield, if it would be possible to introduce the use of out cards and absent folders so that a record can be kept of who has a particular file. She thinks this is a good idea but has asked you to write a memo explaining the advantages.

▶ *What is a miscellaneous file?*

It is important not to tie up valuable space in the filing system by opening files for one-off pieces of information. It may be the case that a business or person has placed an order, sent an enquiry or perhaps made a complaint. In each of these cases, once the matter has been dealt with, the person or business may not be contacted again. It is usual practice to place such paperwork in a miscellaneous file until it has been established whether or not the person or business will generate more paperwork, and therefore a new file will need to be opened.

A miscellaneous file should be placed at the beginning of each new section in the filing system, under A, B, C, and so on (*see* Fig 6.1). Paperwork placed in the folder should also be in alphabetical order. The folder can be used to hold non-routine or special paperwork while awaiting guidance on its full classification or the need for a folder of its own.

DIY 6.2.3

Below, you will find sentences that are incomplete. The sentences are relevant to work already covered. Copy out these sentences and fill in the missing word(s) which you can select from the following lists.

1 AVAILABLE	INFORMATION	FOUND		
2 PRESENT	SYSTEM	EASILY		
3 KEPT	REMOVED	SPAN		
4 STAMPED	READY	LINE	RELEASE	
5 PARTICULAR	JOBS	DOCTORS	SYSTEM	FORWARD
6 DELAYS	REALLOCATE	WORKING	PRIORITIES	TASKS

1 Filing means storing _ _ _ _ _ _ _ _ _ _ _ so that it can be _ _ _ _ _ when wanted. It is important that information is kept securely, but at the same time must be readily and easily _ _ _ _ _ _ _ _ for use.

2 A good filing _ _ _ _ _ _ will preserve and protect information and at the same time _ _ _ _ _ _ _ it in a logical and _ _ _ _ _ _ accessible manner.

3 The _ _ _ _ of time that documents will be _ _ _ _ in the filing cabinet before being _ _ _ _ _ _ _ is ruled by the company's retention policy. Filing cabinets have to be pruned regularly to _ _ _ _ space.

4 Some businesses use _ _ _ _ _ _ _ symbols to show that a document is _ _ _ _ _ for filing. A _ _ _ _ across a document or the word 'file' written or _ _ _ _ _ _ _ on the front page are examples.

5 A bring _ _ _ _ _ _ _   _ _ _ _ _ _ is also called a reminder system or a tickler
file. It is used to provide staff with a monthly, day-by-day account of _ _ _ _
to be done. This type of system would be used by people such as vets,
_ _ _ _ _ _ _ and accountants as a reminder of jobs to be done on a
_ _ _ _ _ _ _ _ _ _ day.

6 Efficiency is about _ _ _ _ _ _ _ to deadlines and reallocating
_ _ _ _ _ _ _ _ _ _. This means reorganising your day to make sure the most
important _ _ _ _ _ are completed first. You should always give colleagues
fair warning of unavoidable _ _ _ _ _ _ so they are given an opportunity
to _ _ _ _ _ _ _ _ _ _ their own priorities.

Completing Element 6.2

To complete this element on obtaining information from an established storage
system you will need to put all DIY tasks in your folder and carry out a final
assessment.

Competence must be proven in dealing with documents classified alphabetically
and numerically. Documents must be located promptly and passed on to the
correct person or location quickly. Delays in the supply of information and reasons
for the delay must be politely explained. File activity must be accurately recorded
and missing or overdue files identified, located and returned to the system.

Claiming credit

Once you have completed your final assessment, you will need to write in your
record book or folder how, when, where and what you have done to prove that
you are competent.

The following is an example of how one trainee completed this claim:

*While on work placement at Coopers and Co for 3 weeks, I located documents
quickly and accurately. I took the documents to the department or person who
had asked for them as quickly as possible. If I could not locate a document I
would ask the supervisor for help and explain why I was having difficulty – this
only happened if staff had forgotten to complete an absent folder. If this meant
there would be a delay, I explained this to the person who had asked for the file.
I completed an assignment at the training centre where I had to record file
movements by filling in an out card. I kept the out card up to date, neat and
accurate. (See work folder for evidence.)*

*A bring-forward system was used by my workplace supervisor to record and
prepare for future visits and interviews. If a workplace visit was arranged it was*

important that she took home the required paperwork the night before so that she did not have to come to work the next morning. To prepare for this details of visits were put into the bring-forward system on the date before the date of the visit.

UNIT 7
Produce text following instructions

■ **Element 7.1**
PRODUCE TEXT USING A KEYBOARD

Performance criteria

- *Instructions are understood before producing text*
- *Text is correctly produced from material provided*
- *Errors in own text are corrected*
- *Work is produced to meet the requirements of the workplace*
- *Produced text is collated as instructed*
- *Text and materials provided are kept as instructed*

To be able to complete this unit it will be necessary for you to type using a typewriter or word processor. Most books refer to the keyboard as a 'qwerty' keyboard. This just means that the keyboard has the keys in a particular order, ie the top row, left-hand side is in the order of q w e r t y. No doubt you have received training on how to use the 'home keys' (the middle row of the keyboard) and all the other keys with the correct finger. It is important that you follow the instructions given by your tutor or given in the manual from which you have been learning.

All skills will improve with practice, whether you are roller skating, ten pin bowling, throwing darts or keyboarding. Keyboarding, in particular, will improve by continually using the correct finger for the correct key. Look at the document from which you are typing, not at your keyboard or hands while you type, and practise frequently. Thirty minutes every day for practice is better than three hours in one day, as it is the continuous practice that improves the skill.

Make and model of machine used:				
Date	Document produced	Time started	Time finished	Errors made

Fig 7.1 Document production checklist

■ DIY 7.1.1

Complete a chart like that given in Fig 7.1 for your folder of evidence. Make a minimum of 20 entries, listing different types of document.

▶ *What is good posture?*

To make certain you do not suffer from strain and injury, you should sit in the most comfortable position for typing. Strain can occur to the neck, back, arms and legs, and can lead to serious complaints. To reduce the risk of RSI (repetitive strain injury), you should use a chair which can be adjusted to suit you. It should allow you to sit with your feet flat on the floor (use a footrest if necessary), and have an adjustable backrest to support your lower back. Desks for typing are generally lower than normal desks, to allow for the keyboard to sit at the correct height.

Your head should be upright, otherwise you will find your neck will ache from constantly looking down at the desk. This means that the document you are copying from should be placed on a document holder, either to the right or left of your keyboard, whichever you find most comfortable.

▶ *Carrying out instructions*

Usually you will be given written documents or corrected typed documents to copy from, but occasionally someone may add a verbal instruction when they are handing you the work. Make sure that you write down any verbal instructions, either on your notepad or on the document itself. Remember to include such instructions when you carry out the work. An example might be, 'Oh, could you do that in double

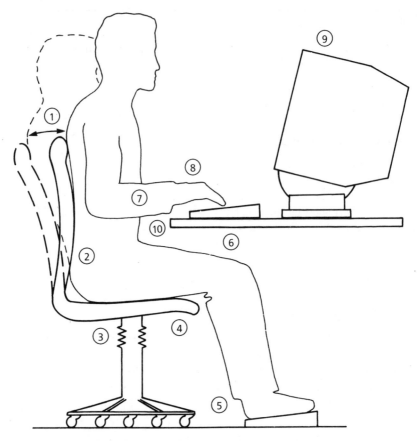

Fig 7.2 Seating and posture for typical office tasks

  1 Seat back adjustability
  2 Good lumbar support
  3 Seat height adjustability
  4 No excess pressure on underside of thighs and backs of knees
  5 Foot support if needed
  6 Space for postural change; no obstacles under desk
  7 Forearms approximately horizontal
  8 Minimal extension, flexion or deviation of wrists
  9 Screen height and angle should allow comfortable head position
10 Space in front of keyboard to support hands/wrists during pauses in keying

line spacing for me – thanks', or, 'Would you do three copies when you type this please?' Verbal instructions are just as important as written instructions, but are easier to forget or overlook if you are not careful.

Instructions may also be given about the size of paper to use. Letters are normally typed on A4 headed (printed with the organisation's

186

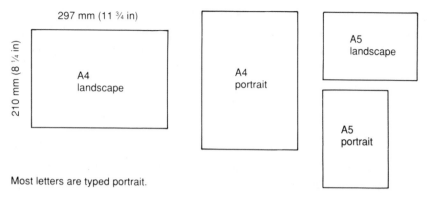

Most letters are typed portrait.

Fig 7.3 Paper sizes

name, etc) paper, although some companies use A5 headed paper. Memos, on the other hand, are commonly available in both A4 and A5 sizes. A4 portrait paper is 210 mm × 297mm, it has 100 spaces across the top and 70 lines down (assuming you are using elite type, which is 12 characters to 25 mm). A5 paper is exactly half this size, and has 50 spaces across the top and 35 lines down. The paper can be used either way: if the smaller side is put into the machine first, this is portrait (as you would draw a person's face); if the longer side is put in first, this is landscape (as you would draw hills or a view).

The most commonly used envelopes are the C5 (229 mm × 162 mm), which takes A5 paper unfolded or A4 paper folded once; C6 (162 mm × 114 mm), which takes A5 paper folded once, or A4 paper folded in half twice; and DL (220 mm × 110 mm) which takes A5 paper folded once or A4 paper folded into three (*see* page 238).

DIY 7.1.2

Different types and sizes of paper are used in offices. Make a list of the uses for A4 and A5 paper sizes in your organisation. In your folder place a sample of A4, A5 and A6 paper, indicating which way is landscape and which is portrait.

▶ *What are correction signs?*

People working in offices have not always received the correct training regarding layout of letters, memos and other documents. When they make corrections to documents they do not always use the approved correction signs. You will get to know each individual's peculiar signs, but if you are unsure at first, always ask. The accepted standard signs should be included as part of your training, and you should always use them yourself when correcting work.

■ DIY 7.1.3

Type out the meanings below and write the correction signs at the side. (If you are not familiar with them, use any beginner's typewriting/keyboarding book for reference.)

Meaning	Sign used in the margin	Sign used in the text
new paragraph		
insert full stop		
capital letter		
small letter		
no new paragraph		
insert space		
take out/delete		
close up space		
transpose (swap round)		
stet (leave as it was)		

Now type out the following paragraph as it is shown and then write the instructions for your typist to follow, making sure the correct signs are used:

there was some uncertainty as to who was responsible. The majority of the group pointed at Jenny as the culprit, but then many thought it could have been Kris Just as a final decision was going be to made, Kelly confessed.

(You will need to indicate full stop, capital letter, transposition, small letter, and insert space.)

▶ *What are abbreviations?*

As well as using correction signs, you will probably find that people also use a variety of abbreviations. These could include:

ack	acknowledge	ref	reference
ackd	acknowledged	sec	secretary

amt	amount	sins	sincerely
amts	amounts	sh	shall
chq	cheque	shd	should
co	company	tel	telephone
del	delivery	th	that
dept	department	tog	together
ff	faithfully	wd	would
fr	from	wk	week
hv	have	wh	which
mth	month	wl	will
recd	received	yr	your or year *(the content of the*
rect	receipt		*sentence should tell you which*
			one to use)

See if you can make sense of this instruction:

Wd you please send a rect to ref 134 and ack the order and chq, then tel and speak to the sec tell her we wl send the next del tog with the outstanding amts fr last wk.

The number of abbreviations in the above paragraph is obviously exaggerated, but people will often use abbreviations when drafting out letters, memos and reports for typing. You should always type the word in full. Never type words that you do not know – look them up in a dictionary and, if you cannot find them, ask. Quite often inexperienced staff will type absolute rubbish, thinking these are words they do not know. You will soon get to know the range of words used by your colleagues, and then you will be able to increase your speed.

▶ *What type of layout should you use?*

As well as making sure the content of your work is correct, you will need to ensure the correct layout is used. Most organisations use a 'house style' that is a particular style which the organisation (the house) has approved and wishes all staff to use. An approved house style is used so that customers receive the same style of documentation, regardless of which department sends it. The documentation becomes part of the organisation's image and, if customers receive documents with mistakes left uncorrected, they will not get a very good impression of the organisation and may look elsewhere to do business in the future. Some organisations are

```
    Reference

    Date

    Name
    Address
    Town
    County
    Postcode

    Dear xxxxxxxx

    HEADING  (if there is one)

    Paragraph xxxxxxxxxxxxxxxxxxxxxxxxxxxxxxxxxxxxxx
    xxxxxxxxxxxxxxxxxxxxxxxxxxxxxxxxxxxxxxxxxxxxxxxx
    xxxxxxxxxxxxxxxxxxxxxxxxxxxxxxxxxxxxxxxxxxxxxxxx
    xxxxxxxxxxxxxxx

    Paragraph xxxxxxxxxxxxxxxxxxxxxxxxxxxxxxxxxxxxxx
    xxxxxxxxxxxxxxxxxxxxxxxxxxxxxxxxxxxxxxxxxxxxxxxx
    xxxxxxxxxxxxxxxxxxxxxxxxxxxxxxxxxxxxxxxxxxxxxxxx
    xxxxxxxxxxxxxxxxxxxxxxxxxxxxxxxxx

    Yours xxxxxxxx



    Name
    Department

    Enc
```

Fig 7.4 Layout for a fully-blocked letter

```
MEMORANDUM

To

From

Date

Ref

HEADING  (if there is one)

Paragraph xxxxxxxxxxxxxxxxxxxxxxxxxxxxxxxxxxxxxx
xxxxxxxxxxxxxxxxxxxxxxxxxxxxxxxxxxxxxxxxxxxxx
xxxxxxxxxxxxxxxxxxxxxxxxxxxxx

Paragraph xxxxxxxxxxxxxxxxxxxxxxxxxxxxxxxxxxxxxx
xxxxxxxxxxxxxxxxxxxxxxxxxxxxxxxxxxxxxxxxxxxxx
xxxxxxxxxxxxxxxxxxxxxxxxxxxxxxxxxxxxxx
```

Fig 7.5 Layout for a fully-blocked memo

extremely fussy about their house style, even stating what size of print and style to use.

You may have covered different types of layout as part of your training. The most commonly used is the fully-blocked layout for letters and memos, without punctuation (except in the paragraphs of the letter). In this style everything starts at the left-hand margin, usually 25mm from the edge of the paper. It is the quickest style to type, as you do not need to work out spacing, and it is the easiest to remember.

The date should always be written the same way, the most common order being day month year (without punctuation), eg 25 May 1994, whether it is typed at the top of the letter or in one of the paragraphs.

The other layout style frequently used is the semi-blocked style. In this style the date is placed on the right-hand side of the letter or memo, and the signature block is centred (*see* Fig 7.6). The rest of the letter starts at the left-hand side.

```
Reference

Name
Address
Town
County
Postcode                                    Date

Dear xxxxxxx

HEADING (if there is one)

Paragraph xxxxxxxxxxxxxxxxxxxxxxxxxxxxxxxxxxxxxx
xxxxxxxxxxxxxxxxxxxxxxxxxxxxxxxxxxxxxxxxxxxxxxxx
xxxxxxxxxxxxxxxxxxxxxxxxxxxxxxxxxxxxxxxxxxxxxxxx

Paragraph xxxxxxxxxxxxxxxxxxxxxxxxxxxxxxxxxxxxxx
xxxxxxxxxxxxxxxxxxxxxxxxxxxxxxxxxxxxxxxxxxxxxxxx
xxxxxxxxxxxxxxxxxxxxxxxxxxxxxxxxxxxxxxxxxxxxxxxx
xxxxxxxxxxxxxxxxxxxxxxxxxxxxxxxx

                    Yours xxxxxxxxxxx




                    Name
                    Department


Enc
```

Fig 7.6 Layout for a semi-blocked letter

```
                        MEMORANDUM

   To                                          Date


   From                                        Ref


   HEADING  (if there is one)


   Paragraph xxxxxxxxxxxxxxxxxxxxxxxxxxxxxxxxxxxxxx
   xxxxxxxxxxxxxxxxxxxxxxxxxxxxxxxxxxxxxxxxxxxxxxxx
   xxxxxxxxxxxxxxxxxxxxxxxxxxxxxxxxx


   Paragraph xxxxxxxxxxxxxxxxxxxxxxxxxxxxxxxxxxxxxx
   xxxxxxxxxxxxxxxxxxxxxxxxxxxxxxxxxxxxxxxxxxxxxxxx
   xxxxxxxxxxxx
```

Fig 7.7 Layout for a semi-blocked memo

For memos typed in a semi-blocked layout the word 'memorandum' would be moved to the centre and the date and reference across to the left-hand side (*see* Fig 7.7).

When starting a new job, it is your responsibility to find out the style required for documents. Do not rely upon your existing knowledge, or training and experience received at college or at previous companies. Some organisations will produce a manual or guide for staff to ensure that they follow the agreed layout for all documentation. If yours does not, ask for examples of past documents so you can copy their layout.

▶ *Guidelines for typing envelopes*

The guidelines for typing envelopes are given by the Post Office and suit the machinery installed to sort letters.

1 Type the address along the longer side of the envelope
2 The first line of the address should start at about one-third of the way across the envelope and half-way down

193

```
                    Mr J L Protheroe
                    Mobley & Co Ltd
                    1 Somerly Close
                    COVENTRY
                    CL3 2UA
```

Fig 7.8 Layout for an envelope

3 Each line of the address should have a separate line
4 The post town should be in capital letters
5 The postcode should be the last line, in capitals, on its own and with one space between the two parts, eg GN3 2NN

If there are any special instructions, such as URGENT, CONFIDENTIAL, For the attention of ..., these should be typed two lines above the name and address.

■ DIY 7.1.4

Type the following letter, using fully-blocked layout, and dating it for today. Also prepare an envelope and mark it PRIVATE. (If you do not have an envelope, fold a piece of A5 paper in half and type on one side.)

Miss N Huggins 20 Yew Tree Cottage New Poptown BATH BA29 3JJ

Dear Miss Huggins Thank you for your donation of £300 to our fund. We have now raised over £5500 for the new roof conversion. It is hoped that work will start once this spell of wet weather has finished.

I understand that you will be coming to Wales next month and we would all be pleased to see you. Please let me know which day would be convenient and we could arrange for you to see the plans and drawings for the work due to be carried out.

Yours sincerely DI THOMAS Executive Committee

▶ Layout and presentation

It may be left to you to decide how to lay out your documents and you will need to ensure that you select the most suitable method for the document concerned. Remember that layout is important because it reflects an image of the business. The most important rule is to be consistent. If you decide to leave two lines between each paragraph in a report, you should not suddenly start leaving three lines. Always look at previously typed documents to see how other staff have laid out the document or ask guidance from your supervisor.

▶ What happens if you make mistakes?

Everyone makes mistakes; the skill is in knowing when you make a mistake and correcting it – so that no one else knows! There is nothing worse than completing a letter or memo, and passing it to your manager to be signed, only to find it comes back with a big circle round a silly typing mistake. If you are using a typewriter, the whole document may have to be retyped.

It is most important to read everything you type before you hand it to the person for signature. You may believe that you 'know' when you have made a typing error, and realise an error has been made at the time you make most of them, but there could still be some that you have not noticed. If you check your work carefully, and produce accurate work then your value to the organisation will increase. Most employers prefer someone who is accurate rather than fast. Proof-reading is a skill in the same way as typing and, the more you read, the quicker you will become at identifying errors.

▶ What is proof-reading?

This is when you read the document (proof) to ensure that it is correct in content and layout. Most people find proof-reading boring and it probably is, but it is an essential part of document production. It is useful to get someone else to read an important document for you, as they will be unfamiliar with the content, will concentrate more and it is likely they will find errors that you may have overlooked. It is common to find that when you are familiar with the document, you end up reading what should be there instead of what is actually there. Of course, someone else can only read the document if it is not confidential. If you are unsure of how a word is spelt, look it up in a dictionary and keep a list of commonly misspelt words to refer to. If you have a word processor, it may have a spellcheck, in which case make sure you use this. However, you will still need to proof-read, as the spellcheck will not find grammatical errors or words that are incorrect, eg 'it' instead of 'is'; or incorrect punctuation, eg a full stop instead of a comma; or words, sentences or paragraphs that have been missed out completely; or words that have been typed twice, eg 'and and' (Some spellchecks can, however, identify double words.)

■ DIY 7.1.5

Read the following passage and identify the 10 errors:

> On many occasions Eve felt that she was over tired. Although her doctor's had told her to rest, she had so much work to finish and the deadline dates keep getting nearer. Their was freight, retail and warehousing instructions to do, as well as all the computer entries to make.

▶ *What is the best method of correcting errors?*

It depends on the type of error and the type of equipment you are using. Obviously, you cannot use correction fluid for an error on a word processor screen! A corrected error should be unobtrusive, which means you should not be able to notice it. If you are using a typewriter you can use correction paper, where you place the paper over the error, type the error again and the error then has a white chalk covering which will allow you to type the correct character over the top of it. This method is unobtrusive, as long as you have the character lined up correctly otherwise the chalk covering misses part of the character and leaves that part uncorrected. However, this method should not be used for major errors, such as changing two sentences around, or taking out a whole sentence.

The other commonly used method of covering errors is correcting fluid. There are two types on the market, water based and spirit based – both are equally good to use. Paint over the error with the fluid, wait until this is dry, and then type the correct character(s) over the paint.

■ DIY 7.1.6

Complete the following sentences:

1 RSI (R . . . S . . . I . . .) can be reduced by using a . . . which can be adjusted to suit you.
2 You should sit with your . . . flat on the . . . and have an adjustable . . . to support your lower . . . .
3 'House style' is a particular . . . which the organisation has . . . .
4 The most common layout used for letters and . . . is . . . - . . . .
5 Proof-reading is when you check the document is correct in . . . and . . . .

Many electric and electronic typewriters have correction facilities on them. The correction tapes will either be similar to correction paper or coated on one side with a sticky substance. The type of correction tape used will depend on the type of ribbon used. Nylon ribbons use correction paper, and carbon ribbons use lift-off correction tape. It is called lift-off tape as this is exactly what it does, lifting the error from the paper. If you look at the correction tape when you replace it you will see the carbon characters are stuck to it.

The disadvantage with this method of correction is that it leaves an indentation in the paper, and the better the quality of the paper, the more obvious the indentation. This is not a problem if another character is to be typed on top, but if it is between two words or at the end of a sentence, the indentation may be noticeable. Some people may object to sending out a document with noticeable indentations.

Some electronic machines also have a line display, which allows you to correct words or sentences before you actually print them.

When major errors occur in typewritten documents it may be possible to retype the one page necessary or to 'cut and paste'. This means that the correct paragraphs are cut out and glued in the correct order around the newly-typed paragraphs. The whole document is then photocopied before being passed to your manager. This method cannot be used for letters and it may be unsuitable for some occasions, as for instance, when your boss wants the original to be sent.

If you do use a word processor, make sure that you proof-read on screen properly, otherwise sheets of paper and time are wasted unnecessarily in printing work that is full of errors. The main advantage, though, is that errors corrected in this way will not appear at all on the printed document.

■ DIY 7.1.7

Type the following memorandum. Remember to proof-read and correct any errors made.

Memo to All Staff from the Office Manager, date for today. It has been agreed that as from the 1 April an extra day will be allowed for the summer holiday. As usual we will close for the first 2 weeks of August. Staff wishing to take additional time must send their request within the next week to the staff unit. (New para) A schedule of leave for each section will be posted on the notice board by the end of the month.

If you are working as a general assistant, it may be that you send documents to the typing pool or clerk typist for typing. When they are returned to you for signature you must check thoroughly before signing and sending them out. We have already covered the skill of proof-reading as part of the last element and the use of correction signs. You should check spelling (look up any words of which you are not sure), grammar, punctuation and content. Ensure that you use the approved correction signs whenever possible as this will make the typist's job easier and you will reduce the possibility of misunderstanding.

■ DIY 7.1.8

Words are often confused and misused. Write a sentence which uses the following similar words. Look up the words in a dictionary if you are not sure of their meaning. If you prefer, you can write two sentences. The first one has been done for you.

sight and site

The sight was unbelievable; the building site looked as if a bomb had dropped.

soar and sore	bought and brought	seen and scene
tire and tyre	check and cheque	gilt and guilt

In addition to receiving documents from the typist you may also have to check computer printouts, handwritten material and numerical data. Apart from checking that the content and facts are correct, you should also make sure that the layout meets the approved house style, especially if you have a new member of staff producing the documents for you. The style and format used by the organisation, or by you if there is no house style, should be consistent. Numbers and calculations should be checked individually against the original and totals checked with a calculator.

■ DIY 7.1.9

Type the following instruction and order, and then check the text and calculations (use a calculator if you wish). Indicate any corrections, using the approved correction signs and then type a correct version.

Please invoice Mr Jones for the following items:	
10 boxes of red pens at £3.50 a box	£350.00
2 boxes of DL envelopes at £5.26 a box	£10.52
20 reams of A4 bond paper at £3.25	£65.50
10 rolls of adhesive tape at 75p a roll	£6.50
5 boxes of correcting fluid at £7.40 a box	£37.00
Total the figures and deduct 5% discount.	

You should be able to find 5 text errors and 4 numeric errors.

If you have any doubts about the content of the text, check it with the author or the supervisor. Do not assume that what you have been given is always right, as many people make mistakes, especially when things are done in a hurry.

To help you check important or urgent documents it is useful to have the assistance of a reader. This is someone who reads the original document while you check the typewritten one or the other way around. If no one is available, you may wish to use a ruler on the original or the copy to make sure that you do not jump a line when looking to and from the two documents.

Any corrections made should be unobtrusive and should certainly not lead to any confusion. Do not forget that your documents are part of the organisation's image and are a reflection of you and the standards you accept.

▶ *When should apostrophes be used?*

Apostrophes can easily be misused. The rules state that they should be used to form possessive nouns, that is to show who or what something belongs to, eg:

Carly's pencil
Natalie's lunch box
Leila's coat

If the noun ends in 's' the apostrophe is placed after the 's' and another 's' is added, eg:

Kris's bike

If the noun is a plural, the apostrophe would still be after the 's', eg:

the doctors' surgery

This would mean more than one doctor; if it were the doctor's surgery, then it would mean there was only one doctor. Some nouns are changed slightly when becoming plural instead of adding 's'. Words such as **child** and **woman** become **children** and **women**, and in these cases the apostrophe would appear before the 's' is added, eg:

the children's socks
the women's handbags

An apostrophe is also used when a letter or letters are missed from words such as don't, you're, aren't, can't, haven't, we've and I've.

■ DIY 7.1.10

Copy out the following sentences and put the apostrophes in the correct place.

1 Jinnys dress lay crumpled under the bed, shell be in trouble.
2 The ladies hats were placed on the bed upstairs, theyd get them later.
3 John and Steven said theyd be late, Id be surprised if they werent.
4 Its never too late to start again, Ive proved it.
5 Marys lunch bag had spilt all over her books.

You should have placed 10 apostrophes in these sentences.

Apart from a dictionary, another useful reference book is a good thesaurus. This gives alternative words with the same meaning, and can help widen your written and verbal vocabulary. A glossary gives a specialised list of words and their meanings and is often included at the end of a technical book, for example those used in your particular business. You will also find a general office reference book useful such as *Chambers Office Oracle* or *The Secretary's Handbook*, or *The Secretary's Desk Book* and *Whitaker's Almanack*.

DIY 7.1.11

Visit your local library and make a list of all the reference books that would be useful to you when working in a general office to assist with grammar, punctuation, spelling, or give general advice on layout and document production. List down the title, author(s) and how it would be useful to you.

▶ *What is collating?*

This means putting the documents in the correct page order. Pages will usually be numbered using arabic numbers, eg 1, 2, 3, or small roman numerals, eg i, ii, iii. You should be familiar with both. If you have 25 copies of a 30-page report to make, it will take some time to put the pages in the correct order. You will need to have a work area where the 30 pages can be placed in separate heaps. Alternatively, you will have to sort the first 10 pages (or however many you can lay out) followed by the second set of 10 pages and then the third. These three heaps would then have to be collated into the final sets. You will need to lay out the documents in a logical sequence, either in page number order or, to speed up the process, an order where both hands can work at the same time. For example, a 10-page document could be laid out as follows:

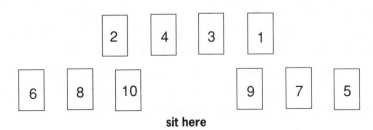

sit here

The left hand will take one copy of page 10 and place it in the space in front, and then the right hand will take one copy of page 9 and place it on top of page 10. Both hands can move at the same time and the document is collated back to front. Complete sets can be stacked away from the work area.

Completing Element 7.1

To complete this element on producing text using a keyboard you will need to put all DIY tasks in your folder and carry out a final assessment.

Competence must be proven in dealing with numbers and text in documents. You should have evidence of proof-reading your work, and correcting by using a dictionary and by consultation with your supervisor. Your evidence may include copies of documents produced by you. When errors have been identified and corrected it is useful to have the first version and correct version as evidence. You will also need to prove that you have collated and distributed documents.

Claiming credit

Once you have completed your final assessment, you will need to write in your record book or folder how, when, where and what you have done to prove that you are competent.

The following is an example of how one trainee completed this claim:

During my training and work experience at Cold Work Limited (March 14–31) I have used a typewriter and a word processor to produce letters, memos, reports and minutes (samples are in my folder). I received verbal instructions regarding the size of paper to use, number of copies required and colour of paper to use. I read through my work carefully before taking it from the machine (or before printing) to ensure that there were no errors. When necessary I used the dictionary to check the spelling (although the word processor had its own dictionary). Any errors found I corrected using the self-corrector key (or I used the delete key on the word processor). Sometimes I could not read the writing very well in which case I checked with my supervisor; he also helped me with the grammar when I wrote my own letters. Whenever possible I made sure that I completed all the work given to me during the day. Sometimes I had to leave work until the next morning, in which case I told my supervisor.

When I had to produce reports I stapled the pages together; I also used the spiral binder for larger reports. The handwritten documents were kept until the final document was approved and then they were thrown away.

I made sure that my stationery was kept carefully, so that the edges of the paper were not folded or creased. Envelopes were kept in boxes on a shelf.

■ Element 7.2
PRODUCE COPIES USING REPROGRAPHIC EQUIPMENT

Performance criteria

- *Produced copies are of the required quantity and quality*
- *Materials wastage is kept to a minimum*

- *Copies are collated as instructed*
- *Document pages are neatly and securely fastened when required*
- *Copies and original documents are distributed according to instructions*
- *Difficulties in achieving targets are promptly reported and the reasons politely explained*
- *Procedures for dealing with problems in operating equipment are followed correctly*
- *Confidentiality of documents is maintained*

▶ *What does reprographic mean?*

Reproducing (making more) graphics (documents, drawings, graphs, etc) means, put simply, making more copies of an original. There are many different ways of making a copy of a document. 'Copying' usually refers to photocopying, and 'duplicating' refers to making copies from a master or stencil, which needs to be specially prepared.

The most common form of copying in an office used to be carbon paper copies. Carbon paper is ink-coated paper which is placed between two sheets of paper, so that typing or writing on the top sheet of paper produces a carbon copy on the second piece of paper. Although some offices still rely on this method of making copies, most now have a photocopier or may instruct their computer to produce a second copy.

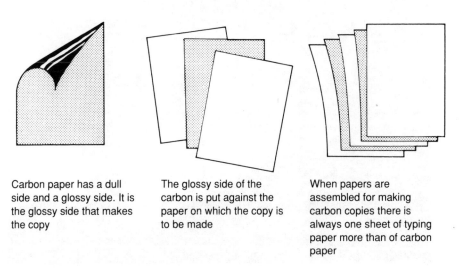

Carbon paper has a dull side and a glossy side. It is the glossy side that makes the copy

The glossy side of the carbon is put against the paper on which the copy is to be made

When papers are assembled for making carbon copies there is always one sheet of typing paper more than of carbon paper

Fig 7.9 Inserting carbon paper for carbon copies

203

▶ *What methods might you be expected to use?*

It will depend on the type of office in which you work and how many copies you need to make. The method chosen must take into account:

1 How many copies are needed?
2 How many pages are in the document?
3 How quickly is it needed?
4 What quality is required?

Offset litho

If your organisation needs to make a large quantity of copies, which are of an excellent quality, it may be worth buying an offset litho machine.

This machine will need a specially trained operator, and the company providing the machine usually arranges for training. The offset litho can produce between 500 and 50 000 copies from one master, called a

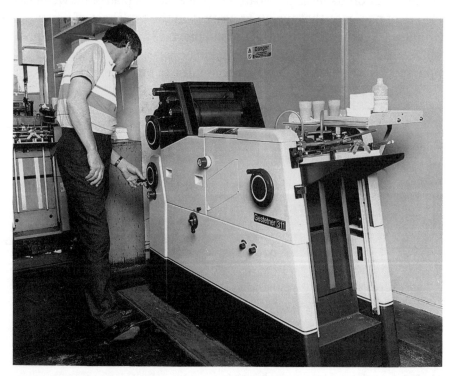

Fig 7.10 Offset litho printer

plate. A plate may be made from paper, plastic or metal. Paper plates are most usual as they are the cheapest, and they can produce between 500 and 1000 or more copies before they start to break. The plate can be prepared by typing or handwriting, but most are photocopied from the original documents. Plates can also be prepared by using special equipment, such as a plate-maker, or they can be professionally prepared by a printer. It is unlikely that you will need to know how to use an offset litho, but you may need to know about the process when recommending to your manager what type of system to use for copying. The copies made from an offset litho are excellent quality, and it is a suitable process for all business stationery, such as letterheaded paper and compliment slips, as well as form letters and circulars, minutes of meetings and staff handbooks, etc.

■ DIY 7.2.1

Test your knowledge so far – write out the following sentences, filling in the missing words.

1 The method chosen to make copies depends on how many . . . are needed, how many . . . are in the document. It also depends on how . . . it is needed and what . . . is required.
2 An organisation may decide to purchase an . . . - . . . if large quantities, at an excellent quality are required.
3 An offset-litho machine may use plates made of . . . , . . . or . . . .
4 . . . plates are most usual as they are the cheapest.
5 These plates can produce between . . . and . . . or more copies before they start to break.

Ink duplicators

These machines are still fairly common and are used by secretaries and general clerical staff. The masters prepared for these machines are called stencils. The stencil sheet is wax, which needs to be cut to allow ink to pass through on to the paper. Stencils can be prepared on the typewriter, where the keys cut the wax; or a scanner can be used which has a stylus to cut the wax; or a stylus pen can be used for handwriting. It is also possible to use heat to burn the wax, but a special wax stencil needs to be used for this. If you use a word processor that has an impact printer (*see* page 79) you will probably be able to make stencils on this as well.

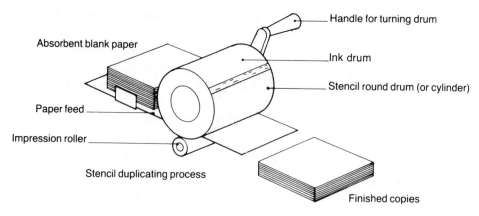

Handle for turning drum

Absorbent blank paper

Ink drum

Stencil round drum (or cylinder)

Paper feed

Impression roller

Stencil duplicating process

Finished copies

Fig 7.11 Ink duplicating process

An ink duplicating machine has a large drum covered in felt, and the stencil has a piece of card at the top with shaped holes cut out, which fit over a section on the drum. The stencil wraps around the drum and is held in place by a holding bar at the bottom. The ink is placed inside the drum and it oozes through the holes in the stencil on to the paper which passes under the turning drum once the machine is started. The paper has to be partly absorbent (a bit like blotting paper) to allow the ink to soak into it and dry quickly, although machines are now available which use ordinary paper and quick-drying ink. Different ink colours can be used inside the drum and an organisation that uses this type of duplicating will usually keep a different drum for each colour. It is very messy to clean all the ink out of a drum and to get the felt spotlessly clean. A different stencil will be needed for each different ink. For example, if you wanted three paragraphs on a page, with the first paragraph in black ink, the second in red and the third in black again, two stencils would be needed. The first stencil would have the first and last paragraphs on it (with a gap in the middle to allow for the second paragraph). All the copies needed would be duplicated with the black ink, and then be allowed to dry. The black ink drum would be taken off the ink duplicator and the red drum inserted. The second stencil would be put on the drum and the copies made would be passed a second time through the machine, and this time with the second paragraph being printed in red ink in the gap left.

Although a duplicating machine does not require specialist training, it can be messy if used by an inexperienced operator. Without sufficient knowledge, changing inks or drums and removing a stencil can be

Fig 7.12 Ink duplicator

awkward. Many companies supplying ink duplicating machines will include training for staff when the machine is bought. The copies made on ink duplicators are of a reasonable quality and suitable for internal use, eg for staff notices, memos or instructions. A stencil will usually produce up to 500 copies easily and some have been known to produce 5000. However, after 1000 copies, the ink usually starts to soak the stencil, sticking to the paper, and the stencil starts to tear. This will result in the ink seeping through on to the copies and producing a mess!

■ **DIY 7.2.2**

State which method, from the ones covered so far, you would recommend for producing the following copies:

1 A copy of an internal memo
2 5 reams of letterheaded paper
3 A staff handbook (1000 copies required)
4 500 copies of a 2-colour leaflet for a local school fete
5 A staff memo (500 copies required)

Computers and word processors

If you are using a computer or WP with an impact printer, you may be able to use carbon paper to take extra copies of your documents – this would be very economical. However, carbon copies are not very good quality and, although they are suitable for file copies, they are not good enough for external use. Many clerk typists will make an extra copy, using their printer instead of using a photocopier. Whether or not this is costing the organisation more will depend on the type of printer used and the type of photocopier available. Some of the larger, more complicated photocopiers are only worth using if you are making at least six copies of a document.

Photocopiers

The most common machine used in offices for reprographics is the photocopier. The facilities available on machines vary a great deal: small machines have very few facilities, and some of the large machines do everything but make the tea! The majority of copiers do not need special paper. The document to be copied is placed on a glass top, which is covered by a rubber and plastic lid, or it may be fed into the machine. If more than 200 copies of a document are required, it may be worth considering ink or offset duplicating.

▶ *What basic photocopier facilities would you be expected to use?*

The basic photocopiers available will carry out the following functions:

- copying 1–99 copies of an A4 sheet
- reducing A4 to A5
- enlarging A5 to A4.

More advanced copiers (sometimes called smart copiers) will also:

- copy using larger and smaller sizes of paper
- copy using both sides of the paper (back-to-back copying, called duplexing)
- arrange the copies in page number order (collate)
- accept card and plastic transparencies
- automatically feed in the pages to be copied (automatic document feeder (ADF))

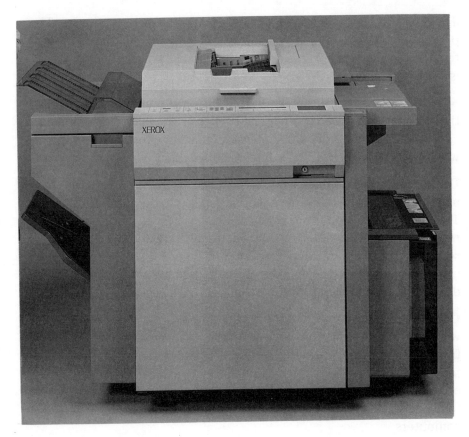

Fig 7.13 A photocopier

- staple the sheets together when the copying has finished
- make colour copies (these machines are expensive and not common in general offices).

Collating

We have already discussed the collating of documents on page 201. This described how to collate manually. If you work for an organisation that produces many multi-page documents, you may have some of the following equipment or facilities available to assist you.

Collator. If you are asked to carry out a lot of collating, it may be worth investigating the cost of a collating machine. Machines that automatically collate, staple and fold documents are also available.

209

Jogger. Another machine which helps in a print room is a jogger. The photocopied documents are placed in the jogger and it shakes them together so that the corners are neatly together before the document is stapled.

Stapling may be an automatic process in some photocopiers. If you do the stapling, you may use a manual stapler or an electric one – take care with an electric ones as it is fast and likely to make you jump when you use it, so keep your fingers out of the way!

Duplexing (back-to-back copying) can be carried out on a basic machine by feeding the same sheet of paper into the machine again. This reduces the amount of paper used, so is cost effective. It also reduces the amount of paper that has to be circulated, which may reduce postal costs (if the document is to be posted to customers, for example), or reduce the amount of space required for filing (if the document is being distributed to staff).

Computers. The most intelligent photocopiers combine computing with copying. Information can be entered on to a computer directly or from disk and stored, and this can then be recalled and automatically printed directly by the copier without having a 'hard' copy (original copy) to print from. It is also possible to network an intelligent copier to allow it to receive and send information to and from distant computers.

■ DIY 7.2.3

Make yourself a copy of the following photocopy record on A4 paper. Use the record to list all the tasks carried out over the next few weeks. You should try to include various sizes of documents, multi-page documents, enlarged, reduced and back-to-back copies, etc.

Date	Details of work	Number of copies	Notes

I confirm that the above work was carried out by ....

Signed .... (Supervisor) Date ....

Sometimes you may be asked to include a picture or diagram in the middle of a document. If the diagram cannot be typed or word processed, the typist will leave a space big enough for the diagram to be inserted. Usually this is done by glueing the diagram or picture in place – your original may look messy, but the copies should look perfect. This process is called 'cutting and pasting'. In the same way, there may be a part of the document that your manager does not want copied and it is possible to put a plain piece of paper over the paragraph or drawing that is not required and photocopy the remainder. This process is called 'masking'.

Whichever type of copier you use, make sure you are familiar with the recommended user instructions. If you are unsure of how to operate a machine, read the manufacturer's manual or ask someone who is familiar with the machine.

▶ *What health and safety points should you remember?*

Any machine using electricity should be away from the wall to allow the air to circulate around it. This helps to cool the machine when it is being used. The electric cable should not trail across a floor where people are walking, eg across a doorway or gangway. It should be switched off at night and the plug taken out. *Never* put any fluids near a copier – not even correcting fluid. Do not be tempted to put your hands inside the machine, unless you know exactly what you are doing. The machine should be regularly maintained, by an expert. This can usually be arranged through the supplier, or if you rent your machine, it is likely to be part of the agreement.

▶ *What will you be able to repair on the machine?*

The type of problem that regularly causes a machine to stop is paper running out or jamming somewhere inside the machine. However, you should not attempt to correct these problems unless you have been shown how to do this by someone who knows. When replacing the paper there is usually a paper tray that needs to be filled. The paper should be taken out of the protective wrapping paper carefully and used the right way up. The label on the protective cover is usually the right way up, or if you pass your finger and thumb carefully along the

Display panel

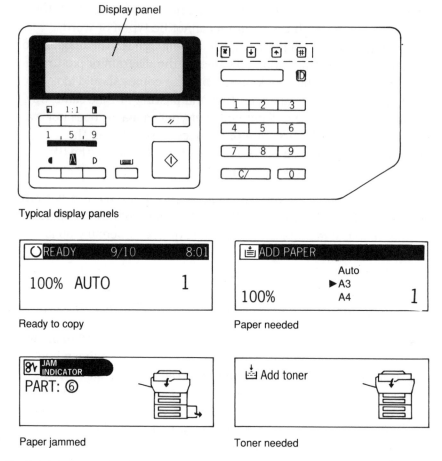

Typical display panels

Ready to copy

Paper needed

Paper jammed

Toner needed

Fig 7.14 Indicator panel on a typical photocopier

edge of a piece of paper you can usually feel which is the 'sharper' side. When the paper is cut at the factory, the edge of the paper is very slightly bent down. The paper should be placed in the machine the same way as it was cut – this will help to reduce paper jams. Most machines have a special sign that flashes when the paper has run out.

A machine jam may easily be put right. If you open the front of a photocopier, there is normally a set of coloured handles or numbered parts. These will indicate where a jam is likely to occur. If you can see the paper, then the position of the jam is likely to be obvious. Otherwise you may have to work through the positions one at a time. Be careful when you remove the paper not to tear it because, if a little piece is left inside, it will probably be enough to jam the next sheet.

Another common cause of the machine stopping, or not producing copies, is when it runs out of toner. This is the powder ink that the machine uses to create the image. The toner is attracted to the drum of the machine like a magnet. The drum rolls the image on to the paper and the paper is quickly heated to get the toner to set. Sometimes when you are unjamming a piece of paper you will find that the toner on the paper is still dry and rubs off on your hands. This is because it has not yet passed through the heat process. Before the toner runs out completely, the quality of the copies obtained from the machine is likely to become poor. You will probably know that the toner is low and will need replacing soon, but a light on the copier will flash and indicate that toner is low or out.

Toner is supplied in cartridges and new ones should not under any circumstances be opened. When removing the old cartridge, make sure that you do not spill any toner on your hands or clothes. If it does get on your hands, wash them in cold water. When the new cartridge is placed into the machine, a strip of paper or foil is pulled back allowing the toner to drop into the machine.

Sometimes, when a document has been corrected with fluid, it has not been given enough time to dry before someone has taken a photocopy. The result is a mark on the glass of the machine and a copy with a blotch on it, where the fluid has spread. Any marks such as this should be removed from the glass with a damp cloth (not a wet cloth), but stubborn marks may need a little spirit, such as thinners, on them. Keep away from the glass anything that may scratch or mark it, otherwise all future photocopies will have a similar mark on them.

■ DIY 7.2.4

List all the facilities on the photocopier that you use. Find out who is responsible for repairs and who you report problems to.

▶ *What if the machine fault cannot be repaired?*

The maintenance engineer should be called to correct any fault which cannot easily be put right. Most engineers will call within 24 hours as they appreciate the urgency of the matter. Make sure that you tell your colleagues and supervisors that the machine is out of action and that there will be a delay in getting the copying finished. This is extremely important, especially if your colleagues have a deadline to meet and need the copies urgently.

▶ How is a multi-page document held together?

There are many different methods of securing documents apart from stapling them. Some need special equipment but others are cheap and as efficient as stapling.

Paperclips

Paperclips come in different sizes, from quite small to huge (up to 50–75mm long). They are quick and easy to use and fairly cheap to buy. The disadvantage with them is that they tend to pick up other documents when they are kept in a pile.

Treasury tags

To use tags, holes need to be punched in the document, either in the top left-hand corner or half-way down the left-hand side. The treasury tags have plastic strips at each end and one is threaded through the hole. Tags are available in different colours and lengths, with longer ones for bulky documents. They are quick, cheap and efficient to use, but are not really suitable for sending documents externally.

Ring binders

Once again, the document would have to be hole punched. Ring binders may have two or four rings and come in different sizes. They are quite expensive and would not be the normal way of securing everyday documents. However, they are extremely useful for items such as staff handbooks or a set of instructions.

Spiral binding

This process needs a special machine which is used to punch oblong holes along the edge of the document, and to open up the teeth of the plastic spiral. The pages are fed carefully on to the open teeth, and when the last page has been positioned the teeth can be closed, securing the document. Metal continuous spirals are also used in this way, except that the spiral is pushed on from the bottom to the top of the document. Electric machines are available that will carry out the whole process and would be a useful piece of equipment to any office that regularly produces booklets requiring binding. The result is a professional look to the document which is suitable for internal and external use.

Flat comb binder

This is a similar process to the spiral binding, the difference being that two plastic strips are used, one with spikes and one with holes. Holes are punched in the document and the spikes are pushed through the holes. The holed strip is then pushed over the spikes and is heat sealed, the document being secured between the two plastic strips. Again a professional look is obtained but special equipment is required that is quite expensive to purchase.

Slide binder

A slide binder is the easiest to use, and is quite cheap, but is not so useful. The binder is made from solid plastic and is slid along the edge of the document (no hole punching is needed). The pages are held

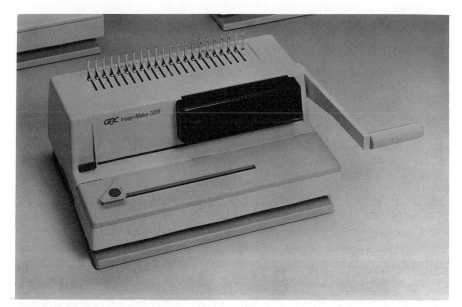

Fig 7.15 A plastic comb binder

firmly but they can be difficult to keep open when reading, as the book would not stay open flat on a desk. Although this is not essential, a plastic tray with guidelines is available, which helps to get the binder on easily and in the correct place.

Heat binding

This gives the document a professional look, similar to a paperback book. The document has a gummed strip placed along the edge and this is put into a heat machine which locks the strip into place. Once cool, the document can be handled without fear of losing the pages. Special equipment is required and this is expensive, so it would not be worth buying unless a lot of binding is required.

If you meet any problems in collating and securing your documents, make sure that you inform your supervisor. You should also tell your colleagues of the delay that will occur in getting the finished work back to them.

▶ *How can you make sure that material waste is kept to a minimum?*

The material used most when copying is paper. To make sure that waste is reduced, follow these simple guidelines.

1 Place the document to be copied carefully on to the glass of the photocopier and make sure it is the right way round. (Use the guide arrows on the machine.)
2 If you need a lot of copies, try making one first to ensure it is all right. Alter the density (lighten or darken the copy) if necessary. When you have a good copy, the remaining copies can be made.
3 If you are copying back-to-back, always try one first, to make sure that the second side is the right way up.
4 Keep a tray for any wasted 'first tries'. These can be used on the other side, or can be cut up for use as rough paper in the office.
5 Use the back-to-back facility whenever possible, as this reduces by half the amount of paper required.
6 Reduce copies whenever possible, such as A3 to A4, but make sure the final document is still easy to read!
7 Do not make extra copies 'just in case'. Only copy the amount required.

8 Do not store the paper anywhere damp, as damp paper will jam in the machine.

9 Restrict staff use to essential work and do not allow personal work to be carried out.

10 Make sure that the document to be copied is suitable for copying. For instance, some coloured papers will not copy, eg dark orange, and photographs do not always copy well; some other documents may be too light to give clear copies.

11 If you have been interrupted while copying, make sure that you are at the correct place before starting again. Quite often people will ask to 'jump the queue' for just one copy, but this can be quite off-putting if you are in the middle of a long and complicated job.

■ DIY 7.2.5

Use as many of the systems of collating and binding listed that are available to you and include these in your folder as evidence. Which methods of securing would you use for the following:

1 A memo with an appendix
2 40 copies of a 100 page report
3 A letter with an invoice enclosed
4 A staff handbook on company policies (pages will be added later)
5 A training manual on how to use the new computer system

▶ How can staff use of copiers be supervised?

Some organisations use a record book to record how many copies are made by each member of staff and each department. This book may be kept by the photocopier operator, if there is one, or it may be filled in by each person using the machine. If it is left to each individual to fill in, the copier counter needs to be checked regularly to make sure that people are being honest. If the counter number and the book record are totally different, another method of recording may need to be found. This could mean employing a photocopier operator who will carry out all requests and keep a log of work carried out.

Some machines may have a special card reader supplied as an accessory. Each member of staff is issued with a 'credit' card that will

217

allow them to make copies up to the maximum credited on the card. The card is inserted in the reader and the copier will then allow users to make copies. The card works in a similar way to a telephone card in that each time the card is used the units are reduced on the card. Once the maximum has been reached, the machine will not allow any more copies to be made. The card will have to be returned to the main office for renewal or replacement.

Another system in use, which is similar to the credit card, is a copier which has a keyboard attached to it. Each member of staff is given a PIN number (Personal Identity Number). This number must be keyed in before the machine will operate. Each PIN number will have a maximum number of copies allowed, this information being stored in the memory of the keyboard. Once this number is reached the machine will not allow any more copies to be made.

Larger organistions may invest in a central reprographic section, which may have a smart copier, and this section will carry out all requests for large numbers of copies (for example anything more than five copies). The costs can be reduced but the time taken to send the document to the repro section and get it returned may be a disadvantage.

■ DIY 7.2.6

You have a new junior starting in the office. Design a 'help' sheet for her to follow when using your photocopier. Include the facilities available, how to reduce and enlarge, how to collate and fasten documents neatly and securely. Do not forget to include a section on reduction of waste and cost.

▶ *Can any document be copied?*

The copying of documents is controlled by the Copyright, Designs and Patents Act 1988. It is illegal to copy documents that are protected and the symbol © is printed, normally on the first page or the back of the first page of the document, or inside the front cover. If you look at the front pages of this book you will find the symbol as well as a statement that copying is not allowed. However, some documents may be copied if it is for educational purposes and others may be copied if the author's permission is obtained first. You should always check before copying that the document you wish to copy is not protected. Obviously if the document has been written by someone in the office it will be all right to copy it. The Act also covers copyright in music and video tapes, records, TV and radio programmes and computer programs.

■ DIY 7.2.7

Your organisation is having problems with the number of excess copies being made by staff. Write a memo to your manager suggesting ways in which the use may be reduced, including your ideas for a new system. Your manager has also requested that you draft a notice for display by the copiers about the Copyright Act (you may need to visit your local library to read a summary of the Act).

Completing Element 7.2

To complete this element on producing copies using reprographic equipment you will need to put all DIY tasks in your folder and carry out a final assessment.

Competence must be proven in dealing with: single-page and multi-page documents, enlarged and reduced copies, and single-sided and double-sided copies. Samples of documents copied should be included in your evidence folder whenever possible.

Claiming credit

Once you have completed your final assessment, you will need to write in your record book or folder how, when, where and what you have done to prove that you are competent.

The following is an example of how one trainee completed this claim:

During my time at the training centre and during my work experience (November – May) I have made plenty of copies (see my photocopy log for details). I have always made sure that the correct number of copies were made and that the quality was as good as possible. I reduced wastage by making sure that the machine was correctly set before using it and by first making one copy of backed documents before running off several. I returned the original copy to the correct person and distributed the copies as requested. I always made sure that confidential documents were kept private and did not let anyone else read them; I did not take more copies than were necessary. I always removed the original from the copier before returning to my desk.

On occasions the machine was out of order and I made sure that I informed the staff immediately that their copying could not be done. I also informed my supervisor if the machine was not operating properly.

The type of machine I used was (fill in the name of the machine you have used).

UNIT 8
Handle mail

■ Element 8.1
RECEIVE, SORT AND DISTRIBUTE MAIL

Performance criteria

- *Procedures for receiving mail are in accordance with organisational requirements*
- *Mail is sorted according to instructions within appropriate timescale*
- *Mail is directed to the relevant person within appropriate timescale*
- *Unavoidable delays in distribution are promptly reported to the appropriate person*

Mail arriving at an organisation may include many different documents. There may be letters, quotations, orders, invoices, enquiries, applications for jobs and advertising material sent by other organisations. It is very important to open and distribute the mail to each department without delay, so that office staff are able to make a start on their day's work as soon as they arrive in the office.

In a large organisation, it is usual practice for mail-room staff to start work before the other office workers in order to make sure that all the mail has been delivered to each department by the time the office workers are ready to begin their day. However, in a small office it may be the case that only one person is responsible for opening, sorting and delivering the mail.

Some organisations rent a private box or bag from the Post Office for an annual fee. This allows the organisation to collect mail or parcels from the Post Office every day, except Sunday. The organisation can collect mail from their box or bag early in the morning to ensure that it has been sorted and delivered to each department ready for action at the beginning of the day. If an organisation has no private box or bag at the Post Office's delivery office, mail will be delivered in the normal way.

▶ *How should incoming mail be sorted?*

Each organisation will have its own procedure for dealing with incoming mail depending on the size and type of business carried out. For example, a large mail-order company that keeps to a strict timetable would employ experienced staff who are able to use specialist equipment. A smaller company may only employ one person who deals with mail as one of a number of responsibilities and, therefore, follows a less rigid timetable.

In both cases remember that all mail is important, regardless of the size of the organisation. Mail which fails to reach its destination quickly and accurately may result in the loss of valuable business.

▶ *How do most organisations deal with incoming mail?*

The following steps are likely to be followed:

1 Sign for registered and recorded delivery items. (Details of these may have to be entered into a Special Mail Register.)

SPECIAL MAIL REGISTER				
Date	Time	Sender	Method of Delivery	Received By

Fig 8.1 Special mail register

■ DIY 8.1.1

Make your own copy of a page from a Special Mail Register. Enter the details of the following post received by you at 9.00 am today:

- recorded delivery letter from Arthur Simmons & Co
- recorded delivery packet from Samuels & Son
- registered letter from Mrs H Chandra
- recorded delivery packet from Sally Bright
- Trakback parcel from HMSO
- Datapost parcel from West Midlands Branch office
- confidential letter to Mr Brice in Personnel.

2 Remove all mail that is marked 'Private' or 'Confidential' and put to one side.

3 Open envelopes, using your finger or a paper knife. Alternatively, a letter opening machine may be used, in which case the contents of the letter should be 'tapped' down to the bottom of the envelope so they are not cut with the blade.

Do not open registered, recorded delivery, personal or confidential mail. This mail is usually taken to the person or department to whom it is addressed for opening.

4 Remove the contents carefully from each envelope, checking that nothing has been left inside. Attach all enclosures to the back of the letter with either a paperclip or staple. Enclosures are indicated at the bottom of the correspondence by the letters 'Enc' or 'Encs'. If the enclosure is not there, write 'NOT ENCLOSED' on the letter.

You or another member of staff will have the responsibility of contacting the sender of the letter to inform him/her of the missing enclosure.

5 Date stamp all the mail – in the case of mail which is registered, recorded delivery, private or confidential, date stamp the unopened envelope. (Some electric date stamps print the time as well as the date.)

6 Some organisations require a record of all incoming mail to be kept, usually in a special file or book. Most organisations will require mail that contains remittances in the form of cash, postal orders, stamps or cheques to be recorded in a Remittances Book. Each day details

REMITTANCES BOOK				
Date	Sender	Type of Payment	Amount £	Signed

Fig 8.2 Remittances book

of remittances received are entered into the book. They are then totalled up and handed over to the Chief Cashier who will sign the book in the 'signed' column. This signature acts as your receipt and transfers the responsibility for the remittances over to the Chief Cashier.

■ DIY 8.1.2

Make your own copy of a page from a remittances book. Enter the following remittances that have been received by you today:

- Messrs Bloggs & Co enclosed a cheque for £26.00
- Mrs A Patel enclosed a postal order for £98.40
- Mr P J Nyland enclosed £28.00 in cash
- Short & Co enclosed a cheque for £118.45
- Trevor Ricketts enclosed a postal order for £10.75
- Ms A Arnold enclosed 48p in stamps.

When you have entered all remittances, total the amount column ready for you to hand over to the Chief Cashier for signing.

7 Date stamp empty envelopes as they may be needed at some future time to give details of when the letter was posted or indicate a return address. Some organisations use these envelopes for their own internal mail.

8 Sort mail. This can be done directly into pigeon-holes or wire trays labelled with details of departments or individual members of staff. Also sort internal mail into the correct pigeon-hole or tray. All mail will then be delivered or await collection.

If the mail is not addressed to a particular department or person, look for a subject heading which may indicate where it has to go; or read through the letter to see if the contents give any clues. If you are still unsure, put the letter to one side and deal with it later. It is important not to hold up the rest of the mail while dealing with a query.

■ DIY 8.1.3

Copy the diagram in Fig 8.3 of mail pigeon-holes.

Here is a list of mail received today. Each item has a number which should be written into what you feel is the correct department's pigeon-hole. If you have any uncertainties, place the number of the item below the pigeon-holes to indicate t.,at you will sort this out later.

(1) Letter addressed to the Accountant
(2) Leaflets regarding stationery supplies
(3) Price list for office supplies
(4) Job enquiry
(5) Urgent letter addressed to Sales Manager
(6) Request for a company price list
(7) Wages query from Southampton Branch
(8) Internal post for the van driver

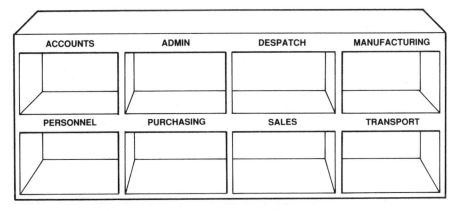

Fig 8.3 Pigeon-holes for mail

(9) Invoice for parts

(10) Registered letter for Administration Assistant

(11) Final demand for telephone bill

(12) Internal post for Manufacturing Manager

9 If a piece of correspondence requires the attention of more than one person or department, either take the required number of photocopies and send one to each department/person concerned, or attach a circulation or routing slip (Fig 8.4) detailing the names of other people or departments who need to see it. Once the correspondence has been seen by the named person or a representative from the department, they will initial and date the slip and then pass the correspondence on to the next person. The last person on the list returns the slip and correspondence to the person who is named at the bottom of the slip by the specified date.

■ DIY 8.1.4

Make your own copy of a routing slip. You have received in today's post a price list from your stationery suppliers but it is too bulky to photocopy. To ensure the

ROUTING SLIP		
Read or copy and pass on in order shown below:		
Name	Department	Initial/Date
Please return to: By:		

Fig 8.4 Routing slip

relevant staff see the price list, complete your routing slip with the following information:

- Mrs B B Hammond – Head of Accounts
- Mr M Ireland – Administration
- Mrs B Harvey – Purchasing Department
- Sally Richmond – Buyer

You wish the original notice to be returned to you by Friday of next week.

10 Once the bulk of the mail has been sorted, go back and deal with any mail that was put to one side.

▶ What should you do with damaged or suspicious items?

When you collect or receive the daily mail, check to ensure there are no damaged items. If any items are damaged in any way there may be a Post Office label to confirm this was done during sorting. If there is no label, point out the damage to the delivery person or contact the local customer care department. Your organisation may wish to claim compensation from the Post Office for the damage and can only do so if they have evidence that the item(s) were damaged before delivery or collection.

Always make sure you treat mail as instructed, if 'HANDLE WITH CARE', 'DO NOT BEND' or 'FRAGILE' labels are used on the item, treat it accordingly. Also look for pictures on packages, such as a broken glass, which indicates fragile contents, or an arrow which is used to show the correct way 'up'. If you do not obey these instructions and damage the item, it is your fault and the organisation cannot claim compensation from the Post Office.

If you are ever suspicious about a piece of mail then do not open, prod, shake or squeeze it. Your suspicions may be aroused if the item has an unusual smell (some explosives smell of marzipan!), if it is of an unusual shape or size, or if it has strange writing, spelling or wrapping – in fact, anything that is 'out of the ordinary' should make you suspicious.

If you are suspicious of an item, the first thing you should always do is tell your supervisor. Your supervisor will then be able to contact the person or department to whom the item is addressed and ask if they are expecting such a package. If the package has a return address, this can be contacted to confirm the contents of the package. However, if there is no such address and your own staff are unaware of the delivery of such a package, then it is wise for all personnel to leave the office, lock the door and contact either security or the police.

Large organisations often use machinery that can scan mail, in the same way as luggage is scanned at airports. Mail and packages can be passed through a type of X-ray machine that produces an image of their contents on a screen. Staff are trained to recognise suspicious contents and to know the procedures to be taken if their suspicions are aroused.

Remember that 'suspicious' does not always mean a letter bomb. Individual staff may be 'under attack' for personal reasons or the organisation itself may be open to attack because of the nature of the work it carries out. Security procedures for mail should never be taken lightly – if you work in a government department dealing with sensitive information, or a fur coat manufacturers, or perhaps a cosmetics company that carries out testing on animals, you would have to take security very seriously!

Remember, if you are ever in doubt, tell your supervisor immediately.

▶ *What should you do if you are unable to deliver mail on time?*

There will always be times when things just do not go smoothly and you may find yourself unable to deliver the mail on time. If this happens, it is essential that you tell your supervisor what has happened immediately. It is only then that something can be done to help you out – if your supervisor is unaware of the problem, you will not be able to get help!

It is important for you to remember that your colleagues will be organising their day according to priorities, some of which will be affected by what is in the daily mail. Therefore, one of your own priorities will be to ensure that your colleagues get their mail as early as possible.

If for any reason you are unable to do this, you should always look to see if any of the day's mail is marked 'URGENT'. If it is, make sure this is delivered immediately with an explanation that the rest of the mail will follow later. You should encourage colleagues to let you know if they are expecting an urgent delivery so that you can make sure it is delivered to them as soon as it arrives on your desk.

■ DIY 8.1.5

Complete the following sentences. Try to write as much as you can to prove you understand what to do.

1 When receiving mail I would . . .
2 The rules I follow when sorting mail are . . .
3 When sorting and delivering mail the time scale is . . .
4 To ensure mail is directed to the correct person I use . . .
5 If there was an unavoidable delay I would . . .

Completing Element 8.1

To complete this element on receiving, sorting and distributing mail you will need to put all DIY tasks in your folder and carry out a final assessment.

Competence must be proven in following the organisation's procedures for receiving routine, urgent and confidential mail. Mail must be sorted and delivered to the relevant person or department within the required timescale, supported by evidence of understanding of location and responsibilities of people in the organisation. Unavoidable delays, damaged and suspicious mail must be reported to the appropriate person.

Claiming credit

Once you have completed your final assessment, you will need to write in your record book or folder how, when, where and what you have done to prove that you are competent.

The following is an example of how one trainee completed their claim:

While on work placement at Coopers & Co for 3 weeks, I did not receive any damaged or suspicious mail. If I had, I would have reported this to my supervisor immediately. If mail is damaged by the Post Office, official Post Office sticky tape is used to repair the damage or the item is stamped to confirm that the Post Office caused the damage. I checked all enclosures and stapled them to the document. If the enclosure was missing I told my supervisor immediately and she wrote on the letter 'No enclosure' and initialled it. I made sure that any cash or valuables were delivered to the correct person immediately. I did not use a remittances book, but covered this in a task (see work folder). I used a paper knife to open the mail. I made sure the contents were not damaged by tapping the contents down first. I used pigeon-holes to sort mail into departments and delivered the mail to the correct department or person as early as possible. During my work experience I did not have any unavoidable delays, but if I had, I would have told my supervisor immediately to make sure all urgent mail was delivered.

■ Element 8.2
DESPATCH MAIL

Performance criteria

- *Procedures for despatching mail are in accordance with organisational requirements*
- *Any enclosures are securely attached and any missing items reported promptly*
- *Mail is legibly and correctly addressed*
- *Mail is despatched within required deadlines*

If you are given the responsibility of dealing with the despatch of mail, you must have a thorough knowledge of the Post Office mail service and its regulations. Mail services are also offered by other organisations such as Securicor, DHL, TNT and Group 4 – you will find other delivery companies detailed in *Yellow Pages*.

The organisation that you work for or train in will choose the delivery service that best suits its needs. Solicitors, for instance, use their own private methods for delivery of important documents between each other, but would use the Post Office for delivery of mail to their clients. A large organisation may use a private delivery service rather than the Post Office if they are able to negotiate a cheaper rate for bulk deliveries. Be aware that there are a number of different companies offering delivery services and that your organisation will be looking for the best service at the lowest price.

▶ *What is the Post Office?*

The Post Office Corporation is now made up of 3 separate businesses: Royal Mail, Parcelforce and Post Office Counters Ltd.

Royal Mail is responsible for the collection and delivery of nearly 60 million items a day to 24 million addresses nationwide. It provides a wide range of special services designed to cater for businesses and private mail users. Royal Mail uses a 2-tier system of service for postal delivery.

▶ *What is the 2-tier postal system?*

The Post Office offers a 2-tier system for the delivery of letters (parcel post is just a one-tier service). First-class post costs more but arrives at its destination within about 24 hours. Second-class post is cheaper but slower, although post should be delivered by the third working day. When preparing mail for despatch it is important to consider costs – mail should be sorted and stamped according to its urgency. It is pointless sending mail by first class if it is not urgently required, as this will only have the effect of increasing the company's postage costs.

Parcelforce provides a nationwide parcel delivery service. It offers a variety of services for business and private users, including Datapost.

Post Office Counters Ltd operates as an agent for many of the services offered by Royal Mail and Parcelforce through its network of 20 000 Post Offices across the country – over 1000 main Post Offices and over 19 000 owned and run by agents.

▶ *What Post Office services are available?*

The Post Office publishes a *Mail Guide* which gives details of all regulations, services and costs. The *Mail Guide*, costs approximately £20. You may find a copy in the library or your place of work. It is updated by inserting replacement pages issued by the Post Office giving details of new services, conditions or prices. There are, however, many leaflets available from post offices that give you up-to-date information and prices on most of its services. Remember that if you are unsure of what service to use for a particular item, post office counter staff are there to help you and will give advice.

The Post Office offers many services in competition with private companies. Therefore, costs may vary considerably and will need to be taken into account when selecting the most appropriate service.

■ DIY 8.2.1

Call in to your local post office and collect as many leaflets as you can on postal services and rates. Leaflets that are particularly useful are: *UK Letter Rates; International Letter Rates; Wrapping up Well; Parcelforce Standard; Parcelforce International; Parcelforce Datapost.* Also collect an example of a Royal Mail Special Delivery label, Recorded Delivery label and a Certificate of Posting. Place all the leaflets, labels, etc, in a safe place – you will need to refer to them later.

Some of the more frequently used services are as follows:

Certificate of Posting

This is the cheapest way of making sure that an inland ordinary letter or parcel, or overseas ordinary letter, has actually been posted. It gives the sender proof of posting and compensation can be claimed from the Post Office for loss or damage. The letter or parcel has to be handed in

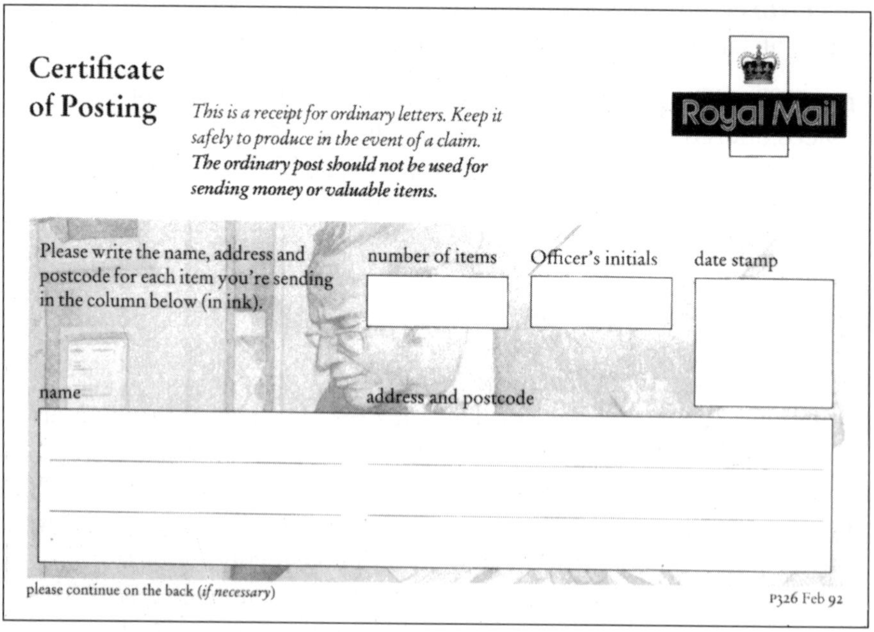

Certificate of Posting

This is a receipt for ordinary letters. Keep it safely to produce in the event of a claim.
The ordinary post should not be used for sending money or valuable items.

Royal Mail

Please write the name, address and postcode for each item you're sending in the column below (in ink).

number of items

Officer's initials

date stamp

name

address and postcode

please continue on the back (*if necessary*)

P326 Feb 92

Fig 8.5 Certificate of posting

at a post office for the counter clerk to complete and stamp a receipt. Delivery is made in the normal way and the item does not have to be signed for by the recipient. Compensation will not be paid if money or jewellery is sent in the ordinary post, even if covered by a certificate of posting.

Recorded Delivery – first- and second-class mail

This service provides a certificate of posting and a signature from the recipient to confirm delivery. It can be used for important documents such as passports, examination certificates and legal documents.

Fig 8.6 Recorded Delivery slip   Fig 8.7 Registered post label

Limited compensation will be paid for loss or damage but this is only to cover for the inconvenience caused. Therefore, this service is not suitable for money or jewellery. If you need a guarantee of delivery next day you should use Special Delivery.

The Post Office provides a blue adhesive label upon which you enter details of both your address and that of the recipient. The top portion of the label is peeled off and affixed to the top left-hand corner on the front of the letter (or close to the address on a packet). The middle portion of the label (which includes barcodes and sender's details) is affixed to the reverse of the letter or packet. The certificate is handed in to the Post Office with the letter or packet, and payment. The certificate is date stamped and initialled as your receipt and must be kept in a safe place as it will have to be produced in the event of a claim or to make an enquiry. When the letter or packet is delivered a signature is collected from the recipient to confirm delivery. If you wish to confirm delivery yourself, telephone the number given on the back of the recorded delivery adhesive label and quote the 13 digit customer reference number on your barcoded receipt. The barcode allows tracking through the Royal Mail network so that progress and delivery can be checked. Recorded Delivery charges are paid in addition to first- or second-class postage.

Registered post – first-class mail only

If you wish to send anything valuable in the post, such as cash or jewellery, you should use this service. The fee you pay will depend on the value of the item being sent. If the item is lost or damaged, compensation up to £500 will be paid according to the value of the item being sent. This service provides you with a certificate of posting and the signature of the recipient when the item is delivered. Letters and packets sent by registered post are handled with special security measures and kept separate from ordinary mail.

The Post Office provides a blue adhesive label which is completed in the same way as the recorded delivery label.

The Registered Plus service can be used for valuable items which require extra security and compensation arrangements. On the back of the Registered Plus adhesive label you can choose compensation up to £1500 or £2200 by placing a cross in either of the 2 boxes. The cost of sending registered items increases according to the value of

234

compensation required. The registered fee is paid in addition to the first-class postage.

Special Delivery

This service is for first-class mail only and can be used for letters and parcels. Special Delivery guarantees next day delivery by 12.30 pm to most UK destinations. Friday postings are guaranteed Monday delivery by 12.30 pm. The Post Office provides a blue adhesive label with barcodes that allows it to track the item through the postal network and check progress and delivery. The signature of the recipient is collected to confirm delivery of the item. If the item is not delivered by 12.30 pm, compensation can be claimed from the 'Double Money Back guarantee', providing a written claim with the certificate of posting is received by the Post Office within 14 days.

Parcelforce Datapost

This service provides delivery of urgent letters, packets and parcels by no later than 12.00 noon the next day. It guarantees overnight delivery within the United Kingdom and speedy delivery to many overseas countries. If an item is not delivered on time, compensation can be claimed. If Datapost is to be used regularly, a contract can be arranged. Arrangements can be made to have mail collected regularly or on demand.

FreePost

This service allows people to send mail to a company free of charge. The Post Office issues the company with a licence to operate a FreePost service, and the words 'FREEPOST' can then be included in the address. The service requires no special stationery, unless first-class service is required, and allows customers sending orders to a company, for example, to do this without having to pay postage. FreePost is often used to encourage people to reply to advertisements – you may have seen it used in magazines or on television.

▶ *What international services are available?*

The service you choose depends on how quickly your international mail needs to get to its destination.

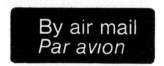

Fig 8.8 Airmail label

Airmail

This service provides a speedy and cost effective method of delivery. Delivery time is usually 3–4 days to cities in Europe, and between 4–7 days for destinations elsewhere. Whatever you are sending by airmail, you should always use an airmail label or write 'PAR AVION – BY AIRMAIL' in the top left-hand corner of your envelope.

Swiftair

This is a priority service for urgent documents and goods. All items sent by Swiftair receive special treatment which speeds sorting and onward despatch to provide a faster service than airmail. A certificate of posting can also be obtained, although a particular delivery time cannot be guaranteed. The charge for Swiftair is paid in addition to the normal airmail postage.

Surface mail

This service is more economical than airmail but slower. Delivery time is usually between 3 and 5 weeks. Letters cannot be sent by surface mail to European destinations.

Fig 8.9 Swiftair label

■ DIY 8.2.2

Your supervisor has asked you to recommend the most suitable postal service for the following items. Choose from the services already explained above which you think would be the best.

1 A letter containing £1200 in cash
2 A second invoice to a company who say they did not receive the first invoice
3 A gold ring worth £500
4 An examination certificate
5 An important contract that has to be in Cardiff by tomorrow morning
6 A letter to Berlin inviting an applicant to attend a job interview in 3 days' time
7 A catalogue company inviting readers to become agents and claim their free gift
8 A non-urgent letter to a penfriend in Japan
9 Routine business mail to overseas customers
10 Children's television programme inviting children to send in their answers to a competition

▶ *How can you help the Post Office?*

First, always make sure you put the right postage on all items. Post Office charges are calculated on the service required, the urgency of delivery, the destination and weight of an item. Up-to-date charges can be found in the Post Office Mail Guide and leaflets, both national and international, which should be used at all times to ensure correct postage is paid. If too little has been paid, the person receiving the item will be asked by the Post Office to pay double the missing amount!

Always use standard size envelopes. The Post Office uses machinery that handles and sorts mail automatically and asks its customers to use envelope sizes that are 'Post Office preferred' – known as POP. You should use envelopes no smaller than 90 mm × 140 mm, and no larger than 120 mm × 235 mm. Envelopes should be oblong in shape, made of paper weighing at least 63 gsm (grammes per square metre) and no thicker than 6 mm, including their contents. The most commonly used envelopes are DL (110 mm × 220 mm), C6 (114 mm × 162 mm), C5 (162 mm × 229 mm) and C4 (229 mm × 324 mm).

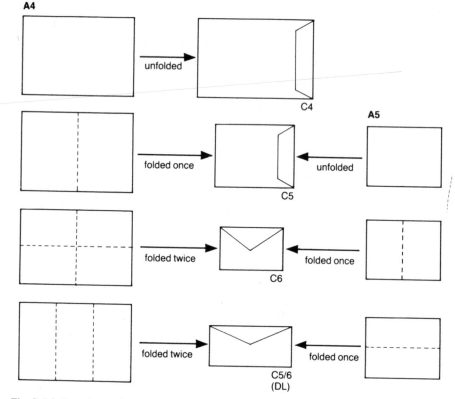

Fig 8.10 Envelope sizes and folding instructions

▶ *How do you fold documents to fit into their envelopes?*

The answer to this question is 'as few times as possible'. Letters and documents should be folded using the instructions in Fig 8.10. Never try to guess where a fold should be, always measure the letter against the envelope to make sure you are folding in the right place. A letter that has been folded and unfolded a number of times before fitting in to the envelope will look scruffy and create a bad impression of the organisation.

■ **DIY 8.2.3**

Practise the correct folding techniques as illustrated in Fig 8.10. Now prepare an information sheet to be used by other members of staff explaining how to fold A4 and A5 size paper to fit into C4, C5, C6 and DL size envelopes. Your information sheet should cover at least one side of A4 paper and should include illustrations as well as instructions.

Regardless of the service used, it is vitally important to address all mail legibly and always to use the postcode. Labels for envelopes should be typed or produced on a word processor. If you have to write envelopes, make sure your writing is 'readable'. Always write the town in CAPITAL LETTERS, and put the postcode on a separate line. If you cannot fit the postcode on a separate line, leave about 5 character spaces after the town and put it there.

In order to help the Post Office sort mail quickly and efficiently postcodes are used to identify the exact location of the addressee. Post Office sorting staff are able to key in the postcode using electronic keyboarding equipment that marks the envelope with a series of dots. Automated sorting equipment can read these dots and will divert the mail to the correct location according to the area indicated by the postcode.

Therefore, if you use the correct postal address and full postcode on all items, you will help to ensure quick and accurate delivery. If you are not sure of a full address or postcode, ask your local Postal Customer Care Unit (you can find the number in the *Phone Book* and in the *Mail Guide*).

▶ *What items must not be sent through the post?*

Dangerous items and substances should not be sent through the post nationally or internationally. The Mail Guide provides a list of items and substances such as aerosols, lighters, asbestos, enamels, varnishes, explosives and prohibited drugs which should never be sent by post. Live creatures such as bees, leeches and worms can be sent provided they are sent first-class in adequate packing, but creatures such as poisonous spiders cannot be sent!

▶ *How should an envelope be addressed?*

Most organisations use a blocked style for addresses on envelopes. The address may be typed directly on to the envelope or adhesive labels which can be peeled from their backing and placed in the correct position on the envelope can be used.

The address should be placed half-way down the envelope and a third of the way in from the left-hand side. Remember to leave enough space for the envelope to be franked across the top and, if stamps are used, the Post Office will need to cancel these out with an ink impression. If you have placed the address too high, the top half of the address may become unreadable if it is franked across!

If the letter is confidential, private or has a 'For the attention of' line, this should be placed one clear line space above the address in capitals.

Note that on both examples the town has been typed in capitals and the postcode placed on a line of its own. If any special instructions are included (for example, CONFIDENTIAL or PRIVATE), these should always be typed in capitals and/or underlined. Special instructions such as 'DO NOT BEND' or a postal label such as 'Recorded delivery'

```
                      Mr J L Protheroe
                      Mobley & Co Ltd
                      1 Somerly Close
                      COVENTRY
                      CL3 2UA
```

Fig 8.11

```
          FOR THE ATTENTION OF MR J L PROTHEROE

          Mobley & Co Ltd
          1 Somerly Close
          COVENTRY
          CL3 2UA
```

Fig 8.12

240

should be placed on the top left-hand corner of the envelope – remember the stamp is placed on the right-hand corner.

Some organisations require staff to mark envelopes with a pencilled '1' or '2' in the top right-hand corner of the envelope to indicate to mail-room staff whether first- or second-class postage is required. However, if the envelope is to be delivered by hand and requires no postage, it is usual to type or write 'By hand' in the top right-hand corner of the envelope in place of the stamp.

■ DIY 8.2.4

Prepare envelopes or paper cut to DL, C5 or C6 size, for each of the following mail items. Special instructions have been shown in brackets after each address. You must ensure that these instructions are placed on the envelope in the correct position. The Registered and Recorded envelopes will each require the correct Post Office adhesive label to be prepared with the relevant peel-off portions affixed to the envelopes.

1 Edwards & Edwards Co Ltd
   12 Solent Avenue
   SOUTHAMPTON
   SO95 9BB
   (for the attention of J Hine)

2 Mr R P Cameron
   48 Dorchester Way
   BRIGHTON
   BR11 9GH
   (Confidential)

3 Miss S Philipp
   Malzstr 90 PSF 361
   0-2000 Berlin
   GERMANY
   (Swiftair)

4 Internal Mail
   Purchasing Department
   (By hand)

5 Messrs Stone & Waring
   39 Allsop Road
   WARRINGTON
   CH27 6AS
   (Registered)

6 Ms S Chandra
   19 Moordown
   COVENTRY
   CV9 8HH
   (Recorded)

▶ *How should mail be prepared?*

All items for mailing should be securely sealed in appropriate sized envelopes, packets or parcels. Mail should be legibly addressed and the correct postal rates should be calculated and applied. Post Office

241

sorting requirements should also be followed. You will find that each organisation has its own procedure for preparing outgoing mail; it is important for you to ensure that you know these procedures so that mistakes are not made.

If an organisation is large enough to have its own mail room there will be a system of regular collection of mail from every department during the day. Trays marked 'outgoing mail' are usually placed in each department so that mail can be collected and prepared during periods of the day when the mail room is not so busy. The mail room will probably advise staff of a final collection time, after which no mail will be accepted for that day. This will avoid a last-minute rush and ensure that Post Office collection times can be met.

In the case of bulky envelopes, these will have to be weighed and the correct postage calculated. The job of putting the contents into their envelopes may be down to individual members of staff who typed/keyed in or wrote them, or it may be done by staff in the mail room itself.

The procedure for outgoing mail should be as follows:

1 Check the bottom of the letter for 'Enc'. If the enclosure is not there, put the letter to one side while you prepare the other mail.
2 Check that the letter has been signed.
3 Check that the inside address is the same as the address on the envelope.
4 If the letter is marked 'Confidential' or 'Private', make sure the envelope is too. Also check that 'For the attention of . . .' information has also been included on the envelope.
5 Fold the letter so that it is creased as few times as possible.

If window envelopes are used, check that the address on the letter can be read through the window. Some organisations mark their headed paper with a small box into which the address should be typed and/or mark the edges of the paper to show where the letter should be folded. This ensures the address is in the correct place to be seen through the window in the envelope.

6 If the letter is bulky or addressed to a country overseas, it may need extra postage. The correct postage can be calculated by weighing the item on a set of scales and then looking the weight up in the correct Post Office Rates leaflet or *Mail Guide*.

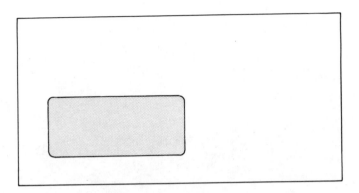

Fig 8.13 A window envelope

7 Affix correct stamps and place letter into one of the following three categories:

- First Class
- Second Class
- Registered/Recorded Delivery – taken to Post Office as a receipt has to be obtained.

All first-class items should be placed in a red Post Office bag and second-class in a green Post Office bag. The mail is now ready to be collected by or delivered to the Post Office. Remember that there will be a cut-off time in the afternoon, usually around 1700 hours, after which the Post Office will not accept post for that day.

■ DIY 8.2.5

Prepare for despatch the envelopes completed in DIY 8.2.4. Write in pencil in the top right-hand corner of each envelope the correct postage required or, if possible, use a franking machine to frank each envelope ready for despatch. Match the item number given in DIY 8.2.4 for each envelope to tell you the service required:

1 second class   **4** By hand
2 first class   **5** Registered (first class)
3 Swiftair   **6** Recorded (second class).

Remember that charges for Registered and Recorded Delivery services are added to the normal postage. Swiftair charges are added to the airmail postage.

Fig 8.14 Electronic scales for weighing post

On a separate piece of paper work out how much it would cost to send the following items using:

1 airmail
2 Swiftair
3 surface mail

- Letter weighing 200 g to Austria
- Packet weighing 1000 g to Pakistan
- Printed papers weighing 100 g to New Zealand
- Letter weighing 125 g to Greenland

Did you remember that letters cannot be sent by surface mail to European destinations?

8 Once the mail is prepared, go back to any items that were put to one side. You will have to inform the person responsible for the correspondence the reason why it has missed the post. Remember that it is not your fault if he/she has forgotten to sign the letter or perhaps left out the enclosure. However, do try to inform them of the problem as soon as you can so that it can be put right, if possible, in time to catch the afternoon's outgoing mail.

POSTAGE BOOK			
Stamps Bought	Name and Town of Addressee	Stamps Used	Special Services
£20.00	2.7.9–	£ p	
	J Jones – Derby	0.48	
	S Ferry – Cardiff	0.97	Reg Mail
	Messrs Pike & Co – Hull	7.40	Parcel
	Smith & Son – London	0.54	Rec Del
	TOTAL	£9.39	
	Balance c/f	£10.61	
		£20.00	

Fig 8.15 Postage book

9 If stamps have been used for the mail, complete the Postage Book. This book gives a detailed record of all letters, packages and parcels posted. It also keeps a check on how many postage stamps have been used. Remember that stamps cost money and are not for private use. Therefore, a receipt (in other words some form of postage record) is completed to identify how the stamps have been used. The Postage Book and the stamps themselves should always be kept safe and secure, usually under lock and key to prevent dishonest use.

■ DIY 8.2.6

Copy a page from a postage book. Stamps bought today – £50.00. Enter details of the mail you prepared for despatch in DIY 8.2.5. Remember to include details of special services used. Add up the total of all stamps used. Deduct this from the £50.00 you started with. The amount left will be carried over to the next day.

▶ *What is a franking machine?*

This machine prints on an envelope, postcard or adhesive label (used for parcels) in coloured ink the value of a stamp, as well as the date

245

Fig 8.16 Franking mark

and place of posting. The Post Office licence number and an advertising slogan can also be included if required. It saves time when preparing mail, makes a record of all postage used and is easier to keep secure than postage stamps.

Franking machines can be bought or hired from manufacturers such as Pitney Bowes and Roneo, but a Post Office licence is also required. There are 2 meters on the machine – one that shows how many postage units have been used to date (ascending register), the other shows how many postage units are left in the machine (descending register). When the descending register is low, this means that more postage units need to be bought from the Post Office.

It is important not to let the descending register run too low – this may result in postage units running out and mail missing the Post Office deadline. Some machines allow a small part to be lifted off and taken to the local Post Office, where a special key is used to open the machine and add units, once payment has been made.

Modern, computerised franking machines are linked to a Post Office computer and have credits added simply by making a telephone call. The Post Office computer automatically prints an invoice and sends it to the franking machine user. Modern machines can use a credit card system which allows credits to be added to the machine by simply inserting a plastic card which is bought from the Post Office.

Franking machines can be locked to prevent dishonest use. The machine has to be set with the day's date each morning before use and the ink roller regularly re-inked. If a franking is incorrect, it should be put to one side and used, if possible, later in the day. Otherwise, the franked item can be taken to the Post Office, which will give a refund, less 5 per cent. If a franking machine is taken to the Post Office for

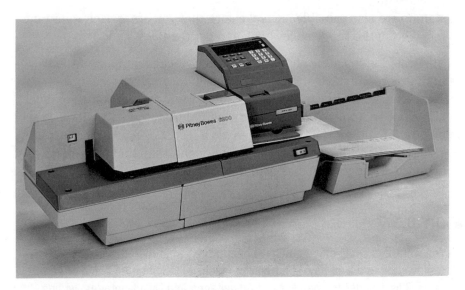

Fig 8.17 An electronic franking machine

credits to be added, a record card is completed showing units used and units purchased.

When franking mail, the counter on the machine can be set to the amount of postage required, so that all items can be prepared easily without the need for the correct value of postage stamps. Franked mail can pass through the Post Office much faster as the franking on each item does not require cancelling by the Post Office in the same way as postage stamps.

However, franked mail does have to be posted in a special way – either handed in over the counter of a post office, tied in separate first- and second-class bundles facing the same way, or posted in a letter-box in a special envelope marked 'franked mail'. Some organisations use red Post Office bags for first-class mail and green bags for second-class mail, and special mail items are placed in a yellow bag.

▶ *What about security?*

Firstly, remember that stamps are worth money and should be locked away until needed. Petty cash is normally used to buy stamps and should also be kept in a special tin box out of sight to prevent temptation. Incoming remittances in the form of cheques, postal orders, cash or

247

stamps are also valuable, so make sure that you enter each remittance received in the remittances book and get the book signed.

The franking machine should also be kept locked and out of the way until it is required. It should only be used for business and not personal use. If a mistake is made, never throw the envelope or label away, but try to use it later or get a refund from the Post Office. Do not be afraid to admit that you have made a mistake. Your supervisor would prefer to get a refund, less 5 per cent, than find out you have been throwing your mistakes in the bin!

■ DIY 8.2.7

You work in a small office and have been asked what the advantages and disadvantages are of having a franking machine. Using an A4 piece of paper make 2 lists under the headings of Advantages and Disadvantages, writing down as many things as you can think of under each heading.

Completing Element 8.2

To complete this element on despatching mail you will need to put all DIY tasks in your folder and carry out a final assessment.

Competence must be proven in dealing with routine, urgent and confidential mail. The organisation's procedures and deadlines for despatching mail must be followed along with standard Post Office procedures. All mail must be legibly and correctly addressed and all enclosures checked and securely attached; missing items must be reported immediately. Knowledge of express delivery services and agencies must also be proven.

Claiming credit

Once you have completed your final assessment, you will need to write in your record book or folder how, when, where and what you have done to prove that you are competent.

The following is an example of how one trainee completed this claim:

While in the College training office I checked the supervisor's outgoing letters for enclosures. I reported omissions immediately. I used DL sized envelopes for the paperwork and Jiffy bags for larger items. Parcels were wrapped according to the Wrapping up Well leaflet. All mail was addressed according to Post Office requirements.

Scales were used to weigh heavy items and the Mail Guide *used to calculate postage. Second-class mail was placed in green bags and first-class mail in red bags ready for collection at 3.00 pm. Registered or recorded items were taken to the Post Office. The postage book was totalled each day and I kept the stamps locked in the petty cash tin in a secure drawer. Confidential mail was always sent first-class and sealed immediately. If mail was urgent it was marked as 'Urgent' and on some occasions a local express delivery company was used.*

UNIT 9
Monitor and issue stock items

■ **Element 9.1**
MONITOR AND REQUEST STOCK

Performance criteria

- *Stocks are monitored and low levels reported to the appropriate person*
- *Stock is requested in accordance with organisational procedures*
- *Stock is handled and securely stored in accordance with organisational requirements*
- *Records are up to date, legible and accurate*

Have you ever heard the terms 'stocktake', 'out of stock' or 'summer/winter stock? The term 'stock' has the same general meaning, whether in a large industrial organisation or a small office. In the *Pocket Oxford Dictionary* it is described as 'Store of goods, etc, ready for sale, distribution, or use, supply of anything'.

In your college or workplace you will find different kinds of stock. This stock is usually kept together in a special place called a storeroom, stockroom, or 'the stores'. The stock is kept here to protect it and to make sure it is ready to be taken out when required. You must always remember that stock is worth money; it is of value to the organisation and you must treat it with great care.

▶ *What types of stock are there?*

The stock held by any organisation will generally fall into one of five categories:

250

1 Raw materials

This type of stock is held ready for use in the manufacture of goods. Sufficient stock of raw materials and components must be held for a regular supply to the production department. Can you imagine what would happen if the production department was brought to a halt because there were not enough raw materials in stock to make the goods? Examples of raw materials would be cocoa in a chocolate factory or cotton and other textiles in a clothing manufacturer's factory.

2 Consumables

These are supplies that are necessary for the smooth running of the organisation, but which are used up in the day-to-day running of the business and do not make a profit in themselves. Consumables may be used up quickly so there must always be a reserve in stock. Examples of consumables in an office would be stationery, such as envelopes, rulers and notebooks.

3 Finished goods

These are the goods that have been manufactured by the organisation and are held in stock awaiting orders from customers. The organisation will want to sell this stock as quickly as possible to make a profit, in order to buy more raw materials and make more finished goods. The organisation will always keep in stock popular lines which sell quickly, so that delivery can be made upon the receipt of an order – this is called delivery 'ex-stock'. Examples of finished goods are cars, bicycles, computers, furniture and carpets.

4 Goods purchased for resale

Retail shops and wholesale warehouses purchase a variety of stock which they display and hope to sell at a higher price than they paid the manufacturer, to make a profit. These outlets usually offer a wide range of stock from which customers can choose as and when they require it. Examples of resale stock would be clothing, food and drink, and electrical equipment.

5 Spare parts

These are required so that they are readily available in the event of the breakdown of the factory machinery, vehicles, plant, etc. Examples of spare parts would be engines, gear boxes, and smaller items such as nuts and bolts, and fan belts.

■ DIY 9.1.1

During the next 2 weeks make a list of all the items of stock that you use when working. This will include such items as pens, pencils, eraser, staples and stapler, correcting fluid, A4 bond paper, envelopes (state the type) etc. Make sure that the description is accurate, eg describe exactly what type and size of paper and envelopes you are using.

▶ *How might stock be ordered?*

The stock used in your organisation will be purchased from suppliers (retail shops, wholesalers or manufacturers). The organisation will send out an initial **enquiry**, perhaps to three or four suppliers, in order to find out which supplier can offer the best deal. In return the suppliers will send a **quotation** detailing the goods required and the price and terms that they are prepared to offer. The supplier may also take this opportunity to send price lists, catalogues and free samples, or arrange for a sales representative to call.

The purchasing department will decide upon the supplier to use and will send out an **order**. When the supplier receives this order, an **acknowledgement** will be sent back to the organisation's purchasing department to confirm that the supplier has received the order. Once the order is ready to be delivered, the supplier will send an **advice note** by post, containing the delivery details for the goods.

A **delivery note**, containing the same details as the advice note, will be sent with the goods. It is the responsibility of the person receiving these goods to ensure that they correspond with those detailed in the delivery note. Any discrepancies must be written down on the delivery note and confirmed by the signature of the person delivering the goods.

An **invoice** will be produced by the supplier for each delivery of goods sent to the organisation. This will give full details of the goods supplied, together with a breakdown of costs, including any discounts (money off) and VAT. At the end of each month the supplier will send the organisation a **statement** which details the amount payable for all the invoices for that month, less any refunds for goods returned or damaged. The organisation then arranges for a **cheque** to be sent to the supplier in settlement of the account.

This process will be used when an organisation is first looking for a supplier of a particular range of goods. Once contact has been made and a suitable supplier found, it is usual for the organisation to place regular orders with the same supplier. However, in the case of an emergency supply being required at short notice, most suppliers will take an order over the telephone. This should, however, be supported by giving them an order number, and an authorised order form should be sent by post or fax as soon as possible.

In the case of smaller organisations you may find yourself being sent in person to collect goods which are urgently required.

■ DIY 9.1.2

Write a suitable initial enquiry to 3 local stationery suppliers (find the names and addresses in a local directory) asking them for a quotation for the following goods:

A4 bond paper, 30 m rolls of fax paper, B graded pencils, DL window envelopes in white and brown.

Make sure that the enquiry has your name and address on it as well as their name and address. As well as wanting to know the price, do not forget to ask them about discounts and how long delivery takes. It is not necessary to post these enquiries to the suppliers concerned.

▶ *Checking*

It is usual practice to check deliveries against the initial order, to ensure that the correct goods and quantities are being delivered. The delivery note (complete with corrections if there are any) will then be compared against the invoice sent to your organisation to make sure the correct amount has been charged.

If at any stage a mistake is identified, this must be reported to a supervisor immediately. It may be that incorrect goods have been delivered, which will need to be returned, or that your organisation has been charged for goods that it has not received. In both cases it may be your responsibility to find these errors and mark them on the delivery note before signing it. Remember that the delivery company uses the delivery note as a receipt for goods delivered and will, therefore, work out your organisation's final invoice based on these details.

■ DIY 9.1.3

Compare the following order forms (Fig 9.1a) with their delivery notes (Fig 9.1b). Make a list of all the errors you find, writing the correct details next to each error.

Often organisations use stationery packs which contain all the relevant documents for one order. Each document is either made from NCR (no carbon required) paper, or will have carbon paper placed between each sheet. When the order details are typed or written on to the top sheet they are automatically copied on to the other sheets – delivery note, stores requisition, accounts advice, invoice, and so on.

This saves time, as the documents do not have to be prepared separately. Sections of information that are not needed on certain forms can be blanked out (for example, it is usual practice not to have price details on the delivery form).

▶ *Why do organisations hold stock?*

It is essential to have a reserve supply of all the goods and materials required for your organisation to operate efficiently. Delays in the supply of such stock will cause hold-ups in production and possible loss of profits if an order cannot be delivered on time.

Another point to remember is that it is cheaper to order goods in 'bulk' and put the excess into stock so that advantage can be taken of discounts and lower prices. However, care must be taken not to over-order. Remember that stock is worth money to an organisation and a storeroom full of stock that is not used for a long time is tying up money that could be used elsewhere.

PEMBROOKE MARKETING SERVICES LTD

115–119 Cavendish Square, Bridport, BR4 9PQ

Order Number: 123890   Date: 12.9.– –

Please supply the items listed below:

Quantity	Description	Cat. No.	Unit Price £	Total Price £
20	Clear display binder	17933	3.39	67.80
15	File boxes	19345	4.29	64.35
5	Blue double staplers	16829	3.99	19.95
10	Paperclips (boxes)	18739	1.79	17.90
5	Bulldog clips (boxes)	18628	0.89	4.45
			TOTAL	£174.45

Authorised by

a.N.Other

PEMBROOKE MARKETING SERVICES LTD

115–119 Cavendish Square, Bridport, BR4 9PQ

Order Number: 123892   Date: 15.9.– –

Please supply the items listed below:

Quantity	Description	Cat. No.	Unit Price £	Total Price £
10	Paperclips (boxes)	17889	1.89	18.90
8	Gluepens 50 ml	12339	0.95	7.60
4	Cork noticeboards	15664	4.99	19.96
5	Desk tidy	20984	4.59	22.95
5	Hole punch, heavy duty	14928	8.49	42.45
			TOTAL	£111.86

Authorised by

a.N.Other

Fig 9.1a Order forms

The Stationery Company Ltd

97 Fontmell Street
Bridport Dorset

Date: 20 September 199–

Order No: 123890   Delivery Note No: 1675
Delivery Address: Pembrooke Marketing Services
                  115–119 Cavendish Street
                  Bridport

Quantity	Description of goods	Catalogue number	Total £
10	Clear display binder	17933	33.99
15	File boxes	19345	67.50
5	Blue double staplers	16829	19.95
10	Paperclips (sm boxes)	18749	17.90
8	Bulldog clips (boxes)	18628	15.12
		TOTAL	£154.45

Please mark errors or damaged goods before signing

....

Do not pay until you have received our official invoice.

The Stationery Company Ltd

97 Fontmell Street
Bridport Dorset

Date: 27 September 199–

Order No: 123892   Delivery Note No: 1897
Delivery Address: Pembrooke Marketing Services
                  115–119 Cavendish Street
                  Bridport

Quantity	Description of goods	Catalogue number	Total £
15	Paperclips (boxes)	17889	18.90
8	Gluepens 30 ml	12329	7.60
5	Desk tidy	20984	25.95
5	Hole punch, med duty	14927	42.45
		TOTAL	£111.86

Please mark errors or damaged goods before signing

....

Do not pay until you have received our official invoice.

Fig 9.1b Delivery notes

▶ *What quantity of stock is usually held?*

This will vary according to the type of organisation, size of organisation, and how much business is carried out. There are also five other very important considerations.

1 Money

You are already aware that stock is worth money and that it would be unwise for an organisation to have too much money tied up in stock. It is also wise to remember that some stock may be perishable and have a limited shelf-life. Stock may become dated and therefore unsaleable, or it may age with time and become unusable. Examples are fashionable clothing, fruit and vegetables, and even paper, which may become yellow in time.

2 Time

It may be difficult, or indeed impossible, to obtain stock immediately and valuable orders may be lost to other organisations who are able to deliver the goods on the date required. You will find that, to prevent this situation arising, most organisations will carry a sufficient amount of stock to ensure that when orders are received they can be fulfilled immediately.

3 Space

The storage of stock is expensive. It uses valuable space in areas which must be maintained, heated, protected and secured. Staff are employed to take charge of stock and insurance must be paid to provide cover in the event of damage. The organisation will anticipate the maximum amount of each item of stock that should be kept at one time to prevent profits being spent purely on storage costs.

4 Sales

The organisation will anticipate the actual quantity of stores, spares, raw materials, etc, it will need to keep itself operational. While it is important not to carry too much stock, it is more important to ensure that there is enough stock available to prevent production being halted and money lost.

5 Usage

It is very important to have a regular supply of the stock that is used most often. In an office you might find yourself needing typewriter cartridges, lift-off tapes, paper and envelopes on a regular basis. A clothes manufacturer would need material, sewing cotton and zips/buttons readily at hand in order to keep production going.

Therefore, it is usual to find that regular orders are placed for high-usage items so that they do not run out.

■ DIY 9.1.4

Write suitable replies in the form of a quotation to the enquiries you have written for DIY 9.1.2. Do not forget to vary the prices, terms and conditions available from the different suppliers. If possible obtain a sample quotation from work, or you may have one available at home.

▶ *Why is it necessary to keep control of stock?*

Small organisations may use a 'visual' system of stock control – in other words, stock is ordered when a need is seen. Larger organisations, especially those involved in manufacturing, use a 'bin' system where all components are given a bin number which identifies the component's position in the storeroom. However, most organisations will use 'stock cards' as a system of keeping an up-to-date record of the stock in hand.

A **stock card** (*see* Fig 9.2) will show details of each item used by the organisation (**1**). Each time stock is delivered by a supplier this will be added on to the record (**2**), and each time stock is issued to a department in response to a **stock requisition form**, this is *deducted* from the record (**3**), thus showing exactly how much is in stock at any one time (**4**).

We have already discussed how important it is for an organisation not to have too much stock or too little stock. To prevent either of these situations arising a stock record card is used to indicate the *maximum* (**5**) and *minimum* (**6**) level for each item of stock required by the organisation.

STATIONERY STOCK CARD

Item <u>A4 Bond Paper</u> (1)   Maximum level <u>50</u> (5)   Bin No <u>100</u>

Minimum level <u>10</u> (6)

Unit <u>Ream</u>   Reorder level <u>20</u> (7)

Date	Receipts (2)			Issues (3)			Balance
	Qty	Inv no	Supplier	Qty	Req no	Dept	in stock (4)
199– Jan 1 3 4 10	 30	 A133	 J Smith & Co	 6 3	 141 159	 Accounts Personnel	26 26 20 50 47

Fig 9.2 A stock card

The stock record card also indicates the *reorder level* (**7**), which shows the stock level (quantity of stock) at which an order needs to be requested so that delivery is made before the remaining stock runs out. It is at this point that a **purchase requisition** is sent to the purchasing department (the buying department) to instruct the buyer to order the stock.

A stock record card will be kept for every item of stock and will therefore provide an up-to-date record of issues and requisitions, reorder levels, and the maximum and minimum amounts of stock required for any one particular organisation, department or office. The reorder level will take into account how long it takes for orders to be delivered together with the 'usage' level for that particular item.

You would expect to order regularly those items that have a high usage level because these are used more frequently. For example, A4 bond typing paper would be used daily in an office and you would need to keep up a regular supply. On the other hand, staplers, although used daily, are long lasting and their usage level would be very low, so that you would find you very seldom reorder these.

■ DIY 9.1.5

Look at the example of a stock record card in Fig 9.3. Notice that the columns give details of date, quantity received from supplier, invoice number, name of supplier, quantity issued to the individual departments, number of the requisition form, name of the department and the total balance left in stock. Colour coding can also be used to help you to identify a particular type of stock. For example, all stationery records may be on green cards, and manufacturing on yellow cards.

Anything coming into the organisation will be shown under the heading **Receipts**, and anything going out of the stockroom will be shown under the heading **Issues**.

STATIONERY STOCK CARD

Item <u>D L Brown</u>   Maximum level <u>15</u>   Bin No <u>22</u>
<u>Window envelopes</u>   Minimum level <u>2</u>
Unit <u>Boxes of 50</u>   Reorder level <u>4</u>

Date	Receipts			Issues			Balance in stock
	Qty no	Inv	Supplier	Qty no	Req	Dept	
July 7							10
10				2	A242	Accounts	
27				3	S333	Sales	
Aug 1				1	G201	Reception	
20	12	P131	Parsons				
Sept 2				5	P342	Personnel	

Fig 9.3 Stock record card

As you can see, this stock record card is incomplete, because the figures have not been added to or deducted from the total. Please copy the card on to a piece of paper and fill in the missing details.

It is important that your calculations are correct. If they are not, you may find yourself in trouble for ordering stock that is not required or even worse, not ordering stock that is required. Imagine how you would feel if someone found that the organisation had run out of A4 typing paper but had 20 staplers in stock!

■ DIY 9.1.6

You are in charge of the Personnel Department's (20 members of staff) stock cupboard, which is a small walk-in cupboard in the corner of your office. You have just reorganised it so that the items used most often are near the door and bulky items are on the floor towards the back. On the lines below show where you have located all the stock items. Make sure you include all the items that you have listed in DIY 9.1.1. In addition you have been asked to store: 20 litres of duplicating fluid (highly flammable) and 2 typewriters (old electric ones). These must be shown on your chart too.

Shelf 1 _____

Shelf 2 _____

Shelf 3 _____

Shelf 4 _____

Shelf 5 _____

Floor _____

▶ *How is stock stored?*

You should now be aware that stock is a valuable asset to the organisation and must be kept in perfect condition. The type of storage required will depend upon the kind of stock and the size of the organisation. Large organisations will have a stockroom or department with staff employed to take charge of the stock; whereas a small organisation may have a stock cupboard with only one person in charge of the keys. What you must remember is that, however large or small the organisation, it is essential that the stock is stored correctly.

Every item of stock must be stored neatly and be easily accessible when required. Shelves should be labelled so that it is easy to find what is needed, and the stockroom or cupboard should always be kept locked. It is important that the stockroom or cupboard is kept dry at all times to prevent paper-based stock from becoming damp and going mouldy. Large or heavy items should be kept low down and, when new stock arrives, it should be placed at the back or at the bottom of the existing supply so that older stock is used first.

It is important that you treat hazardous stock with care. Any liquids that are dangerous or inflammable, for example thinners, glue or duplicating fluid, must be kept in a separate area, and staff must never smoke in this area or in the stockroom itself.

■ DIY 9.1.7

Complete the following sentences as fully as possible to show that you understand the procedures for monitoring and issuing stock items.

1 If I find that stock levels are becoming too low I report it to ...
2 When stock is required by me I request it by . . .
3 I make sure my stock is secure by . . .
4 Stock items that need careful handling include . . .
5 The correct lifting procedure for heavy items of stock is . . .
6 The records that should be kept in connection with stock control are . . .
7 It is important that these records are up to date and accurate, otherwise . . .
8 It is also important that the records are legible, if not . . .
9 Hazardous materials that I may come into contact with include . . .
10 When stock is missing or damaged I report it to . . .

▶ *What would you do if you had too much stock?*

Too much stock is called a surplus, and as you know stock is equal to money in an organisation. If you have a surplus it means that you have money tied up in unnecessary stock and that it is taking up expensive space that may be used for other things. If you have a central stock department, you may be able to return the surplus and get a credit for the money for your department. If it is stock that you have ordered directly from the supplier yourself, you may be able to return it for a credit (as long as the stock is not out of date). If there are other departments in your organisation you may be able to exchange or transfer some of the surplus stock to them. This will still save the organisation money as the other departments will not need to order. It will also free up some of the storage space in your stock area.

▶ What happens to stock which is out of date?

Some stock will have a 'use by' date on it. When this date arrives, it does not necessarily mean that the stock is no good. However, it should be used as quickly as possible. Such stock may include replacement toner cartridges for photocopiers and printers. If the quality of the stock has decreased so much that the item cannot be used then it should be thrown away.

An item that frequently becomes out of date in organisations is the stationery with letter head. This is because organisations change their name, address, telephone or fax number. Sometimes the names of the directors or executives are printed on the headed paper and reprinting is necessary when the staff changes. It is important that the old paper is taken out of circulation but it should be recycled whenever possible. Some printing companies will accept the return of the old paper, otherwise local organisations may arrange for recycling. If there is only a small amount of paper it may be possible to use it for messages, printing draft documents, etc. If it is used within the organisation it is important to cross out the printed headings, so that no one uses it for external use by mistake. Old letter head should not be thrown in the bin as it may be found and used by imposters for fraud or deception.

If you frequently have stock which goes past its 'use by' date, it could mean that you have surplus stock or that the stock is not being rotated correctly, ie that the oldest items are not being used first. This may occur if the new stock is always put at the front of the shelf. Always make sure that new stock is put at the back and existing stock brought to the front to be used first.

▶ How are stock levels checked?

Stock levels are checked at regular intervals by a process called **stocktaking** or **reconciliation**. This means that every item of stock

STOCK INVENTORY RECORD SHEET				
STOCK		QUANTITY		
Description	Unit	Date	Date	Date

Fig 9.4 Stock inventory record sheet

in the organisation is counted to calculate how much money is tied up in the value of the stock. This stocktaking produces a document called an **inventory** (*see* Fig 9.4). It is the stocktaker's job to check that the balances of stock shown on the record cards are the same as the amount of stock actually in the stockroom, and that every issue of stock has a requisition form to support it – if it does not, then this means that the stock has been taken without authority.

It is possible to keep an up-to-date record of stock levels by using a computer, which is what is done by the barcode reading tills you see in supermarkets. The computer will deduct from the total stock level every time an item of stock is taken out, and add to the stock level every time stock is replaced. This is a very good method of keeping a check of the stock, but one disadvantage is that the figures it gives you are those that it has calculated to be correct. It cannot take into account theft, pilfering, damage, loss, etc, unless these details are fed into it.

Therefore, you will find that manual stocktaking still has to take place at least once a year so that the actual value of stock can be entered into the organisation's annual accounts sheet. It is during this stock-take that damaged stock, or perhaps stock which has become obsolete (out of date) and is no longer required, can be 'written off' and its value deducted from the organisation's assets. Some organisations will have a sale to reduce the amount of 'written off' stock which they hold.

▶ *What legislation is there relating to the receipt of goods?*

When you or your organisation buys goods or services, you are called a 'consumer'. Do you know that there are a number of 'consumer laws' to protect you? Possible dangers that may be encountered are:

- misleading advertisements
- dangerous goods
- incorrect description of goods
- incorrect weight or size
- goods not suitable for their purpose
- goods paid for but not delivered
- poor quality, making goods unusable
- incorrect price information giving idea of a bargain
- businesses getting together to keep prices high
- credit terms not showing exactly how much you pay
- persuasive or pressurised buying that you later regret.

There are a variety of organisations set up to give advice and provide consumer protection. These include the British Standards Institute (BSI), the Consumers' Association and the Citizens' Advice Bureau. However, as a consumer you are also protected by law – this protection is in the form of a number of 'consumer laws'.

Sale of Goods Act 1979

This Act sets out the conditions under which goods can be bought and sold. The goods must:

- be legally owned by the seller
- suit the purpose for which they are sold
- fit their description
- correspond with samples
- be capable of use for the purpose intended.

The buyer has the right to return the goods and have the money refunded, or to claim compensation, depending on the particular breach of law involved.

265

If someone tried to sell you 'Big Ben', or wellington boots which let in the water, or A3 paper instead of A4, then they would be in breach of this law and you could take legal action.

Weights and Measures Act 1963 to 1979

These Acts make it an offence to give a short (too little) weight or measure, even by accident. Local authorities employ trading standards officers to enforce these Acts, and as part of their work they regularly visit shops and other premises to check the accuracy of scales and other measuring devices used. As a consumer you would be protected when buying goods such as potatoes, petrol or a pint of beer in a pub.

Trade Descriptions Acts 1968 and 1972

It is an offence to describe goods or services for sale in a false or misleading way. This applies to verbal as well as written descriptions, and suppliers must ensure that advertisements do not contain wrong information about goods for sale.

As a consumer you must be told the origin of the goods, ie where they were made, together with the original price of an item which is now being offered at sale price.

Unsolicited Goods and Services Act 1971

This Act protects you if you are sent goods that you did not order. If you inform the supplier that you do not wish to keep the goods, it is the supplier's responsibility to collect these goods from you within 30 days or the goods become your property. Alternatively, you need do nothing other than to wait for six months, after which time the goods will also become your property.

Fair Trading Act 1973

This Act set up an Office of Fair Trading under a Director-General of Fair Trading. It has very wide responsibilities concerning unfair trading practices which affect consumers. It is the responsibility of the Office of Fair Trading to ensure that trade is carried out according to the law.

Completing Element 9.1

To complete this element on monitoring and requesting stock items you will need to put all DIY tasks in your folder and carry out a final assessment.

266

Competence must be proven whilst being observed over a period of time monitoring stock levels in your own work area and requesting stock to refill levels when necessary. The stock you look after should include office consumables and small items of office equipment such as staplers, scissors and hole punches.

Claiming credit

Once you have completed your final assessment, you will need to write in your record book or folder how, when, where and what you have done to prove that you are competent.

The following is an example of how one trainee completed this claim:

During my work placement at Turner & Co I was responsible for looking after the stock cupboard within the department. I worked for one month and I had to rewrite many of the stock cards as they had not been kept up to date. I started by making a list of all the equipment and stationery kept and then counted the items available. Where possible I reconciled the amount with the stock card but most of the time the amounts were different. Some of the stock was old and damaged. After checking with the supervisor, I arranged for it to be returned to the central stores. I then rearranged the cupboard so that the items used most of the time were in the middle and the less used items were put at the top and bottom (although I made sure all the heavy items were at the bottom). People requiring stationery or other items completed a stationery requisition (see examples in my folder) and it was signed by the supervisors. I then issued the stock requested and made sure that I entered the amount on the stock card. When the quantity of items of stock got too low I made out a stock requisition for the central stores and gave it to my supervisor to sign. These stocks were sent up once a week; when I received them I entered the new amounts on the stock record cards. When I left I handed the work over to one of the junior assistants.

At my part-time job in the supermarket we use an electronic system of stock control which automatically reorders items when they are low. A printout of the items ordered is made by the computer at the end of the day and this is checked by the supervisor and kept on file until the delivery arrives from the central depot. I have used this system of stock control and ordering for the last 9 months.

I also carried out some research sheets at my training college (see my folder) which check on my knowledge of stock control procedures.

■ Element 9.2
ISSUE STOCK ITEMS ON REQUEST

Performance criteria

- *Requests are responded to promptly and accurately*
- *Issue of stock is in accordance with organisational procedures*
- *Stock is handled in accordance with organisational requirements*
- *Records are up to date, legible and accurate*
- *Damage to stock is promptly and accurately reported to the appropriate person*

▶ *How is the stock ordered within an organisation?*

You should now be familiar with the sequence of events leading up to the delivery of goods to an organisation, and how such a delivery is recorded on the stock record card. However, as a member of an organisation, you will need to be aware of the procedures required in order to request supplies for your own working area.

Most organisations use **stock requisition forms** which are completed by the person needing the stock. These forms are usually countersigned by the supervisor and then passed over to the Stock Controller, who will arrange for the items to be taken from the stockroom.

If the Stock Controller identifies that stock is low and needs to be reordered from the supplier, then a **purchase requisition** would be sent to the purchasing, or buying, department to inform them that the minimum stock level had been reached and that new stock should be ordered immediately. It is the responsibility of the purchasing department to ensure that the stock is ordered, and also that the correct quality has been ordered at the best possible price.

Remember that every time stock is issued to a department it should be *deducted* from the stock record card, and every time stock is delivered by a supplier this should be *added* to the record card. The stocktaker is employed to check the figures of stock received against stock issued to departments or sold to purchasers throughout the organisation, in order to calculate the total value of stock in hand and discover any mistakes.

You will find that the stock you are most likely to be called upon to order frequently in an office will be stationery. Stationery is classified as a consumable item of stock and is used in the administration of the organisation. It may be kept in the General Office, with a member of the office staff being responsible for it.

Items of stationery could include paper, envelopes, typewriter ribbons and lift-off tapes, paperclips, pencils, glue, pens, and so on. The value of this type of stock is very high and great care must be taken to control its use and ensure that staff are not requesting it for personal use, or storing unnecessary quantities.

■ DIY 9.2.1

Copy the form in Figure 9.5, or you may be able to obtain a copy of a stationery requisition from work. You need to request the following stationery supplies for use in your office. Complete the form correctly and do not forget to sign and

STATIONERY REQUISITION	
No	
Date	
Quantity	**Description**
Signed	Storekeeper's initials
Department	
Authorised	....

Fig 9.5 Stationery requisition form

date it. The next requisition number for your section is 321. The items you require are: 1 stapler, 1 box of staples, 1 red pen, 1 blue pen, 1 stick of adhesive, 30 window envelopes size DL brown, 1 ream of A4 bond paper coloured blue.

▶ When should stock be issued?

This will depend on how frequently you receive requests. If your colleagues ask for small items all the time you may find it interrupts the flow of your other work. If it interrupts to such an extent that you start getting behind or you do not meet the deadlines set then you will have to speak to your supervisor. It is better if a set time of the week is put aside for stock control and issuing. People soon get to know that they should put a request in regularly for items that they require. Obviously if there is an urgent request then this should be issued when requested. Do not encourage staff to help themselves from the stock cupboard as they may take more than is necessary and will possibly spot other items that they can order which they had not needed up to that time. If you are responsible for the stock cupboard then you must remain in control. After issuing the stock requested it is a good idea to tidy the cupboard and have a quick check to see if any of the items are getting near to the reorder level.

▶ What hazardous materials might you be in contact with?

Hazardous materials are any that may cause unsafe conditions for staff. The majority of the time stock, handled correctly, will not cause a problem. However, there have been cases of fumes overcoming staff. Fumes may come from some toners, adhesives and solvents, correction fluids, cleaning materials and duplicating fluid. If these items are stored and handled correctly there should not be any accidents caused. Always check that the lids are secured and that the items are stored in an upright position. They should not be stored where they are likely to be kicked or knocked over. Never over-order on these items or hold a surplus of stock – this will only increase the hazard.

When issuing items such as toner cartridges, the manufacturer may recommend that the cartridge is only handled by someone wearing gloves and these are usually supplied inside the box with the cartridge.

Check when issuing these items that the gloves are supplied and if not, supply some to the person requesting the item. In some organisations office staff are not allowed to replace the cartridges in the printers or photocopiers because of the hazard. However, even if specialist staff are available to replace the items, the office staff may be expected to supply the cartridge.

Completing Element 9.2

To complete this element on issuing stock items on request you will need to put all DIY tasks in your folder. In addition competence must be proven in dealing with requests for stock promptly and accurately. Stock should be issued and handled in accordance with the organisation's procedures. Records should always be kept up to date, legible and accurate. If damaged stock is found this should be reported promptly and accurately to the correct person. The type of items dealt with should include office consumables and small items of office equipment, such as staplers, scissors and hole punches. Ideally you should be observed in the workplace over a period of time carrying out these duties. In your folder you should have examples of stock issue records, records of action taken with damaged stock and copies of stock requests. You may also have a statement from your supervisor stating exactly what work you have carried out for this element.

Claiming credit

Once you have completed your final assessment, you will need to write in your record book or folder how, when, where and what you have done to prove that you are competent.

The following is an example of how one trainee completed this claim:

When working at Turner & Co for work placement I issued stock when requested by the staff. I always made sure that they had a signed stock requisition form before getting the items required. I was told not to issue more than one bottle of correcting fluid at a time and had to tell one of the staff to see the supervisor when they wanted 3. I kept stock record cards for all the items and each time I issued stock I made an entry on the correct card. I also made sure that the total column was completed. My writing was neat so that in the future other people can read it. When stock was damaged I reported it to my supervisor.

My supervisor has observed me carrying out these duties for the last few weeks and I have completed a work record form which has been signed by her (see my

INDEX